The Road through the Isles

The Road through the Isles

JOHN SHARKEY

Drawings, diagrams and maps by
KEITH PAYNE

WILDWOOD HOUSE

First published in Great Britain in 1986
by Wildwood House Ltd
Gower House, Croft Road,
Aldershot, Hants, GU11 3HR England

Text © 1986 John Sharkey
Drawings, diagrams and maps © 1986 Keith Payne

Cover photograph by Keith Payne

Sharkey, John
    The Road through the Isles.
    1. Western Isles (Scotland)—Description
    and travel—Guide-books
    I. Title
    914.11'404858   DA880.W4

ISBN 0 7045 0498 7
Typeset by Tellgate Ltd., London WC1
Printed in Great Britain by Billing and Sons Ltd, Worcester

Contents

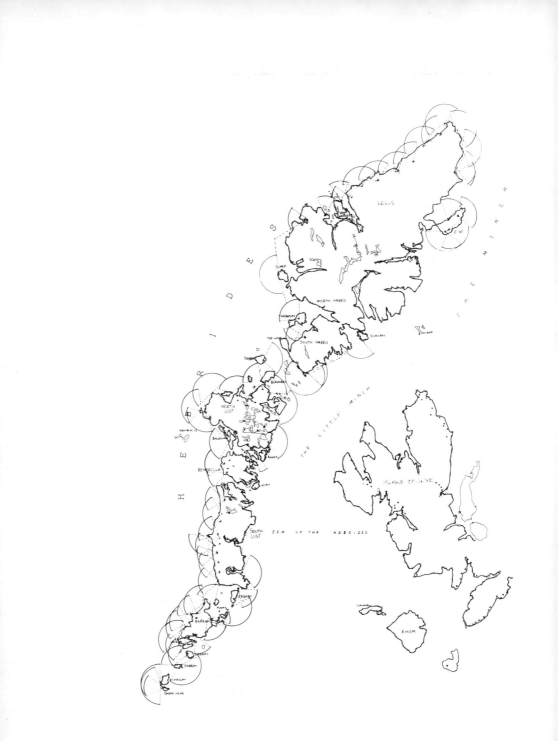

Distribution of the Duns and Brochs of the Outer Hebrides with arcs of intervisibility

For Annie MacLeod of Callanish, Isle of Lewis, and the late Nan MacKinnon of Vatersay. Dedicated also to the bards, storytellers and travellers who made this work possible.

Seo ant-àite mu dheireadh,
an t-àit aonaramach gun fhradhare bheann
far an èigin stad is fuireach
ged nach eil ar n-àilleas ann.

This is the ultimate place,
the lonely place without sight of hills
where it is necessary to stand and wait
through our desire is not in it.

(first verse of *An Ceann Thall*, The Farther End, by Sorley MacLean, Cannongate Press, 1981)

This work is the result of a rare collaboration between writer and artist from our journeys around the isles in all weathers. The constant help and encouragement of Ron Curtis since our first meeting at Callanish cannot be overestimated. Special thanks are due to Patrick Ashmore of the SDD(AM) for his helpful suggestions after reading an early draft and to Peter Warby for typing a later version of the manuscript; also to Peggy Angus of Barra and Lord and Lady Granville of North Uist for their generous hospitality.

To echo William Blake who said that his authors lived in paradise, ours were very much a part of the Hebrides. Both for the manner in which the book took shape alongside the conversations of fellow explorers such as Lynne Wood and Jill Smith and to the many islanders who helped with endless goodwill and stories without any withholding of their ancient store of knowledge for 'that which does not evolve is knowledge that will not survive', our grateful thanks.

Variations in the Gaelic placenames are common in the printed literature since the eighteenth century. Here the Ordnance Department spellings are used unless there is good reason to do otherwise. Heights of mountains are taken from Ordnance Survey maps and given in metres; most others measurements are given in Imperial units.

The Little Book of Barra

Stone of the Pass of the Mouth

Barra

Nearly 50 years ago a handsome publication called *The Book of Barra* was compiled by John Lorne Campbell, 'to give the reader some idea of the social and economic history of a small Hebridean island during the last four-hundred years'. It included excerpts from early travellers; accounts of the customs, literature, religion, and the Gaelic schools; and the verbatim evidence taken by the Crofting Commission later in the 19th century on the abject conditions of the people. The influence of Norse on local place-names and a lively contribution by Compton Mackenzie on 'Catholic Barra' were included, as well as a bibliography, and lists of the fauna and flora, the names of the Proprietors, Ministers, Priests and population figures from the first official census in 1811. It certainly collated most of the available information about Barra, for which the following account is deeply indebted. Although the emphasis, here, is on the folk stories—particularly those relating to the ancient monuments—recent social changes are also woven in, making the book of interest both to the armchair traveller and to the visitor following the single main road around the island.

In outline, Barra has a slightly erratic appearance, resembling a giant tortoise swimming in the sea, with its extremities jutting out at the corners and the road looped like a ribbon on its hump. Confined to this narrow, 14-mile capillary, the car traveller skirts the trackless interior cluster of heather-covered hills that usually give an impression of softness—although composed of Archaean gneiss with small intrusions of pegmatite. Amid the rugged, uneven, peripheral spread of landscape towards the sea, startling white beaches around Borve Point and Traigh Mhor near Eoligarry stand clear against a backdrop of seemingly endless water and sky, making it difficult to resist the charm of what many consider to be the most serene and beautiful of the larger Outer Isles. Along the eastern coast road the contrast is not so marked, although numerous wide headlands are constantly opening to reveal vistas of rounded islets protruding from the sea and the peaks of the Cuillin Hills of Skye on the far horizon. Barra is five miles wide by eight in length, and its compactness and relative accessibility throughout make it ideal for the individual hiker, unlike the interminable boggy interior of the loch-strewn Uists, the mountainous terrain of Harris, or the vast peat cover spread over Lewis. Clambering over its rocky hills may be taxing and uncomfortable, especially during the abundant rains of autumn and winter, but on Barra one has only to reach the nearest high ground for refreshing glimpses of the surrounding ocean. There are superb views of the smaller isles to the south from the summit of Ben Tangaval (433m.). From Heaval (363m.), the plethora of isles to the northeast have that rounded quality of glaciated rock and pervading aspect of aloofness characteristic of our birdseye view of scenery that predates the human influence. There is an old proverb here that the sands of the western machair shift every 200 years. From the evidence of inundated settlements and the rise and fall of sea-levels due to climatic changes, it is clear that some or even all of the larger Hebridean islands may have been depopulated in the past.

The endless road of Barra can be traversed metaphorically by way of the architectural remains from prehistory to the most recent past. Neolithic chambered cairns, Iron Age fortifications, early Christian chapels, mediaeval castles, ruined shielings, blackhouses that here and there are still used as byres or for storage, and even the rotting industrial waste around Castlebay harbour, have become part of the landscape for outsider and resident alike. Each period piece, of course, has particular interest for the specialist but as a whole they tend to blend into a nostalgic configuration of nature which the tourist industry promotes wholeheartedly as part of an archaic heritage that has little connection with the life of the islanders. The general deterioration of the majority of the ancient structures throughout the Hebrides may add a romantic background to holiday snapshots but unless some positive steps are undertaken soon to ameliorate the continuous erosion by wind and rain, most may well become archaeological 'sites' rather than structures embodying any life history.

The immediate needs of travellers emerging from the overheated interior of the ferry from Oban on the Scottish mainland onto the wet or blustering quay of Castlebay, for a hotel room or the more homely bed & breakfast are well catered for in the nearby Tourist Information office. Here, they have up-to-date lists and prices of accommodation available throughout Barra, although during the height of the summer season prior booking is advisable. On four days of the week, but never on a Sunday, the Oban ferry does the triangular trip to Castlebay and Lochboisdale in South Uist, with a short stopover in each harbour of half-an-hour; the accompanying unloading and reloading of cars and freight usually attracts its share of interested spectators, including both locals and visitors. Run by Caledonian MacBrayne, who have a complete monopoly of inter-isle trade with ships, lorries and even their own quays, the service is efficient and regular except during the most severe weather conditions. The fare in the cafeteria on board is plain to the point of dullness but the most nourishing, wholesome and reasonable dish is a bowl of hot homemade soup and bread rolls. The large and varied repastes so lovingly described by travellers of yore are now merely sidelights of social history; while inflation and the high cost of travel have put paid to the drunken revelry of pre-war day-trippers, who could take advantage of the ever-open bar with the added benefits of sea air and the sight of some of the most beautiful islands in the western hemisphere. However, in season there are special rates for drivers taking their cars on the round trip from Oban, up through the Isles, and returning via Stornoway to Ullapool on the mainland.

Castlebay has a small cluster of shops curving up from the quay to the modest Catholic church and nearby hotel. It was once the centre of a fish-curing industry that began a century ago when James Matheson, Proprietor of Lewis, encouraged the development of the herring drifters known as the 'Anstruther Build'. The rusted sheds and broken concrete remains testify to the effects of the depletion of the herring stock—although apparently during the inter-war years Barra was even more prosperous than today, for according to the castle boatman there was enough work locally 'for every man and dog'. Flat and shell fishing remain the traditional occupations of the islanders, with capital encourangement from the Highland and Islands Development Board. On quiet evenings when the trawlers and boats are moored within the shadow of Kisimul Castle, the ancient stronghold of the clan MacNeil, the harbour is indeed a haven of tranquillity. The large school complex and the spread of new houses around the curve of the bay, giving the town a prosperous air, are indicative of the recent upward trend in the population recorded in the 1981 census, although Barra has experienced a persistent decrease—from over 2,500 in 1911 to only 1,200 today. The circular road around Barra is the hub of island life, linking Castlebay with Brevig, Northbay, and the air service at Eoligarry. The sandy runway of Traigh Mhor, once famed as a cocklebeach, is covered by shallow tidal water twice a day, a charming touch that belies its direct connection with the outside world. The essential utility of the motor car and of the ubiquitous TV, the increased range of the electricity supply and of the telephone: these are playing their part in the island's development, which has also seen the spread of bungalows between the townships around the coast. The material benefits are obvious from the daily influx of the white bread vans, oil tankers and lorries full of building materials disembarking at Castlebay and the other points of entry to the Hebrides—Lochboisdale and Lochmaddy in the Uists, Tarbart on Harris, and Stornaway on Lewis—but the hidden costs to the indigenous culture of the Isles will doubtless be assessed sometime in the future.

The traditional history of the island, like that of Ireland and of the West Highlands, is an accumulative mixture of legend, genealogy, poetry and petty gossip. The MacNeils claim an ancient lineage going back to Niall of the Nine Hostages, an Ulster king who ruled during the early centuries after Christ, and Barra itself is named after Finbar, a sixth-century Cork bishop, so the connections between the two islands have always been marked. After the Reformation in 1560 both doggedly maintained their Catholic religion in spite of persecution, ridicule and the lack of franchise. Towards the end of the 18th century it was stated in the General Assembly of the Church of Scotland that out of 20,000 Catholics in the Highlands not more than 20 owned land worth £100 a year and that in the commercial world there was not one Catholic of eminence. The 1829 Catholic Emancipation Acts helped to change this state of affairs but still the heritage of being second-class citizens, bonded by a common language as well as the innate conservatism and self-reliance of islanders, produced a close link that is still maintained today. There is also the 'feel' of Barra itself, which is one of those undefined aspects not given to sensible explanation—but anyone who has travelled through the southwest of Ireland will immediately recognise what I am referring to, as well as the small dark racial type common in both places.

The tradition of fact and heresay over many years' storytelling of the ceilidhs, (or gossip-houses, the original meaning of the word) amalgamated local preoccupations with the flotsam of outside history and politics into a kind of folk history, that was eventually served up as literature by travellers, antiquarians, folklorists and natural scientists. Donald Munro, as High Dean of the Isles, visited them in 1549 and was the first to write an account of the Hebrides, followed in 1582 by George Buchanan, a well-known scholar and historian. Martin Martin's was the only early account written by a native. Born in Skye, he was ordained a Presbyterian minister and for a time was tutor to the young James VI of Scotland, before spending five years travelling and researching his *Description of the Western Isles* (1703). Walter MacFarlane, an antiquarian, wrote his *Geographical Collections* between 1713–22, while other 'outsiders' commenting on the life of the islands included such distinguished writers as Thomas Pennant (1771–5), Samuel Johnson (1775), James MacCulloch, a geologist (1819), Alexander Carmichael (1880) and W.C. MacKenzie (1903). The 19th-century mania for collecting and preserving local lore had reached its peak when Carmichael and others realised that as the Highlands and Western Isles were being depopulated a vast repository of oral tradition was in danger of being lost forever. His work, which has been collected in the five volumes of *Carmina Gadelica*, is a classic of its kind. His perceptive vision, unfailing sympathy as a listener, and sheer hard work influenced those who followed his example and contributed to the archives of the School of Scottish Studies. Many of the old stories remain as quaintly contemporary as ever, and since the weather has not changed much nor yet the character and disposition of the islanders, it is no surprise to hear a tale repeated today in much the same form as the original. For instance, the one about MacNeil refusing even God himself when asked to skipper the Arc of Noah, as he had a galley of his own to sail, was told verbatim by a local fisherman in Castlebay as a topical joke to be shared by two people standing in the rain rather than as a serious anecdote of island history.

Kisimul Castle, Castlebay

Built on a rocky inlet in the entrance to Castlebay harbour, the castle with its freshwater well was the stronghold of the MacNeils of Barra up to the 18th century, when the 41st Chief, Col. Ruaridh, moved his residency to Eoligarry House. The roof timbers burnt down and much of the masonry was removed to serve as ballast in boats which had shed their cargo of potatoes from Ireland. However, in the 1950s Kisimul was rebuilt and renovated by Robert Lister MacNeil, an American architect who had bought the ruined castle and 2,000 acres of land. His son, Ian Roderick, the 46th Chief, is continuing the renovation with financial support mainly from the MacNeils in America and Canada. This and the small chapel at Kilbar are probably the sum total of private preservation of ancient monuments in the whole of the Hebrides. The castle now looks much as when Martin Martin saw it in 1699 but failed to gain admittance because an officer thought he might spy out the inner defences while the Chief was abroad. These days a local boatman does the journey to the castle twice a week if anyone wishes to explore it.

The original building nucleus is the oblong tower, from which a stone curtain was built to form an irregular-shaped enclosure measuring internally 100 feet by 68 (30 x 21m.). At two places in the north and northeast angles of the enclosure the curtain rises above the general level, giving a vantage point over 30 feet above the rock. The later buildings— Chapel, Watch-tower, Great Hall, Tanist House, Kitchen House and Marion's addition next to the well—were placed in the form of an ellipse against the inner curtain. In front of the entrance is a tiny harbour protected by an outwork built on the rocky spur. The walls of the tower are 35 x 28 x 6 feet thick (12 x 8 x 2m) and those of the curtain are crenellated with 'weep-holes' for drainage at the level of the parapet. There is some disagreement as to the date of the tower, but it is usually thought to have been constructed around the time of the MacNeil Charter from the Lords of the Isles in 1427, though other experts say it was built during the 13th century or even earlier.

St. Clair's Castle, Tangasdale

Just over a mile outside the main town, on the western road around the island, is a ruined square tower standing on an inlet at the upper end of the loch nestling under the curve of Ben Tangavat. Marked on the Ordnance Survey (OS) map as Dun Mhic Leoid, its present name stems from a Victorian novel based on the oft'times rather eirie setting. According to a booklet produced by the present MacNeil, it was Ian Garbh,

Castle St. Clair and altar (foreground)

brother of the legendary Marion of the Heads, who built it as a dungeon. The wooden floors have gone and as there are no signs of a fireplace or staircase and only one entrance high on the first floor, the original three-storey building has been the subject of speculation as to its use. In the collection of *Stories from South Uist* by Angus MacLellon (1961) there is a long convoluted narrative surrounding the building of the tower by a grandson of the Duke of Monteith at a time when the gentry were supporting the King of France against the English. The ruin is now 15 feet high (4.5m) but immediately below the water level are the remains of extensive flat levelling that might have been the foundations of a larger building or even an earlier dun site. Among the wild flowers and mint growing around the bottom of the tower are nesting gulls, terns and ducks, as well as a pair of mute swans that are usually seen gracefully turning around the loch.

There is an iron gate by the road that leads to St. Columba's Well, just above the east shore of the loch, and the path is well marked with 50 varnished white stones and six black ones painted with a white cross to represent the 'stations' of the rosary. The custom of the Priest and the faithful moving slowly down to the well, praying together at each stone on the Sunday nearest the 6th of June, the Saint's day, was recently inaugurated by the local parish priest. Known as Tobar nam Buadh, 'Well of Virtues', it is kept clean and tidy by a local crofter. The Rev. Edward MacQueen, who visited Barra in 1794, referred to it as a medicinal spring famous for its curing qualities. Nearby are some large stone blocks said to be the remains of an outdoor altar used during Penal Times, that may also have been connected with the ceremonies associated with healing wells and pilgrimages that were popular throughout Scotland until the last century in spite of constant pressures and protestations of Church ministers.

St. Brendan's Chapel, Borve
You cannot miss the motel further along the road as it is an unfortunate example of modern angular concrete construction. However, the weather will often ensure that one need not be bothered too much by ungainly architecture, and the bar provides welcome food and refreshments—

although the invidious presence of a TV set permanently switched on will doubtless make one more determined than ever to regain some of the beauty of the sandy machair and the sea washing around Borve Point. Between it and the road is a four-foot-high smooth black standing stone gradually sinking into the sand. The Royal Commission for Ancient Monuments' survey in 1914 listed another ten-foot stone nearby as being overturned. Its top is now barely visible.

Snails at Borve

None of the locals knew of this second stone, yet for some curious reason this site is listed as 'standing stones' on the OS map and tourist information sheets. The foundations of St. Brendan's Chapel are hardly visible, either, at the Point, although the broken quernstone seems to have taken the place of a 'cup' that, locally, was believed never to run dry. This is a single two-inch-diameter depression in a small block of dark gneiss which, when located near the fence leading into the old burial ground, had no moisture in it: but then, this was during one of the best summers seen in the Isles for years! The wall of the burying ground on the west side was curved to incorporate the much older foundations of Dun na Cille just above the shore line by a sheltered landing place behind Borve Point. 'Borve' is an Old Norse term, common on the western coasts of the Isles, meaning 'fort' or 'castle', and is usually a good indication of a favoured site of ancient habitation. Here on Barra, 1,000 years prior to the arrival of the Norsemen, lived the 'dun-makers'—there are three such sites listed in the immediate vicinity—and over two millenia prior to them, the chambered cairn builders. St. Brendan is said to have preached here on his journey across the North Atlantic, and the chapel was later built in his name. Brendan came from southwest Ireland, and his journey up the western coast was thought to be mythical, but recently the explorer Tim Severin duplicating the conditions of the period in an open hidebound boat, sailed this route to the Faroes, Iceland, and then to Greenland. There is also a tradition that Brendan preached to the people from the back of a whale, but this is obviously a spin-off from the common run of stories relating to his fabulous voyage. Since then the burying ground has interred countless generations of Borve folk, and even the tiny harbour used as a shelter by fishing craft until recent times has fallen into ruin. Yet sitting on the rocks by the sea, all these relative time-periods count for little in the constant rhythm of nature itself in an endless minuet of sky, water, wind and rock.

Don Cuier, Allasdale

A mile to the north, this round stone fort was built on a natural promontory overlooking Seal Bay—with its

permanent family of bright-eyed dogheads bobbing about—
and the Greian headland. It is about 30 feet (9m.) in diameter
and reputed to be a broch, there being the remains of a gallery
on the southwest curve of the rock walling which is now
nearly 12 feet high (3.6m.) in places and 14 feet (4m.) thick.
Excavations in 1956 revealed clay pipes, Iron Age implements
and shards of 'craggon' ware, an indigenous crude pottery
used for cooking and storage utensils, that was still being
made in the Isles until late last century. As a ruin without its
outer wall structure it is difficult to visualise as it might have
looked originally but it certainly commands a wide spread of
the sea.

Other forts were situated close by Dun Chlif to the north,
while at Scurrival at the topmost point of Barra is a ruined
broch that once commanded the Atlantic approaches with a
broad view of South Uist and the Sound of Fudday to the east.
On that island another dun extended the visible spectrum over
towards Skye. South of Borve Point the intervisible chain of
defensive forts extends to Dun Ban, and then across to Dun
Birualum on Vatersay and as far south as the spectacular cliff-
top fortifications on Mingulay and Berneray. There is an old
dun site at Castlebay, and it may be possible that Kisimul
Castle was built on earlier fortifications. So for a distance of 50
miles the exposed coastline of the most southwesterly reaches
of the Outer Isles was protected from potential aggression.
The distributive map of these galleried duns or small brochs,
duns and promontory forts confirms this pattern of
intervisible siting. There did not appear to be a need to guard
the eastern side of Barra so closely, although there are a
number of ruins here as well, probably because the currents
running through The Little Minch between the Uists and
Skye were a fairly effective barrier. Furthermore, the western
side of Skye as well as the smaller Inner Hebridean Isles were
also ringed with forts, and these continued up the mainland
coast as far as Cape Wrath, around the Orkneys and
Shetlands, and down the east coast as far as the Moray Firth.

The actual construction of the forts—there were about four
basic types, set on natural promontories, flat headlands and
loch inlets—reveals that these were not haphazard creations
but rather the well-structured results of building engineering

that had obviously utilised local labour working from 'blueprints'. It would appear that there was a highly organised and economically powerful society, probably centred on Orkney, that could plan and site defensive structures around nearly every mile of a thoroughly indented coastline in response to a threat of outside aggression. However, no evidence has so far been uncovered of any fighting, and as the structures are thought to date from around the turn of our era, it is likely that the people responded to a threat of a possible Roman invasion in much the same spirit that the Napoleonic forts were built around southeast England and again nearer our own time during the wars against Germany when concrete bunkers, mine fields and rolls of barbed wire completely surrounded every inch of the accessible coastline of Britain. The influx of refugees into Britain after Caesar's naval rout of the Celts near the Bay of Morbihan and his subsequent action of putting Amorica to the sword showed his intentions clearly enough. However, the Pictish autocracy were not to know that his assassination soon afterwards would put off the plans for Roman colonisation for at least a century.

Chapel Ruins of Kilbar, Eoligarry
Beyond the turning north at Northway but before one reaches the air terminal is a unique wooded valley called Drochaid Ruadh. Because it is narrow and steep there is a heartening mixture of mountain ash, larch, scotspine, broom, scrub oak, bramble, and that most peculiar species of plantain, the monkey-puzzle tree. A first-time visitor to the Isles may not be immediately aware of the almost complete absence of trees, apart from a few unimaginative military-style plantations and clumps of ash and bramble on the little isles, that fortunately are in the middle of lochs and so escape the destructive nibbling of the sheep. Even on a sunny day this valley has an odd feeling, an air of eerie tragedy, that may account for some of its sad stories. Clach Mhor stands on a prominence above it. A vast natural boulder (30 x 20 x 15 feet), it was said to spell doom for Barra if it ever fell over. However, it seems that the island can rest assured because the base around and beneath it appears to have been packed with supporting material. It was probably originally a 'logan', or 'rocking stone'. Nearby is a

Doorway, Cille Bhara

recent memorial grave set under a six-foot-long stone. From here there is a fine view southwards over the peninsula of Adrveenish and beyond to Bruernish.

A narrow strip of collapsed sand dunes separates the east and west coasts with the road past the airfield to Cille Bhara and the nearby small ferry service to Ludag in South Uist. The sands where the plane lands were called Cockle Strand, and it was here that games and horse-racing were held on St. Barr's feast day, the 25th September, until as late as 1840s, when poverty and emigration finally took the heart out of such pastimes. As part of the celebrations, a wooden effigy was carried in solemn procession around the island. Martin mentioned that it stood on the altar of Cille Bhara but as he was not allowed to see it, being a Presbyterian minister, his description is necessarily vague. Its whereabouts since are a mystery, though in keeping with the romance of Hebridean heritage, there are always those who will profess to know the location of such treasures, but they will not be telling the likes of outsiders.

Within the curved walled burial ground, St. Barr's Chapel still has its eight-foot-high (2.6m.) north and south walls

Runic Carved stone, Cille Bhara (National Museum of Antiquities of
Scotland, Edinburgh)

largely intact. The rest is shapeless and grass-covered, while the only striking architectural feature that remains is a rude triangular-headed doorway set in a semi-circle of drystone. This design is a feature of the remaining windows, though a third one in the south wall has collapsed and another at the east end, reported in 1929, has completely disappeared. Inside the open ruin, by the doorway amid a tangle of overgrown grass and weed, is a blackened stone measuring 14 inches by 8 (35.5 x 20cm.) with a circular hole hewn into it. A few yards to the southeast is another chapel in even worse condition. During the 19th century, Muir, in his 'Ecclesiological Notes', wrote that there were four ruins within the walled enclosure resembling those at Howmore in South Uist. The remaining chapel is St. Mary's, which has been renovated by the local people and re-roofed with slate in place of the grass and reed thatch that was once uniformly used throughout the Isles. A worthy effort, though unfortunately their reconstruction of this tiny chapel with flat-headed windows and a curious raised half-floor and poor-quality 'builders' pine' supporting the roof, lacks craft or subtlety. This is not helped by the conglomeration of kitsch and religious replicas that surrounds the four ornamental medieval grave slabs set two by two along each wall on the raised floor. The long swords surrounded by Celtic interlacing make excellent rubbings. Known as the Crusader Stones, they once stood outside in the burial ground and are somewhat similar in design to those at St. Clements, Harris, through the finest here is in a class of its own with a three-lobed leaf-pattern surrounding a long sword blade and headed in a complicated Celtic 'Knot of Eternity.' At the other end of the chapel is a fibreglass replica on a concrete plinth of the Runic Stone that is now displayed in the Museum of Antiquities in Edinburgh. The original greenish slate was found outside in 1865. It has a mixture of Nordic and Christian design forming a decorated cross with four plaited patterns. The border is an S-scroll developing into a square-keyed motif, which is also found on church stones at Kells and Monsterboise in Ireland. Similar examples of the runic lettering on the reverse side have been found on Arran and at Maeshowe, Orkney. There have been various interpretations of the runes, but the one pinned on the wall reads: 'This cross has been raised in memory of Thorgeth, daughter of Steiner.' 'Stein' means 'stone', so the final word might actually refer to the carver himself. The faith and devotion of the Barra people should be given some regard, especially as this little chapel of Mary has been reconsecrated. It was hoped that the authorities in Edinburgh would return the Runic Stone to its original setting, away from the sterile and ridiculous display of fibreglass casts and actual Pictish stones from all over Scotland, stuck close together in a sandpit in the Edinburgh Museum.

Dun Bharpa, Craigston

The easiest way to get to the only chambered cairn that is still standing in anything like its original form is through the Borve Valley and up the cattle track past Craigston. However, for those who also wish to explore the interior of the Isle it is possible to get there from almost anywhere off the main road, with the help of some map reading. It must be emphasised that, when walking over rough hilly or boggy terrain anywhere in the Hebrides, one should be prepared for rapid changes of weather; even on a bright day and on such a seemingly small island as Barra, waterproof clothing, stout footwear, and something to eat, are a very good idea. A compass is advisable, too, if you don't want to get completely lost.

To get some idea of how the hinterland was utilised prior to our times, one can do no better than begin at Dun Cuier and follow the burn up the valley towards the jumble of whitish-grey boulders on the far hill that may have been building material from a chambered cairn because of its massive diameter and height (75' x 10'). Nearby is another mound of considerable size, the site of an aisled house known as Tigh Talamhanta, marked as such on the OS map and roughly contemporary with the erection of the duns. Along the banks of the curving stream are extensive ruins of shielings and old cattle enclosures. As one gets deeper into the silence of these hills, broken occasionally by the harsh cry of the hoodie crow and sweeter note of summer birds, among the peat and heather, an older resonance begins to take hold. It is almost as

Dun Bharpa

if the shrill voices of long-gone woman and children become tangible in the wind through the silent glens which were once used extensively for summer grazing. The yearly communal activities of tending the stock, making cheese and carding wool were part of the life cycle of women, with their children in attendance. Other favoured locations were the south-facing slopes of Ben Tangaval and directly across the Sound of Vatersay around Caolis; meanwhile the men were at the fishing or perhaps working at seasonal jobs on the mainland. Peat cutting and collecting as well as the sheep fank twice a year are still family and community activities, and the close social bonding through their expression of deeply held religious feeling — mostly Catholic up to Uist and the Wee Free Church of Scotland dominant through the Long Isle of Harris and Lewis, where the Sabbath is strictly observed — helps preserve much of the resilience and independence of the islanders. However, when one looks at the changing traditional roles — for example, the men took over the weaving after the Great War and made it economically viable, and later the woman began to neglect bread making and garden produce in favour of mainland mass-produced cellophane-wrapped food — it is not very surprising that during the long winter months of inactivity, the depression known as the 'Lewis Blues' affects mainly the womenfolk, who are confined to the house and the doubtful solace of the television set.

Dun Bharpa was constructed on the rising ground behind Beinn Mhartainn. Now set within lichen-covered boulders that form the solid mass of the seventeen feet high steep-sided circular cairn (86' diameter) are a ring of uprights. Some of the 17 large stones, up to six feet (1.8m.) in height, have been displaced or lean away from the cairn itself, but the majority seem to be in their original positions. The entrance to the central chamber is on the east side, a distinctive feature of many of the Hebridean round cairns, where some large portal stones protrude in parallel fashion. About 200 yards (60m.) to the northeast by the new stock fence is an 11-foot-long (3.5m.) recumbent stone, shaped like a hammerhead, that may once have been an outlier or marker for the horizon. Excavation has shown that such cairns were used for communal burials from between the third and second millenium BC. However, this may not mean that they were constructed primarily for funereal purposes as many of the small pre-Reformation chapels now contain so many grave slabs in their interiors, that one could well argue that they were built as tombs rather than temples.

Less than half-a-mile to the west of Dun Bharpa is the largest stone monolith on Barra, prostrate on the peat in the middle of a pass between the hills called Beul a'Bhealaich. In its original setting this magnificent 16-foot (5m.) standing-stone faced east and west on the ancient path through the middle of the Isle, creating a resonance that is certainly lacking today. The feeling is difficult to define in words but almost certainly palatable in the alternating silences and wistful moaning of the winds through the Pass as one lies full length on the white grained stone. Perhaps it could be re-erected under the supervision of the Ancient Monuments Branch of the Scottish Development Department so that once again it might become the solitary guardian of the old route across the island.

Pass of the Mouth

It was the singer and storyteller, Nan MacKinnon, who told us how the large flat stone in the Pass became associated with the Devil's Hoofprint. It has a large hollow cup in the centre, a common feature in many prostrate stones throughout the Isles, probably due to the erosion of its crystal nodule that may once have had an active role as a sound conductor. However, the 'Judas' as she called Satan had persuaded so many of the angels to leave Heaven that Michael was worried it might even become deserted. So the gatekeeper turned to God with the bad news, who then ordered him to close them immediately and prevent any more leaving for this other paradise on earth. However, when the angelic band arrived here they found nothing but water and rock, and after circling the earth a few times eventually landed on Barra. The indented spot where the Devil first alighted is still marked on the face of the large stone.

> For not of the seed of Adam are they,
> Nor from Abraham father came away,
> But of the Proud Angel they are the seed,
> Extruded from heaven with all its breed.
> (No. 234 in *Highland Poems*, translated by G.R.D. MacLean, SPCK London 1963)

According to Archie MacDonald, a storyteller who died some years ago, the flat stone was used as a 'Stone of Judgement.' Wide enough to hold man and pony without either touching the common earth, it was here that the MacNeil of Barra heard the claims and complaints of his clanfolk once a year and dispensed justice. It presents an extraordinary image of the power accorded the clan chief, whose herald could proclaim from the parapet of Kisimul Castle: 'Hear, O ye people, and listen O ye nations, the great MacNeil of Barra, having finished his meal, the princes of the earth may dine.'

The Pass at one time had been renamed Bealach a'Ghugain, in honour of Fr. Duggan, an Irish Franciscan missionary who, disguised as a trader with two helpers, one to row and the other to officiate at openair mass, travelled around Barra and South Uist for five years during the mid-17th century. The name for the Pass never caught on but from Fr. Duggan's letters home we get a glimpse of the harsh life then. Often going without food or on a megre meal of barley and oaten bread with a little cheese or salt butter because the people were too impoverished to provide any better. And if he managed to get some meat in the homes of the gentry, 'it was so unpalatable and so disagreeably served that one does not relish it'. He was continually astounded at the devotion of the islanders and he baptised a great number of children and adults. Some were over 80 years of age which gives some indication of the length of time that the Barra people maintained their faith without a priest after the Reformation outlawed them a century earlier.

John MacPherson (d. 1955), a postman from Northbay, had his stories collected together by J.L. Campbell in a delightful book, *Tales of Barra told by the Coddy* (1960). One of these was about the last time the fairies were seen somewhere close to the Pass of the Mouth. The mother of a postman from Balnabodach on the east coast was dying but as it was dark, her son was afraid to cross the hills to Balnacraig (Craigston) where the priest lived. As soon as it was light he set off and when he reached the Pass he saw a lot of little men and women running in and out of a rock at a place called Glair Ghlas ('Green Valley'). At first he thought they might be real folk, but as it was so early in the day he decided they must be fairies. He hurriedly collected the priest, and as they were returning related all that he had seen on the way over. Well, said the priest, it is many years since I have heard of any fairies on Barra and I am satisfied that what you saw must be they. So that was the last time any fairies were seen on the island.

A sequel to this story, concerning the eminent collector Alexander Carmichael, was related to us off-the-cuff and without any prompting by Nan MacKinnon. It was about the time when Carmichael paid him a visit, bringing a bottle to whet the whistle of the postman. As the bottle was emptying fast without any mention of the wee folk, the exasperated collector finally said, 'and when was the last time you saw the fairies of Barra?' The old man paused and, pointing to his tattered bagpipes on the chair, replied: 'Last night and will you look at what they left.' Her inflection on the penultimate word carried so much emphasis, bringing together the undertones of the story, that she fell about giggling as soon as she finished speaking.

It was a touching example of a vanishing art. The performer in full flight accentuating delicate nuances of word and meaning, making her listeners follow each inflection until that final encapsulation, like an indrawn breath, brought us down to earth again into the small front room of her tiny cottage by the sandy shore of Vatersay Isle. It was Nan MacKinnon's physical presence that was important, and no amount of recording on tape or transcribing on paper can compensate for her loss. This remarkable 80-year-old lady passed away a month later in June 1982 while we were on Lewis. An appreciation with some of her songs and stories was recently issued in *Tocher* No. 38, the magazine of the School of Scottish Studies in Edinburgh whose archives contains much of her work recorded over the past 25 years. Still, without her and other storytellers such as Donald MacDonald and John MacPherson, Barra and the Hebrides are all the poorer. The ceilidh during the long winter evenings was an age-old ritual exchange of news, gossip and stories that kept everyone in a community in touch with each other as well as those on other isles through the extended family networks. It was in such a social context that the traditional storytellers thrived. Not only are they dying off fairly fast but the cultural mileau which gave their lore resonance and meaning is rapidly being eroded by television, to which each viewer responds as if an island unto themself. As a symbol of individual isolation and a hidden medium of change, the goggle-box might well affect the Hebrides as a whole in the same invidious manner as the introduction of money during the 19th century that eventually destroyed the community on St. Kilda.

One of the reasons for journeying up through the Outer Isles from Barra Head to the Butt of Lewis was to visit all the ancient sites, using this firsthand experience to compare and collate as much as possible the other available information so as to create a revised version of the old publications that would take into account natural changes due to erosion and weather, and also to assess how far traditional values have shifted in relation to recent material changes. It is unlikely in the foreseeable future that the weather itself or even the character of the people will alter for, as I have said already, many of the anecdotes related by past travellers can still be heard today. What *is* altering though is the archaic and tenuous infrastructure that once sustained their vigorous cultural and spiritual life. Over 100 years ago, Alexander Carmichael travelled the Isles collecting and translating their songs, prayers, blessings and poems because they were then on the wane. It was a time of massive emigration to foreign cities and exile in alien lands. You can travel a long way these days without hearing any voices raised in prayer. Ask about the old times and the traditional stories and you may well be told very politely that the old one who knows them best is in another township or on the next isle—which is how we first heard about Nan MacKinnon.

Standing stones, fairy mounds and early ecclesiastical sites are silent indicators of a very ancient source of power. Travelling from island to island, spending time at them and attempting to intuit or isolate an essence that makes each place different from its neighbour, one begins to sense an overall quality of loss. Psychic damage and cultural senility are extreme effects of the changes that have been taking place in one of the last outposts of our Celtic heritage and where the language is still strong. The final phase is quite noticeable. For example, on the ridge above Breivig is a nine-foot-high (207m.) standing stone which is listed in the archaeological guides as yet another isolated megalith from the Neolithic period. Some time prior to 1915 its ten-foot neighbour had been overturned for a wager and now lies nearby broken in two parts. When close to the one standing, its exceedingly dark aspect might be explained by the fact that it is surrounded by heavy iron spikes that were driven into the ground to hold the connecting wires of an old radio mast. The military have moved on from here to higher ground further up the coast and erected a much taller tower, but have left behind their old radio-shack still full of cables and the like. Early last summer I crossed the Pass of the Mouth to visit the eastern side of Barra on my way back to Castlebay. Wandering southwards close to the edge of the hills I reached the stone at Breivig to find some sheep standing motionless and looking towards the

Standing Stone at Breivig

shack. I then heard the sound of bleating and fortunately was on hand to rescue the lamb that had been trapped inside. The door which usually swings in the wind had closed-to behind it. There is a story, connected with this area, of a hunter who had married a fairy but with subsequent disastrous consequences. The military leave behind no such fairytales. Their disregard for any beauty and harmony in the natural landscape is a constant sour note in keeping with their unmistakable presence and the outlandish steel edifices constructed along the whole length of the Hebrides.

The Bishops' Isles

All the isles of the southern Hebridean archipelago were in times long past part of the far-flung diocese of the Bishops of Man and Sodor. A permanent legacy from this era of Norse occupation of the western seaboard is retained in the place names of headlands, townships and islands. South of Barra the group all bear the suffix 'ay', an Old Norse expression for 'island', pinpointing particular descriptive qualities which, in terms of possible identification or as points of reference to the seafarers of that time, could not—in some cases at least—be bettered today: Vatersay (Water-Isle), Sandray (Sand-Isle), Lingay (Heather Isle), Pabbay (Hermit or Priest's Isle), Mingulay (Bird Isle), and finally Berneray (Bjorn's Isle), the most southerly and windswept often taking the full force of North Atlantic gales. The battle of Largs in 1263 forced Norway to cede the Isles to the Scots. Later, after the Battle of Bannockburn, MacDonald, King John of Islay, took the title Lord of the Isles as a mark of deference to his father-in-law, Robert the Bruce, first Stewart King of the Scots. This was the beginning of a long friendship between the ruling house of the Stuarts and MacDonalds that lasted until Prince Edward Charles tried to rally the Highland Clans behind the Stuart cause in 1745.

The Gaelic language reasserted itself and there appears to have been a revival of religious fervour with church architecture and the establishment of centres of learning, poetry and the ancient bardic traditions. There had been similar revivals in Wales, Ireland and parts of England so such centres as Temple na Trionaid in North Uist which was endowed and rebuilt by Amie Ruaridh, the first wife of John, had more than local renown. In fact it was at this monastic institution that Don Scotus, the medieval philosopher, was educated. The Lordship ruled the entire western seaboard of Scotland and granted land charters to chiefs of direct Donald descent such as ClanRanald of the Uists and others including Mac Neil of Barra. However, at the end of the 15th century the Lordship was abolished by James IV, King of Scotland; thereafter, many descendants of the indigenous northern settlers formed powerful clans. It was from this period onwards, with the constant changes of loyalty and acrimonious division—'every chief for himself and his clan'— that the romantic colour and blood of Highland history grew. Often styled on the former insular tradition of the Lordship, each powerful chief was surrounded by a retinue of clansmen. He had his own judge, known as the 'breive', his musician, a harper or piper, and he was eulogised in the Commonplace books—which recorded the geneology and exploits of the clan—by the seanchaichean (professional poet-historian).

The islands, big and small, were like pawns in a shifting power game, to be exchanged as part of a marriage contract or taken by force to consolidate an ambitious chief's waning prestige, or used as political leverage by the Kings of Scotland. After the battle of Culloden in 1745, when the Highland army was defeated by the English, among island chiefs only the Catholic ClanRanald actively supported the Jacobite cause; Parliament disarmed the clans, banned Highland dress and heritable jurisdictions. Many families emigrated to Canada, but those unable or unwilling became the confused victims, almost like children without parents, as islands were eventually sold piecemeal by the acreage to pay off the creditors of bankrupt lairds, such as the Mac Neil of Barra, and were then acquired by mainly absentee landlords. Up to the time of the clearances early in the 19th century, the island people—having been forced off the good land—clung to a way of life embittered by harsh weather and poor soil in spite of mainland indifference or interference.

Depopulation has continued up to the present as the fragile interdependence of these small communities falls apart due to economic pressures in a world far removed from them. Mingulay, for example, was depopulataed entirely in 1909 when everyone moved to Vatersay. And even here, the population has dwindled from the 240 recorded in the 1931 census to about 100 today, with the island in every sense a satellite of Barra (much as the latter is economically dependent on the mainland of Scotland for its survival)—and this in spite of the introduction of a regular ferry service, of a community co-operative, and of good grazing for the stock (the sheep are actually fenced in on the high ground). The high cost of importing goods and services and the low return on the cattle every year is rapidly making the small croft redundant in terms of present-day economies.

Crofting, legalized under the Crofters Holdings (Scotland) Act 1886, was initially forced on the islanders by the lairds and their tacksmen late in the 18th century to ensure a ready labour force for kelping. Each worker was given a small plot of land known as a croft on which he could erect a shelter. The potash market collapsed at a time when the population of all the large islands had risen enormously. Forced immigration seemed a perfect answer to many of the absentee landlords, who had no stomach or inclination to deal with the problem: the people were seen as an impediment to making the islands into deer and game reserves or to turning them over to large sheep farms. However, even for those who tried to help their tenants the problem occasioned by overcrowding, lack of food and natural resources seemed insurmountable. Horrendous tales are still told of the brutal slave conditions under which a large part of the old population of the Uists and Barra were shipped to Newfoundland when Col. Gordon acquired the islands in the 1850s, the government of the day having rejected his suggestion of turning Barra into a penal colony. Later, his wife, Lady Gordon Cathcart, tried to set up emigration schemes to deal with subsequent overcrowding, and needless to say such moves were not very popular with the local people. As absentee landlord, she refused to give over any good land to the peasants and cottars (tenants who occupied a cottage in return for labour), and by the end of the century conditions among the poor people of Barra had become so bad that the government intervened and in 1901 bought 600 acres to turn into small croft farms. But even this was not sufficiently ameliorative and Vatersay Isle was the only single farm left on the Gordon Estate that could be broken into crofts. Negotiations dragged on for a few years until one cottar took the matter into his own hands, moved from Castlebay and erected a dwelling within a day. During the following year six others joined him and, taking advantage of an old Scottish law that allowed a person to take possession of the adjoining land if a house could be built between sunrise and sunset and a fire lit by nightfall. Nevertheless the men were arrested and brought to trial in Edinburgh. When they were sentenced to prison for six weeks there was such a public uproar throughout Britain over the plight of the Hebridean islanders that the men were quickly released. Such is the saga of the Vatersay raiders which is still referred to locally with great pride. It was a struggle for land that lasted more than a decade until, in 1909, the Conjested Districts Board bought the whole of Vatersay, dividing it into crofts and selecting 58 tenants to settle there. The census, two years later, showed that there were nearly 300 people living on the island.

Both the advantages and disadvantages of the crofting system are much in evidence here. The size of the island and its relatively fertile machair enables it to have a cattle-based economy rather than one dependent on sheep subsidy and supported by fishing or occasional work—although unemployment is very high throughout the Hebrides. But in a recent survey it was shown that over 90 percent of all Hebridean crofts were so small they needed only a few hours attention per evening in contrast to the small percentage of large farms that were self-sufficient. Ironically enough the sheep that were first introduced to clear the people have now become their main source of income through government subsidy, even though these animals destroy every soft sweet root that emerges from the ground. So the nibbling sheep, bad weather and poor soil are not only accepted hazards but also, for the majority, the most tangible aspects of their deep emotional attachment to the islands. Recent legislation has enabled those who wish to, to apply for their land to be 'decrofted', but the hidden benefits from farming and rating subsidy on croft lands have meant that few are willing to take the step towards ownership, especially as land holdings are so small, and as there is little possibility of making a living from

them. The wheel turns, for the old arguments about social
viability versus economic feasability of maintaining islanders
on their barren land, are again surfacing with the introduction
of the £56-million five-year Integrated Development
Programme for the Western Isles (IDP) passed by Parliament
in 1982.

Berneray
The more usual boat trip from Castlebay during the summer
months (see the post office window for details) is to Mingulay
but the skipper may be prevailed upon to continue to
Berneray for a short visit after the passengers interested in
bird-watching or exploring the dunes and green hills have
scrambled up onto the wet rocks, to be collected on the return
journey. However, even for those with a nervous disposition
like myself, peering over the sheer cliff edge of Barra Head
with a drop of over 600 feet to the churning seas below, and
observing the constant moving gallery of puffins, guillamots,
shags, razorbills, gulls and rock pippets, is not to be missed
and infinitely preferable to the serenity offered within the
stratified clefts on the west coast of Mingulay.

Coming in towards the broken pier, Bernaray looks like an
overgrown grey whale with a Victorian lighthouse stuck to its
head. Even the recent concrete helipad has an anachronistic air
within the sparce heather covering this rocky wilderness.
According to one of the builders, it took six weeks to
construct because of the rough weather and it was the
loneliness that he most remembered, 'for there was nothing to
do except look at the sea or chase rabbits'. There is a steep hike
of a mile and half up to the cliff promontory. Beyond the high
granite wall surrounding the lighthouse an area has been
hollowed-out in front of the cliffs to a depth of about ten feet,
probably where the stone was hewn to build the 60-foot-high
(18m.) tower of the Barra Head lighthouse in 1833, as well as
the keeper's houses and the wall itself. One moves cautiously
here to peer down on the delicate puffins or search out for the
surprising blackbird who seems to be using the deep gullies to
amplify the notes against the rising echo of its song. The
lichen, egg-shells and even the seals below are mottled with
the same whitish-grey camouflage splattered by the nesting

gulls down the sheer rock face. The sharp spray in the wind, the moving waters below, and the cacophony of bird sound make one's head spin. Looking at the sea from this ahuman perspective, two lines from the 'Hill of Dreams' by Fionna MacLeod aptly describe its turmoil: 'For ever there the green is spun/The white across the surface run.'

It is almost a relief to sit on the slightly lower promontory above the Sound of Berneray among the scattered ruins of the Dun Bristle fort on the soft ground massed with sea pinks. Across the water is the great hump of Geirum Mhor (Big Sea Horse Isle) where there is supposed to have been another fort, although it is thought the remains may have been shielings, which leaves one wondering just what kind of people would have lived there. The short answer is those who were born here, but on the level of human consciousness such proximity to the neverending byplay of natural elements is a state that is surely beyond our understanding now. Down near the jetty at MacLean's Point there are the remains of a large walled enclosure with outlines of beehive structures, and a small rectangular stone setting that may have been an old chapel— for nearby in the burying ground is a two-foot-long weathered slab with a small cross incised on one face. Berneray, now, is bereft of human company, for the lightbeam is automatic. As Jack, the last keeper, who left in 1980 and now lives on Barra, says: 'it was the micro-chip that put us out of business'. The tradition of a light burning on the most southerly rock of the Outer Isles is very ancient, for it was said that nuns once kept a vigil and a chapel lamp burning here for those in peril on the rough Atlantic seas.

Mingulay

In the days when the isle was under the patronage of MacNeil of Barra, the rent was collected in the form of oil derived from the plump young sheerwater birds killed just before they left the nests. No one was allowed to hunt the birds before MacNeil's galley arrived at the end of the summer to claim the 20 barrels of oil (his 'fachaich') from the inhabitants, each levied according to the size of his croft. MacNeil, in return, would supply them with a milch cow if one had been lost during the year or would arrange partners for the bereaved, or even take the aged back to live at Kisimul Castle.

There is a story that one year when the galley came to collect its annual tariff of bird oil, the crew were disturbed to find no one greeting them so they sent the youngest who also happened to be the biggest of them, ashore to ascertain the cause. He shouted out to the boat that all the houses were empty except the last one in the village, which still had its dead inside. 'In that case', one of the older men called out to him, 'if it's a plague that killed them all you've got a stomach full of it already, so you better stay where you are.' The boy's father, Kenneth MacPhee, wondered what had happened to his son and demanded an answer from the MacNeil. The chief told him what had happened, and said he should pick his own men to go to Mingulay and it would be theirs free of rent as long as their descendants lived. The hill that the lad climbed every day for six weeks to see if the boat was returning is still called Ben MacPhee. A nearby shelf was named MacNeil's Bed, for here he rested while the men burned down every cottage so that nothing remained. New houses were built and their families lived there rent-free until Col. Gordon bought Barra in 1850. The remains of the rebuilt village still visible above Mingulay Bay are now in a very dilapidated state.

It's a good story and clearly one that has often been repeated and recorded. Nan MacKinnon's version (in *Tocher* magazine), like many such folktales, explains both the name of the nearby hill and the later discovery of ashes and ruins when church foundations were being dug.

The inhabitants of the Scilly Isles off the Cornish Peninsula are also 'newcommers', and—like those evacuated from Mingulay early this century who claimed descent from MacPhee—their common ancestors came from the mainland of Cornwall around the 16th century. St. Kilda, too, has had many speculations about its mysterious early inhabitants. However, the dependence on fowling and scaling the huge sea cliffs is well attested there as well as on Mingulay. The narrow rock chasms and vertical stacs of Arnamul and Lianamul just off the west plateau, as well as Biulacraig's sheer 700-foot (213m.) rock face, have excited comment from chroniclers since the 17th century. At one time Lianamul was connected to Mingulay by a rope bridge; although Martin Martin makes no mention of this, he does say that the chief climber was called a 'gingich', meaning a big fellow of strength and courage, who pulled up the rest of the fowling crew on a horsehair rope. Neil Munroe's novel, *Children of the Tempest*, describes a climb up these stratified cliffs with their gullies and caves.

The bird activity hereabouts is endless and the colonies are much the same as on Barra Head. From the caves below Lianamul, seals barking and the cries of the birds on the wind sound uncannily like unruly kids in a school playground. On the upward slopes are a large number of curved overgrown stone structures that could be used as windbrakes, but they have the feeling of grave mounds, especially those with upright stones at their heads. Other ancient remains can be found but only with some difficulty. An old ruin of a chapel long obscured by sand drifts is reputed to be on a knoll at the northwest end of the Bay, while at its other end a structure called 'The Cross' is thought to have been a stone altar. St. Columba is also reputed to have visited here to bless the well, although there is no historical evidence. On the southern slopes of MacPhee's Hill there is said to be the remains of a dun, while below the brow is a broken monolith which, if standing upright to its height of seven feet (1.8m.), would have been a prominent marker for many miles out to sea.

Sliding around on the wet rocks to get back into the skiff with the boat at anchor in the Bay is often no fun for many of the elderly visitors, although after a few hours here it is usually done in good fun. Just off the Bay itself there is a blowhole and in stormy weather its sounding spray was once thought to be the snout of a fearsome monster that lived in a nearby cave. Here, around the turn of the century, a boat crew was said to have been pursued by a creature described as 'a waterhorse but not like a waterhorse'. The shining white quartz rock that hangs down under the roof may be the source of the eirie 'light' said to come from its mouth. A more mundane explanation of the light may be the thick shoals of sand-eels which abound here and which, massed together, would shine and sparkle in the sunlight. Trawlers from Castlebay have now begun commercial exploitation of the sand-eels which are often so dense they break the nets, but which, once out of water, die. The catch is processed as meal and exported for fertiliser—which may at first seem a good proposition. However, the odds are that yet another species may be trawled out of existence, with dire results—for the sand-eels are the main source of food for other fish.

Pabbay

Above White Bay, Bagh Ban, on the east side are vague traces of an old chapel on top of a 20-foot-high (6m.) sandy burial mount, pockmarked with small rounded stones that stick out from all sides. Near the summit are two cross-incised slabs, the largest of which is four foot (1.2m.) high with a cross potent measuring eight by six inches (20 x 15cm.) carved within another cross, eleven by eight inches (28 x 20cm.). Lying downwards on the slope is another four-foot-long stone slab carved with a set of Pictish patterns. This carving was originally found by Fr. Allan MacDonald of South Uist in company with the Scottish archaeologist, Joseph Anderson, around the turn of the century, and it is the only one of its kind discovered to date in the Outer Hebrides. The main carving has been described as showing 'Vrods and crescent above a flower symbol'. Slightly off centre and to the top of the crescent shape is a crude cross that was carved by a different hand and probably later in time for the symmetry of the original design in relation to the overall shape and size of the dioritic stone was disturbed.

On many of the Pictish carvings a number of symbols are repeated in different parts of Scotland, particularly in the northeast where the majority have been found. The animal and fish representations were probably connected with a form of animal magic, a tradition that goes back to Paelolithic times. Many of the more obscure mathematical symbols and those like the comb and the mirror were probably sacred rather than secular, for at certain periods in the early Celtic church much attention was given to the accoutrements of Bishops; there were even special combs used during the service, Cuthbert's at Lindesfarne becoming a relic reputed to have healing properties. The deciphering of their carvings (which may be more than heraldic tribal emblems, the interpretation favoured by archaeologists) is just one of the

Carved Stones at Bagh Ban

many baffling aspects of these mysterious Picts. Another curious feature of the carved stones which remains unremarked is that nearly all of them have been moved from their original standing positions in the distant past, as well as the more recent removals to museums. The exact position of the Pabbay stone is conjectural (although a photograph taken in 1902 shows the long face of it pointing roughly in a north–south direction), and comment on the possible relationship between the mound and the stone even more so. However, the two main symbols—the crescent shape of the moon and the flower—are indicative of the growth of plant life. Within the top crescent, two circles may represent the waxing and waning of the moon, while the right-angled 'arrows' pointing in a downward direction, the seed. At the bottom is the crescent shape repeated, which may also indicate the mount itself with two plants emerging to form another circle before separating. So by carving out the full magical scenario to ensure the transfer of vital energy of one form to another, said to be the core of animistic belief, and placing it on the mount in order to capture the power of the moon to encourage the growth of life, a complex pattern of thought emerges from this seemingly simple design. The · understanding of the movements of celestial bodies in order to influence the natural earth energies is a closed book to most of us, so the inability to recognise or appreciate the full gamut of meanings inherent in these ancient symbols should be confronted rather than ignored. Likewise, elemental properties shaped in the form of mounds, standing stones or emerging from wells and springs were venerated in a manner whose depth of meaning, colour and feeling is far beyond us now, but in places like this mound on Pabbay there is still an inkling of that presence.

Recorded in the Castlebay church is an account of the tragedy that led to the exodus of the people of this small isle. On the 1st of May 1897 a fishing boat sank with all hands lost. The remaining families moved almost immediately. Nan MacKinnon told us about her grandmother standing on a rock in the bay collecting carageen, a seaweed then used for cooking, while the men were out fishing. Cutting the wrack with her sickle, she saw a half-fish half-woman creature, smooth and mottled without scales but with a tail similar to a mackerel, in the dark waters beneath. She was so startled that she cut her finger badly and then watched the mermaid swim through her blood as it mingled in the swell. This was clearly a bad omen and she knew the men would not return. The story had an almost dreamlike lucidity, the sight of the half-human creature in the sea swimming through the bloody water with the foreknowledge of death and then the equally sudden demise of Pabbay itself as their home. Fishermen tend not to land there, now, although it is used by a group of crofters from Barra for grazing sheep. They return en masse a few times a year on one of the larger fishing trawlers—the men, women, children and dogs all making a grand day of it after Sunday Mass.

Our own day-trip to Barra Head to begin the journey of the book at Berneray, certainly gave us a glimpse of the precarious nature of these fisher people's lives and the cheerful volatile manner in which they help each other in times of stress. The engine had failed with about ten of us in an open boat floating in the Bay and after an hour with the weather coming up, one such group of crofters leaving Pabbay picked up the distress signal. They had spent the day dipping sheep, sheering and selecting the young rams for meat. The trawler was a yelping mass of excitement as they tied up alongside the small boat and quickly decided that a tow was the best way to get us all back to Castlebay. Without such a strong sense of community, life would be intolerable if not well nigh impossible here on the fringes of the everchanging Atlantic ocean.

Sandray

It is hard to imagine anyone living on this steep hill jutting out of the sea for over 600 feet (182m.) but apparently it was farmed until the 1930s. Perhaps its good fishing loch helped the inhabitants eke out a subsistence living. The Old Norse name (Sand-Isle) is most apt for the lower slopes are covered with blown sand giving it a soft white fringe and allowing a profusion of wild flowers to blossom. A dun site is marked on the OS map and through it runs a long alignment linking ancient sites on a southwest/northeast axis, which appears to be a common throughout the long sweep of the Hebrides.

Beginning at the chapel site on Berneray, the alignment runs to Dunan Ruadh on Pabbay (Red Fort, which is a natural arch through which the herring boats sailed in calm weather); then to the dun on Sandray; to the tiny isle of Uinessan off the extreme east side of Vatersay and the church where Marion of the Heads was buried; then through the standing stone at Breivig on Barra, and on to the dun site near Bruernish at the northeast end; then across the Sound of Barra to finish at the ruined castle on Calvay Island at the entrance to Lochboisdale harbour.

Vatersay
Because of the ungainly shape of the coastline and the triangular spread of the road ending at the three main settlements at Caolis, Uidh, and the Vatersay village, it is a difficult place to explore on a quick visit. However in the vicinity of each there are some interesting examples of ancient monuments, and with the regular ferry service from Castlebay a few times a day it is worth the attempt to come to terms with its rather grave expansive terrain and the vast spread of the ocean, which is always in view. Beyond Uidh and the extreme eastern headland is the tidal isle of Uinessan. Six feet from the corner of the ruined Caibeal Mhore nam Cearn (Chapel of the Heads) is small granite slab incised with a simple cross. The area is strewn with quartz crystals, a peculiarity noticed around many other early holy places by the sea. The chapel itself is thought to have been supervised by Fineola, the wife of Gilleonan MacNeil, who received the charter to Barra and Boisdale in 1427 from the Lord of the Isles. She was known as 'Marion of the Heads' for sinister reasons. One story has her throwing the heads of her stepsons into the freshwater well in Kisimul Castle so that her son could become Chief—although Nan MacKinnon maintained that the name came from Marion's liking for cow's tongue, with a new beast being slaughtered for every dinner. Marion was eventually buried in a cairn against the outer wall of the chapel facing towards Canna, which she had inherited from her first husband. The weather was so bad, the bearers stood the coffin upright and covered it with stones. Mary MacLeod, a 16th-century bardess, is said to have been buried face

downwards at Rodel in Harris, so whatever significance there was in the deviation from the usual practice in the burial of famous Marys of the Isles, it seems to be related to their deep devotion to the Virgin. During the late medieval period her cult flourished throughout Christendom, and on Barra it has continued to the present. During the 1954 Marion Year, a large marble statue of the Mother and Child was erected on Heaval, 1,200 feet (364m.) above Castlebay.

On the way down to the village there is the gaunt wreck of a fighter plane from World War Two and a granite memorial to the tragic foundering in 1852 of the 'Annie Jame' with a large number of emigrants aboard on their way to Canada who never survived the storm. The cattle grazing on the machair are a welcome sight. Noticeable too and quite unusual in the Hebrides, the sheep are kept fenced in on the highest slopes, which allows a wide variety of flora to proliferate. The sand dunes of the narrow isthmus immediately beyond the new community centre are covered in wild flowers during late spring and summer. King cups, primroses, marsh orchis, ragwort, butterwort, birdsfeet trefoil, cuckoo flowers, daises, calandines, violets and cotton grasses were noted during a random walk towards the remains of the dun about a quarter of a mile west of the dusty collection of small houses above the sand dunes. Further over towards the southwest corner on the slopes of Ben Rulibrech is a sheltered hollow that was once used as a 'cuithe', or stock enclosure, which contains a five-foot-high (1.4m) stone that appears as if it were part of the main entrance. It has been noted as a 'standing stone', but because of its shape it seems unlikely that it was ever meant to be viewed in isolation from the enclosure, which also has the remains of three other 'portals'. A number of similar rectangular structures can be found elsewhere in the Hebrides, either with the portal stones or the midpoint of the walls set fairly accurately on the cardinal compass points. Beyond here on the final slopes above the sea is a broken monolith. Now covered in grey lichen and split in two halves, each six foot (1.8m.) high but of enormous girth with one stump still protruding from the earth, this megalithic giant would have been an impressive territorial reminder to those people who first sailed around these Isles over 4,000 years ago.

On the road to Caolis from the new jetty in Cornaig Bay the ruined circular broch, Dun a'Chaolais, is full of loose stones and without much of its original outer walling. However, among the debris portions of a gallery constructed of large lintels can be seen, as well as a small oval cell. There is another ruin of a fort, Dun Birualum, on the extreme west side, accessible at low tide only—but the beautiful beach, Traigh Varlish, should not be missed. Spending time on any of these small islands induces a degree of heightened awareness of the sudden changes of air and temperature. Movements of birds and animals seem to become languid, as if the creatures are aware of the lack of people. Even a shift of the clouds or a pause in a squall changes the mood. And the clear nights leading up to a full moon have to be seen to be believed, for the moonlight, especially in winter, makes everything visible with a strange silvery glow for almost twice the length of time the sun is out. On first arriving in the Hebrides, the contrast between the mainland and the large islands is as marked as when one moves to a smaller isle, and so it continues until you may be lucky enough to reach a rock totally enclosed by water so that—by merely looking around—you can see everything there is to be seen at a glance. It is at such moments that understanding begins to dawn. For people who were content to live on these small islands, nature's rhythms and perceptions were such an inherent part of their lives that even the lilting speech reflected the constant motion of natural phenomena.

Fuday

Among a plethora of isles off the northeastern coast of Barra, such as Hellisay, Gighay, Orosay, Fiaray, Lingay and Fuday, the last-named is the biggest and most interesting historically. Said to be the final stronghold of the Norse in the Isles after their defeat at Largs, it also has a 'Well of the Heads,' which connects the place to the infamous Marion. It is located near the shore by Cordale Bay with its flat cover stone still in place—for the locals apparently feared that it would inundate Fuday if misused. Famed as an oracle well, and like most oracles the 'heads' would probably give obscure and often contradictory advise, it was also said to have been used by

MacNeil who, when wanting favouring winds for sailing his biorlinn, would simply stir the well with his Chief's wand. This distinction has also been claimed for a well on Gighay when MacNeil's boat was becalmed.

One of the stories told by the Coddy from Northbay concerns an illegitimate son of the MacNeil who gained the 'love' of a Norse princess in order to learn about the island's defences. Later he led a raid and slaughtered every last one of the Norsemen on the island. The last three had their heads cut off and thrown into the well, hence its name, Tobar na Ceinn. The small cairns that are such a noticeable feature of the northern headland are said to be their graveplaces. At the south end of Traig na Reill there are the scanty remains of an Iron Age 'Red Fort', and stone cists with human bones inside have been reported exposed near here after severe gales.

There is no normal access to Fuday or any of the other small isles but one of the fishermen out of Eoligarry can usually be prevailed upon to take one across and to return later on the turn of the tide. Except for the small flock of sheep and the rabbits hopping about among the short grassed hills and the spiky marron of the dunes, the 'I am monarch of all I survey' feeling is wonderful. It brings back a bit of adventure into one's life, especially when scanning the sea for that boat hours later and worrying if this was the actual prearranged pickup spot rather than a half mile down the beach.

Eriskay

One wonders what the exile brought up on the Eriskay Boat Song might feel on returning here without any close ties of living kinship. Its charm is said to be hidden rather deep, and it is not the most prepossessing of isles for the casual visitor either. There is a frequent but small ferry service from Ludac across the Sound in South Uist. The road curves among its stony terrain, and houses look as they have emerged from the rock. At the time of the clearances it was considered such a poor deal that the evicted tenants from the best lands were magnanimously allowed to settle here. However, with a good harbour fishing became their main source of livelihood, which it still is today. Another speciality of Eriskay are the patterned jerseys with narratives built-in to the design, available from the cooperative shop. The church of St. Michael's at Rhuban, built in 1903 from money raised initially by Fr. Allen MacDonald, is an extraordinary example of Catholic kitsch. The overall design has Spanish influence, the bell comes from a German battleship sunk in Scapa Flow, and the altar was made from a local wreck with a lifeboat from the aircraft carrier 'Hermes' standing on golden anchors and great coils of rope. A small, whitish-grey pony may still be seen here; though once quite common on Barra, the breed, born black, is now near to extinction. The football pitch and the island rubbish compound are at either end of the beach, where the famous convulvus, a sea bindweed (*Calystegia Soldanella*), blooms pink during July. Its common name is Prince Edward's flower, as the islanders believe that the King brought the plant with him in 1744 when he first landed on the beach to begin his unfortunate attempt to claim the crown. He also left the recipe for making Drambuie behind him.

On Stac Islands, off the southern end of the main Isle, is Weaver's Castle. This was once a stronghold of pirates who harassed all shipping from this impregnable spot—so the name may originally have been 'Reaver's Castle'. There is a story by the Coddy that this MacNeil kidnapped a beautiful girl who then fell in love with him and became his mate in every sense, helping him with the wrecking and plundering. Eventually, the reaver and his lass were captured and executed on Eriskay. A completely different sort of tale has been compiled from the notebooks of Fr. Allan MacDonald, who was interested in ghosts and hauntings, and occult phenomena. Between 1895–97 he recorded instances of premonitions of death, uncanny noises and strange lights in the night, flying balls of fire, ghost pipers, the washer women, mysterious voices and, of course, haunted dwellings. Ada Goodrich Freer, on her journey around the Isles at the turn of the century, as a representative of the London Society for Psychical Research, is said to have got on well with the priest, and in fact much of the material on second-sight which she used in her writings in the *Folklore Journal* (Vol. 10 and 13) apparently came from his conversations and notes. From his *Traditional Ghost Stories*, two examples give the sense of the uncanny that still often prevails on many of the small islands.

During the spring of 1887 a bird with a terrible scream was observed to fly across Eriskay from time to time during the night. None of the inhabitants ever saw its like before. Angus Johnson told Fr. Allan that he heard it at his house and what was more it seemed to be pushing against the door and making as much noise outside as possible. The autumn of that year was sadly memorable for an epidemic of measles which killed many of the young children, among them the only daughter of Johnson, who had told his account of the strange bird long before her illness. On the night of Christmas 1890 a singular phenomenon was seen from Eriskay by several people. In the sky towards the east above Fuday was a revolving bright light that continued to appear and then disappear like the beam of a flashlight. White and bright, it was seen on three separate occasions. It was thought it might have been a lunar reflection from some distant lighthouse. I experienced the same phenomenon myself on Rousay in Orkney over 20 years ago. The beam of light across the ground was so bright that it seemed as if there was a lighthouse revolving from the top of the hill illuminating a flickering path right out to sea. It was a clear crisp night with much the same conditions that produce Aurora Borealis and the moonbow effect when its light is actually convex to the curve of the sky rather than to the ground. Yet I still remember the uncanny silence of it and the fact that the light appeared to rise from the ground into the air so that one was surrounded by a column of intense light for almost a minute, to be then absorbed by the darkness as the beam moved around the island. There seems little doubt that this was much the same phenomenon as was seen from Eriskay, although over the distant isle of Fuday.

In 1941, a 12,000-ton cargo ship, *SS Politician*, hit the Hartemul rocks on its way to America with a cargo of a quarter-million bottles of whisky aboard, and eventually sank in the Sound of Eriskay. The rescue of the cargo by the local people with any kind of vessel that could possibly float, and the subsequent attempts by the Inland Revenue to retrieve such ill-gotten gains, have been fictionalised in Compton MacKenzie's *Whisky Galore*. The hilarious film of the book was shot on location in Barra. Skin divers continue to bring up the occasional undrinkable curiosity from the sea bottom, and one of the proudest displays to be seen on a kitchen dresser and mantlepiece hereabouts is one of those long squarish half-pint bottles encrusted with shells and seagrime.

Dun Briste on Barra Head, Berneray, looking towards Mingulay

In Praise of the Uists

Standing Stone, Pollacher, S. Uist. Barra in the background.

South Uist

Long and narrow, this island is only eight miles across at its greatest width, yet the bog-strewn rugged eastern area presents the usual forbidding obstacles to casual exploration. Geographically it is similar to the rest of the Hebrides with numerous lochs, inlets, skerries and broad stretches of unrelieved peat moor. Indented by a series of substantial sea lochs that were probably utilised more in the past than at present, with the exception of the coastal area around Loch Boisdale, it is largely uninhabited. Along the western coast of its 22 miles length is a fair stretch of good machair land, and travelling on the main road with its contiguous habitations, old and new, means that it is difficult to avoid a north/south movement. However, a glance at the map will show a host of minor roads, and tracks branch off the A865. To explore the most interesting of the ancient sites demands a constant to-ing and fro-ing from this narrow highway. South of Daliburgh, for instance, is one of the best examples of an 'aisled-house', at Kilpheder among the sand dunes close to the sea. Castle Calvay is not much to look at and almost impossible to see close-to due to its situation on the craggy top of an island, but the journey to North Glendale and then the mile trek over a hillside is worth considering because of the constant presence of the sea below. Dun Trossary is visible from the main road, nearly opposite the schoolhouse at Garrynamonie. Now part of a massive concrete sheep fank, from its profile and jumble of fallen stones – there is one nine-foot-high standing stone – it was clearly originally a Neolithic chambered cairn of some importance. For those with an eye to the ironies of local history, the walled garden in the now deserted Kilbride might be the place to begin after stepping from the ferry at Ludac. It was built by the MacDonald of Boisdale, who was the first to introduce the potato and the manufacture of kelp into Uist in 1745, and who is remembered as an obsessive tyrant who cleared the tenants from their land with great brutality. Dun Trossary can also be a starting point for a leisurely jaunt around the slopes of Easaval (250m.). And if you want to follow the journey of this book, then the six-foot-high (1.8m.) lichen-covered standing stone at Pollachar, marking the old landing spot from Barra, is where to begin.

If the folk songs of an area can be defined as the unwritten history by and of unfamous people then the great headland between Loch Boisdale and the Sound of Eriksay is favoured indeed. It may not have been the most amenable in terms of terrain and weather but for those who once lived there it appears to have provided most of the needs for mind and body as well as the inspiration for their songs. North Glendale is still inhabited but on the track over the hills to South Glendale there are enough ruined habitations to show that it was once a thriving community in spite of its bleakness and poor soil. Even as late as the 1930's, Margaret Fay Shaw recorded and translated many of the songs from its elderly members – but now the place is filled with windy ghosts and grey memories. Amid a landscape dominated and dotted with grey igneous rocks are the crumbling remains of stone walls and outlined strips of raised pasture. Known as 'lazy-beds', they were initially built-up and fertilised with dried sea wrack, and then turned by the foot plough, a cas chrom, to plant oats and potatoes. The old blackhouses have collapsed and the scattered townships are in ruins. Usually drenched in mist from the cold encircling sea, the headland has its own special atmosphere.

One of the songs from her book, *Folksongs of South Uist* (1955), with its chorus 'O I love Uist of the high hills/The land of heroes who were strong and hospitable/Who won honour for ClanRanald' points up the picturesque vision they held of themselves. 'In Praise of the Uists' presents an image of the locals as a valiant people – in fact, not altogether that different from what is printed in today's tourist brochures, except *then* it was the islanders themselves who were praised rather than heaps of old stone! Ormiclate Castle is still roofless but its crumbling masonry has deteriorated so badly that it ought to be repointed before it adds an unfortunate footnote to its short-lived history.

You who travel over to Uist by boat
Will find history on your route
And will strengthen your health.

You will find men there kindly and generous;
You will see beauty there in bloom.
Between Iochdar and Pollachar
The sun does not shine on a more beautiful place.

You will go to Lochboisdale on the 'Staffa',
A fair village and safe haven.
Who ever went there but was happy
And constantly praising its inhabitants?

You will see Eriskay of the flowers
Planted there by Prince Charles.
And the ruin of Airigh Mhuillinn
Where Flora MacDonald was born.

Though Ormiclate Castle is roofless,
Often the bard's voice was heard there,
Raising a lay to the valour of champions
Who won honour for ClanRanald.

The girls of Uist are pretty,
Like the glitter of sun on gold;
Though you will not understand 'a Laobhra' ['by the book',
    the Bible]
They will address you in well expressed Gaelic.

Loch Skiport is a pretty township
Where I myself lived for a while;
Where I and my bonny children
Raised a Jubilee Cairn to Queen Victoria.

But if you go northwards to Iochdar,
Far north to the edge of the shore,
Take care when crossing (the ford)
That the tide will not drown you.

The rather pedestrian translation into English gives no hint of the rhythmic lilt of the original song written by a schoolmaster from Loch Skiport who later emigrated to Canada. His final note of warning against the dangers of the quicksands when crossing the tidal estuary no longer applies for a bridge was built during World War Two to link South Uist with Benbecula. Iochdar, now called Eochan, is on a minor road off the A865 and if one continues around the top of Loch Bee, it eventually becomes a track across the dunes. Between the entire length of the loch and the sea are the red 'Danger Area' signs, for it is frequently used by the military.

Lochboisdale.

Apart from the solid-looking comfortable hotel which serves an excellent breakfast, there is little of interest here, although the town is being modernised as a proper ferry terminal. Formerly an old crofting village, it has always profited from the wide estuary's safe anchorage for boats during bad weather. Now dotted with sailing yachts during the summer, the town—as the entry point for the Caledonian MacBrayne ferry—has become part of the three-mile ribbon development along the entire length of the road to Daliburgh with houses, schools, modern shopping facilities, some small factories, hotels, garages and a hospital.

Although it is only about half a mile north of the road, the chambered cairn at the top end of Loch a Bharp may take a considerable time to get to because the terrain is really boggy. Also marked on the OS map are a number of stone crossings across the Loch that should be approached with care during the rain periods, and even on a dry day Wellington boots are advisable. However, for all that it is worth the effort because the cairn is in a state of good preservation. The large ring of upright stones that supported the smaller packing material of the circular cairn is now covered with grey-green lichen, and some large impressive slabs up to nine foot (2.3m.) long surround the central chamber so the interior of this megalithic structure is visible. But it was the notion of sacred space, the axis mundi connecting earth and heaven, that was probably important for the people who built and used such solid architecture that has stood for at least 5,000 years. So a few

Chambered Cairn at Loch a 'Bharp

minutes' rest by the trickling waters of a small burn, below the field from where the top of the stone cairn is visible, will not only be refreshing after the plod through the bog but should also put one into the proper mood before crossing the stepping stones into this ancient domain. I do admit that on the heather-covered hillside it is almost impossible now to imagine the setting with any kind of grandeur, but a few hundred yards to the northeast past a 12-foot-high (3.6m.) pointed stone is a natural rock plateau. This may have been a ceremonial spot, as the top of the cairn is visible within the grand sweep across the shallow valley that leads down to Loch Boisdale and the open sea.

Admiral Boyle Somerville visited here in 1909 as part of his research into the connections between celestial alignments and ancient sites. He suggested that there were possible solar orientations from the round cairn, north to Ben Shuravat and south of Easaval, but that there was, however, 'an interesting orientation to the sunrise of the day of the winter solstice about which there can be little doubt'. This was by means of a large spherical boulder that can be seen from the Bharp clearly against the sky, resting on a flat crest of a ridge of hills about two miles away. Somerville thought that either the boulder was moved or even that the cairn itself was built on a rather low-lying area so that the sunrise behind it, on probably the most imortant day of the year for the ancients, would be visible from inside the central chamber. A similar phenomenon has been shown to exist at Newgrange, near the River Boyne in County Meath, Ireland. Over the main entrance a substantial stone slot or box was discovered that allows the sun to beam down the 60-foot-long (18m.) inner passageway and flood the central chamber soon after it rises on 21st December.

Just over two miles north–northeast of the Barp is a low underground passageway that joins up three ruined stone beehive houses. The tunnel is over 30 feet (9m.) long and was built of drystone walling up to about three feet high, and then corbelled over with irregular slabs. This souterrain is situated at Beal a Choalais, a pass at the base of the southern slopes of Stulaval, and from which there is a sharp descent to the rocky coast. The flattish bogland must be traversed for at least half the journey, but once on the slopes of Clett (188m.) the ground is firmer with a rakish climb to the pass. The site is about 300 yards north–northeast of Loch nam Arm. As always with these underground passage constructions, one marvels at the extent of human ingenuity in overcoming a variety of problems to do with the terrain, materials and the need for shelter and storage. They are found mainly on the hilly eastern side of the Uists.

Aisled-House at Kilpheder

The narrow road past Kilpheder becomes a track on the dunes, and a few hundred yards after it fords a small stream a ruined circular structure can be seen surrounded by a sagging wire fence. It was excavated by T.C. Lethbridge in 1952 at the behest of Werner Kissing, who has lived on Uist and other isles for many years. When I met him recently, this thin gaunt man was practically blind but could recall quite clearly his first visit to St. Kilda in 1906 with his mother, a German Countess. He handed out white gloves to the children for their first communion. His marvellous photographs of the islands and

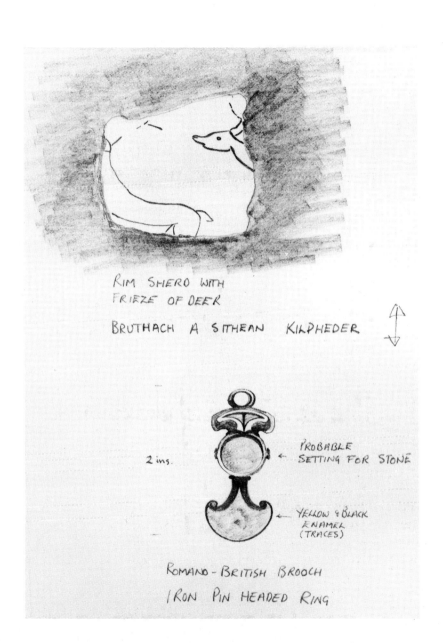

RIM SHERD WITH
FRIEZE OF DEER

BRUTHACH A SITHEAN KILPHEDER

PROBABLE
SETTING FOR STONE

2 ins.

YELLOW & BLACK
ENAMEL
(TRACES)

ROMANO-BRITISH BROOCH
IRON PIN HEADED RING

Artifacts found at Kilpheder. (National Museum of Antiquities of Scotland, Edinburgh)

islanders are now in the archives of the School of Scottish
Studies, Edinburgh. He also illustrated Lethbridge's book,
The Painted Men (1954), that unfortunately has never been
reprinted. It vividly recreates the life of the ancient hunters
and gatherers and herdsmen who once lived hereabouts.
From the huge quantities of bird and animal bones, pottery,
and bone spindles, bobbins and pins found locally, the house
has been dated to about the second century AD. Its circular
complex was built on hard sand but in time became covered
by blown sand, which probably gave rise to the confusion
between the souterrain, or true underground house, and the
wheelhouses found buried in the sand. There are at least eight
radial stone piers that supported corbelled roofs making up
separate chambers that opened onto a centre courtyard which
was unroofed and contained the fire-area. The whole complex
would have been about 20 feet in diameter, and with the
remains of the midden pilled up around the outer wall, the
roof could have been used quite extensively as in some of
North African communities. A mile to the north, at a place
called Sithean a Phiobarie ('Fairy Hill of the Piper') are the
remains of another aisled-house, and Lethbridge thought that
all such sithean were possibly once wheel-houses. However,
since his time despoliation of some of these 'fairy mounds' has
revealed large amounts of bones, pottery and other midden
but no significant stone structures beneath them.

Sir Lindsay Scott, who excavated some of these ancient
habitations in the Hebrides, was of the opinion that the brochs
and duns were merely one element in a whole culture and that
an intellible account of the builders involves, 'a study of the
wheelhouses which are closely related structures revealing a
nearly identical material culture'. Since then, Dun Cuier on
Barra was excavated by Alison Young, and the pottery shards
and bone artifacts were similar to those recovered from Dun
Scurrival, a fort a few miles to the north. As well as the refuse
from the shells of oysters, scallops, mussels, limpets, cockles
and whelks, bird bones and general household midden of the
period, the remains of broken moulds for making penannular
brooches indicate that metal was also worked. Bone dies,
rather like those used for dominoes, were also found and are
similar to those found in the earth-house at Fosigarry in North

Uist. The finds by Lethbridge at the Kilpheder aisled-house conform to this general picture. From the mounds of refuse left behind at these sites it would seem that the people who lived in aisled- or wheelhouses were co-existent in time with—or may have even been—the dun builders. The general distributive pattern of fort and habitation sites along the western machair adds strength to this supposition. The gradual unfolding of an understanding, of fleshing out these nameless groups who seemed to live almost entirely on shell fish, is an unequivocal triumph for archaeologists patiently working at different sites during the past 30 years.

The Old Kelp Factory at Boisdale

It was while hunting in vain for a low fairy mount along the flat coastal area about a mile north of the Pollachar Inn that we first became intrigued by a gaunt structure outlined against an azure skyline quite early on a summer's morning. Any such point of focus in this nondescript landscape commands attention. Even though the old seaweed factory had closed down only three months before, it had already acquired the derelict appearance of an industrial tomb. The weather in the isles is not kind to any material less durable than stone, and the metal gates flapping open to wind and rain had already begun the process of corrosion that would eventually reduce the vast rectangular corrugated building to yet another picturesque ruin. Overhead huge curved dryers stretched the length of the shed and back again in a U-shaped loop. Loose electricity cables hung down from the walls. In the still pools of oil and water gleaming on the concrete floor, a variety of metal junk lay scattered around. The oppressive silence and shades of light through the large doors gave the impression of being in a set from a moody Expressionist film but with an eirie feeling of time itself transfixed. Wandering among the stinking mountainous heaps of brittle tangles heaped by the maws of the rusted drying machines, it was difficult to ascertain if the industrial hum had really ceased—as one half expected at any moment to see a line of ghost workers march in to pull some hidden switch that would set the place in motion again.

The sign on the clean concrete wall outside, 'Alginate Industries', brought us back to earth. Kelp is a byword for exploitation in Hebridean history and the almost casual closure of this factory that had been operating for 30 years with the sacking of over 50 men is but the most recent instance. No one seemed to be making a fuss over it. The islanders appear to accept such misfortunate passively. An American company had taken over this and five other factories in the Western and Northern Isles, and when 'Head Office' decided that greater profits could be made by importing cheaper powder from the Argentine, where the weed is actually dried in the heat of the sun, they closed down four of the plants. Apparently an engineer from the Falklands was flown over because the machines there dry the wet wrack by a more modern method, but little could be done with the antiquated Hebridean dryers to make them more efficient. The dried powder is used in a variety of manufacturing and chemical industries—including producing the froth on top of a pint of beer! We learned this and the meagre details of the fate of the factory from one of the redundant workers who had been employed here since it opened and, I suppose out of habit, still rode over on his push-bike. As we stood by the roadside near the derelict building chatting to the man with bicycle clips on his neat serge trousers, the Falklands War was taking place in the South Atlantic, and I am sure that none of the British soldiers were aware that with every pint of beer consumed aboard the naval flotilla, they added that 'extra' to the Argentine economy.

The kelp used was the large tangles, *Laminaria Digitata* and *Laminaria Saccharina*, that are cast up in such quantities on the flat coasts, particularly after storm weather. The black and bladder wracks were collected on the tidal shores of the east coast. The term 'kelp' was also used to describe the alkaline ashes of the weed when burnt in kilns or pits along the foreshore. MacDonald of Boisdale first introduced the method here from Ireland in 1735. Having begun in a modest way with spasmodic collection by the local people, as a windfall from the terrible gales, the collecting—being less dangerous and more reliable than fishing—became organised and the drying process was refined until it became a skilled job to fire the kilns and produce quality ash with a good percentage of potassium chloride, potassium sulphate and sodium chloride. It helped stem the flood of emigration from the Western Highlands and Islands. The price per ton gradually rose, first during the American War of Independence and later in the Napoleonic War, because barilla, then used as soda-ash for glass, soap and linen, could not be imported. In 1750 kelp fetched £1 per ton but by the end of the century it had risen to £20 per ton, falling to half that figure when European hostilities ceased in 1822. All the island lairds and their factors, the tacksmen, took full advantage of the kelp boom: for example, the proprietor of North Uist was making £14,000 a year at the peak, which even in those days was an extraordinary profit for little or no outlay. It was during this period that the crofting system took hold, for to ensure a ready supply of hands for intensive collecting at the beginning of spring, people were given a small piece of land in return for their labour. And even though the tenants received relatively good wages when compared with other workers and trades of this period, the system of barter (there were no shops and no tradesmen)—food in return for their work— operated through the tacksman. So apart from creating a new class of gentry with little social conscience and great expectations from far-flung islands that, for most people of that time, could have been off the coast of Africa rather than western Scotland, and helped by their factors (powerful middle-men whose word was absolute law), it also set into motion a chain of cause and effect that continues even now.

Crofting is the most intractable economic problem in the Hebrides today, for though most crofts are only the equivalent of a large garden in a mild climate, each plot has become fixated as part of a deep emotional bond. It is always easy to be wise with hindsight but essentially what occurred was that the times of collecting and drying the kelp coincided with both the periods of planting and the beginning of the fishing season, so the former was neglected and the latter declined during the half-century when living conditions radically improved for many people. However, as the price of potash began to drop so 'rents' were raised to compensate for the fall of the tacksmen's profits and each plot of useless land began to assume for the tenants an importance it never previously had. During this period the population of the Isles

increased a hundred-fold and by 1840 was reckoned to be
90,000, over three times its present total. The clearances and
forced emigration that followed were yet another grim repeat
of Hebridean history.

Almost at the same time as the kelp industry collapsed,
whisky-distilling, which had been a booming cottage
industry, was made legal under the provenance of large-scale
manufacturers. The herring shoals, too, deserted the inland
lochs during the 1830s and the potato that had first been
introduced to Uist by the same MacDonald of Boisdale a
century earlier had the blight in the 1840s, causing starvation
here as in all the outlying non-industrial areas of Great Britain.
For many people it seemed as if the hand of God had turned
against them. In the wake of the uncompromising message of
the Wee Free preachers the people of Skye, North Uist, Harris
and Lewis willingly threw their musical instruments and
books on bonfires to atone for the evil that had been wrought
on them. And once again they were being moved from their
homes to make room for large sheep farms, for wool had
become the new panacea of the gentry that would take care of
all their money problems.

It was against such a background of relative stability
followed by sudden unrest from a universe beyond their small
island world that many families refused to leave. Living on the
extreme rocky headlands where there was no possibility that
such land could be needed for man or beast, they began to eke
out a pitiful existence close to the earth and wedded to the
fierce elements that surrounded them. Even today, the
headland south of Lochboisdale feels almost a place apart from
the rest of Uist and it is here that one begins to appreciate both
the mysterious imaginative quality that gave birth to the
songs and the haunting melancholic air so characteristic of
Hebridean music.

Giant's Grave, South Lochboisdale

It was Donald MacDonald, a local poet, who showed us the
site of the Giant's Grave near his home. We had been directed
to him as someone conversant with the old tales, and as soon
as we arrived at his cottage in the late afternoon, he said: 'I was
just about to sink into my boots, lads'. It turned out that while

we were exploring the aisled-house near Kilpheder, he himself was not too far away at a funeral of his best friend. In fact we had visited the burying ground at Loch Hallan, after leaving the deserted kelp factory, and even saw the open grave without putting too much thought on it. For those who are attracted to graveyards this one is a classic. Its exposed and almost inaccessible position near the army firing range between the loch and sea, as well as the enormous spread of graves with the timely reminders of ancient weathered crosses, wrought-iron rococo-work and the garish cheerfulness of modern stonework, gave one the creepy feeling of entering a forest of memorial remembrance. Of course it is nothing on the scale of Père-Lachaise cemetery in Paris, but for the dedicated connoisseur this little resting place by the sea, like quite a few others in the Isles, might well be worth a visit.

While we were having a lukewarm cup of tea from a cracked mug I picked up Fay Shaw's book from the table and Donald recited 'In Praise of Uist' in the original. He himself wrote only in Gaelic and even though he quoted by heart some of the great Elizabethan and Romanic poets, he felt that his own work was somehow inadequate because his poetry could only be paraphrased into English. The legacy of cultural imperialism that was so forcefully imposed on the Western Highlands after the defeat at Culloden, when the native tongue was forbidden by law, continues to undermine the islanders' confidence in their language and traditions over 200 years later.

As we walked through the croftland over the strong, almost gaseous-smelling bog, towards the peat workings on the lower slopes of Easaval, Donald recounted the story of the Giant. The last mortal occupier of Castle Calvay, isolated on a rugged isle at the mouth of the sea estuary, was a giant named Iain Breschid, or John the Pox, for his face was pitted and ugly. He was a pirate who terrorized the people, but after he kidnapped a beautiful girl they decided they had had enough of his bullying. Setting fire to the windward end of the castle with a great quantity of heather, they rescued the maiden by standing on each other's shoulders until they could reach the room where she was held captive. Iain escaped by leaping

Giant's Grave

across the gap between Calvay Isle and the mainland, but after running for a few miles he lay down to rest in the lee of the hill at this very spot beyond South Lochboisdale. While he was asleep a Barra-man pushed a huge boulder on top of him and the place where he was crushed to death is known as Beallach Iain—John's Gap. Some weeks later, while Keith was drawing the Giant's Grave, a little woman came over the hill, squatted down between the large boulders and like a child talked of the treasure that was buried underneath. Her clear blue eyes and the ruddy complexion of her cheeks peeping out from behind the megalith made the rainbow that magically appeared in the sky directly behind her, dull in comparison. We had met this elderly fairy on the same day as Donald the Poet, and under equally curious circumstances. The final glimpse of her going over the hill, carrying a sack of peat on her shoulder like a spry young woman, embodied all the qualities of resiliance and unearthliness that pervades this lovely southern headland below Loch Boisdale.

Standing Stone, Beinn a Charra

This is the largest standing stone in South Uist. Seventeen feet (5m.) high by six feet (1.8m.) broad, it had sat high on the south-facing slopes of the hill completely dominating the surrounding terrain for miles in a wide arc to the sea. Recently, however, this 'monarch' has been surpassed in glory beneath a gleaming white concrete water-substation. No one could reasonably accuse the Western Isles Authority of lack of thought or consideration because there is a good road leading up to this white bunker, with car-parking facilities from which to look down on the top of the standing stone to the coastal stretch beyond. Nevertheless a very subtle displacement has taken place, for the ancient power-stone of the island is in fact now visibly awkward in its present configuration and psychologically redundant. The same thing has happened on Barra and on other Isles too. A function of these old stones perhaps was to help draw up the natural energy from a particular confluence of springs deep inside the rock and disseminate it through the environment, whereas the new structures are nothing less than glorified 'header-tanks' storing water from a very wide strata. It is in fact a radical shift in attitude from an older recognition that the vital properties of nature could be harnessed for people's benefit and in harmony with the land, to the modern withdrawal from anything harder than turning on a water tap.

Many of the other monuments are in a deplorable state through natural erosion and neglect, but a levy on the vast sums spent by the Military and Western Isles Council, construcing excellent roads to service installations, might help to conserve some of the ancient heritage of the Hebrides. In general such roads have no other purpose except ease of access without houses or crofts nearby. The sop to the tourist trade in signposting an ancient site, rather than having a 'No Entry' sign, is actually part of a new public-relations policy. It blankets questioning about initial decision-making, siting, cost and – most important of all – the real purpose behind such installations. Perhaps in centuries to come, if they have survived, the proximity of these outlandish-looking structures to megalithic remains may produce a crop of nutty theories about the connection between 20th-century

Standing Stone, An Charra

technology and the remnants of fringe religion, citing the 'typology of construction', 'common processional routes', and possible 'ritual connections', as proof.

Two miles to the southwest the megalithic complex beyond Loch Bornish has almost disappeared from view. If it had not been for a local man who showed us the actual spot with only a few inches of a six-foot-long stone showing, the odds are that it would have been completely covered during the next big storm. It is now partly dug out and marked with a stake, but the remaining standing stones have long disappeared under tons of blown sand.

Less than two miles to the north along this coastal strip is another important landmark in local history, Ormiclate Castle. The crumbling masonry from the high walls that are usually full of nesting birds, make it now something of a hazard. It took seven years to build. The French-born wife of Allan MacDonald apparently refused to live in the nearby house because, she said, her father's hen house was in better condition. When it was completed in 1708 by a French architect and imported masons, it was the finest building in South Uist. The main three-storey block (70x25 feet/21x7m.) had a 20-foot-square wing projecting southwards. However, as the chief residence of the ClanRanald, it was gutted by fire seven years later when the contiguous single-storied kitchen caught alight as revellers were roasting a whole venison to celebrate the coming victory on the eve of the battle of Sherrifmuir. MacDonald was killed there the following day. Thereafter the MacDonalds moved to Nunton, in Benbecula. The original seven-foot-wide double fireplace with its two splendid chimneys, one inside the other, is now exposed in the old kitchen. Beneath the original ceiling-timbers there is a wonderful atmosphere full of old junk, nets, hooks for meats, a smoking cabinet in the chimney and a large anvil used as an altar to marry many desperate lovers, but that practice stopped about the same time as at Gretna Green when the necessary pre-requirement of 'reading the bans' for three weeks was altered in England.

Repairs are urgently needed to prevent the walls from collapsing. One would have thought that there were at least a few energetic descendants of the MacDonalds who could start a preservation fund to repair and even perhaps restore it as the MacNeils of Barra did with Kisimul Castle. The farmer nearby was quite worried in case someone got hurt, and said that he actually stopped two people with a long ladder from attempting to remove the armorial panel over the large main entrance of the castle. When asked to cease such vandalism they merely replied that the old ruin was about to fall down anyway and they wanted the panel as a holiday souvenir. The farmhouse is thought to be the oldest on Uist, and it was here that the Prince was supposed to have met Flora MacDonald, before he left for Skye disguised as her maid. After the defeat at Culloden, he had returned to the Outer Isles a fugitive, with a price of £20,000 on his head. Nearly every natural cave, hovel and house in South Uist has a story about him hiding from the redcoats. The house where Flora MacDonald was born is also in a ruinous state, with a memorial cairn next to it just off the main road at Mingary a few miles south of the castle.

Far be it from me to suggest that all these ruined buildings should be restored to please future generations of tourists, but in fact they are often the only extant visible evidence of early building. Proper signs and more information would help local people as well as outsiders to gain a perspective into the confused sagas of the past, and to appreciate more the structural and architectural qualities of their own heritage.

Chapel Ruins at Howmore
Though scheduled as an ancient monument, a glance at the state of the masonry, the weeds and nettles inside, and general dilapidation throughout the chapel ruins at Howmore, might make even a philistine pause and wonder why the remains of such valuable sources of history are left to crumble away. Once a mediaeval priory of international repute, it was destroyed like so many other early ecclesiatical establishments after the Reformation in the 16th century. The ruins now comprise the remains of Chaibel nan Sagairt and Chaibel Diarmud, both about 20 feet (6m.) long; the three–foot–wide north wall of Teampull Mor, which is all that is left of a rectangular structure that was over 60 feet (18m.) long; and the gable wall of St. Columba's Church and St. Marys, also 20

feet long, which is in fact outside the old burying ground.

Muir in 1847 recorded a group of five chapels inside the grounds but on a second visit found one of them completely removed. 'The missing one was a very characteristic building, the smallest of the group, with a very narrow rectangular window and a short sloping doorway in each end. Externally it measured only 17 feet in length.' Against the inner gable of Chaibel nan Sagairt can be seen an armorial panel with figures carved in relief showing a lymphed with a rudder, central mast and sail, a hand with a cross, a castle, a lion rampant and a bird on a thostle ship. The ancient chiefs of ClanRanald were buried here at Howmore, and in fact, the name 'howe' is derived from Old Norse, and means mount, barrow or place of sacrifice. Three hundred yards (273m.) from the chapel complex is a large elongated mount with a built-up stone cairn and a boulder on top.

A small river meanders through the sands around here, making Howmore one of the most restful places in Uist. An added bonus for the impoverished traveller, student, cyclist or hiker, is the tiny hostel with a thatch roof, run by the Gatliff Trust. Founded for the encouragement of adventure among

Ruined chapels, Howmore

the young and the always-young-at-heart who visit the Outer Isles, the old cottage offers simple, cook-it-yourself facilities at cheap rates for anyone caught out in the frequent stormy weather and not able to find or afford a bed and breakfast for the night. As well as the one here, Gatliff hostels are located at Lochmaddy and Claddach Baleshare on North Uist, Berneray in the Sound of Harris, and at Rhenigidale and Kyles Stockinish on Harris.

A refreshing night at the hostel might also give one the urge to explore some of the ancient sites that can be found in the immediate vicinity. This suggested route is almost a circular three-mile walk over a variety of terrain from the coast to the uplands with constantly changing vistas. It is only when one leaves the main road that the feeling of remoteness can seep through the sensory pores, for essentially the islands have not changed all that much even with the introduction of motorized traffic. From the ruins go north along the track through the sandy area by the sea to just beyond Caistell Bheagram. This 12-foot-high ruin, reputed to be a prison, once had an encircling wall but this is now reduced to its foundations on the edges of the small circular isle in the loch.

Turn right at Drimsdale, formally a farm that was once tenanted by the brother of the famous poet, Alexander MacDonald, and then cross over the main road, go through a gate and follow the track to the sluice gates by the edge of Loch Druidibeg. Continue on the left-hand grass-covered tractor path as far as possible and then over another gate, across a stream and straight up the hill towards a small group of cairns. On one of these gorse-covered mounds is a small standing stone. From this vantage point, one can either go down to the peat diggings at the edge of the loch for a closer look at Dun Daouill, reputed to be one of the best-preserved islet forts in South Uist, but unfortunately you need a boat to explore it, or go southwards to the chambered cairns on the side of Haarsal. A five-foot-high triangular-shaped stone is still upstanding from the delapidated cairn called Glac Hukarvat. The central chamber is a jumble of slabs but the circular ring that once supported the smaller stone material making up the cairn is discernible from about a dozen uprights with a rough diamater of 60 feet (18m.). At the end of the seven-foot (2m.) chamber passage was a crescent-shaped forecourt. This additional embellishment of the round cairn is generally thought to indicate a more elaborate pre-burial ceremony by people who were probably later in time and whose distinctive 'horned' chambered cairns with elongated covering mounds have been found in Northen Ireland, around the Clyde and up the Western Isles. The smaller cairn material is now scattered around the bottom of the original knoll, especially to the southwest where there is an interesting six-foot cubed white quartz block which is beginning to split in parts with grass protruding from the gaps. The summit of Haarsal (139m.) allows a fine view in all directions. Below to the west is the A865 with a telephone kiosk, shop and the side road back to Howmore.

For the car traveller a visit to the Loch Druidibeg nature reserve alongside the Lochskipport road (B890) should not be missed. In fact there is a path from Stilligarry across the Reserve which joins this road. Stillgarry itself was once the home of the MacVurichs . . . bards to the ClanRanald, until they died out over a century ago. A family of poets and historians, known and honoured throughout Scotland, they were originally descended from the Irish poet, Muireadach O'Dalaigh. In 1213 the poet killed the tax-gatherer of the O'Donnell (of north-west Ulster) and even his apology was of no avail so he had to flee.

> What reason for such wrath can be?
> The rascal bandied words with me.
> I took an axe and cleaved him down
> Small matter for a Prince's frown.★

O'Daly was chased around Ireland until he finally escaped in a boat to Scotland. He then went to the Holy Land on the Fifth Crusade with a Scottish contingent of the MacDonalds, and later, when he returned, begot the MacVurich line. A poem by him, 'On the Death of his Wife' (included in Edna O'Brien's *Some Irish Loving*), recounts his sorrow, after 20 years' companionship, on losing his wife who had bornehim 11 children. He returned to Ireland when he was an old man.

★ Robin Flower, *The Irish Tradition*(O.U.P., 1947), p. 86.

Loch Druidibeg is one of the main breeding grounds of the greylag geese. The small herd of red deer are a common sight splashing over the numerous inlets. Many immature swans spend their first seven years here. The mute swan pair for life and then choose a small loch to themselves. These graceful creatures have a mythology and aura all their own; watching them glide through the water, it is easy to be caught up in the melancholia that surrounds many of the stories about the transformation of children into swans. Modern textbooks might question the fact, but many old people believed that these birds actually sing. Perhaps it is a bit like the seals singing I heard one night by the shore at Pollachar, hard to pin down from its reverberation on the water. One old couple who had spent their lives by Loch Aoineant gave this example to Carmichael, putting the sound of the swans into a human song.

gu bhi gi	gu vi gi
gu bhi go	gu vi go
gu bhi gi	gu vi gi
guile mhór!	loud guile!
na h–ealachan!	the swans!
guth na h–eala	voice of the swan
guth an eoin	voice of the bird
guth na h–eala	voice of the swan
air an lón	upon the water
gu bhi gi	gu vi gi
gu bhi go	gu vi go
gu bhi gi	gu vi gi
guile mhór!	loud guile!
na h–ealachan!	the swans!*

On the way north towards Creagorry, a township with hotel and shops on the other side of the causeway in Benbecula, you will pass by a vast statue of the madonna and child, called 'Our Lady of the Isles', on the slopes of Rueval. Ironically enough, on top of the hill is a missile tracking station which is used by the Rocket Firing Range on the far side of Loch Bee.

A visit to the souterrains at East Gerinish will take you off the main road and past some interesting modern

* Vol. 4, p. 25, of *Carmina Gaeldica*.

developments around Loch Carnan. There is a deep sea harbour and modern pier used mainly by the Ministry of Defence as an oil-supply depot. The hydroelectric station is further east at Holmar Bay and as the road passes over the head of Loch Sheilavaig the salmon traps used for fish-farming are visible. At the end of the road there is a track that forks left towards Loch Dubh for about half-a-mile. From a rise just before the loch, the souterrains are visible within a well-protected gully. Sections of the passageways can be discerned among the uneven ground as well as the original walling close to a high rockface. There is a tradition of a tunnel here and at the top is a large depression, now blocked-up, which could have been a smokehole or airduct. The best examples of such underground passages in South Uist, however, are just over three miles south of here as the hoodie crow might fly, among the rocky wilds of Glen Usinish.

The most fascinating aspect of these structures is that they seem to combine the underground walled passage of the true souterrain interconnecting beehives houses with the radial type of house construction that is well illustrated at Kilpheder. There are a number of different sites here. One is on the spur

Entrance to earth house, Loch Sheilavig

of a hill overlooking the sea with a marvellous view of Usinish
Bay and the headland called Newton's Leap. Nestling into the
side of the hill are the remains of supporting pillars producing
the effect of a high curved facade almost in cross-section.
Inside the best-preserved of the individual rounded chambers
is a low stone lintel under which one can crawl into the curved
well-built passageway. It is locked at one end, and the other
end is a bit of a wet squeeze, but it leads into the upright dome
of a hidden stone chamber. The heather had been burnt off the
hill making the extensive ancient settlement more evident.
There are clumps of nearly a dozen circular ruined beehives.
One or two are almost complete except for the roofing, with
thick drystone walling about five feet (1.4m.) high with stone
cupboards on the insides, and a general internal diameter of
six feet (1.8m.). The second complex is a half-a-mile to the
northwest and utilises a huge natural boulder to facilitate the
construction of the stone-walled passage. Inside the
souterrain is a seven-foot-high (2m.) corbelled chamber.
There are also remains of beehive-house constructions
outside. The third complex is nearby but you have to go
around the cliff and over the top to a cave. Here there is
another souterrain leading to a hidden beehive chamber.

There are many ways of getting to Glen Usinish and all of
them present much the same difficulty because of the wet
boggy terrain and the fact that wherever you walk from, you
will have to slog that distance back. From the main road there
are a number of tracks, due east, that lead to the central
uplands area slightly to the north of the highest peak in South
Uist, Beinn Mhor (620m.). Unless you want to get a view of
St. Kilda, over 40 miles out in the Atlantic, or the
breathtaking and often quire forboding brown curved
shoulders of Hecla (606m.) two miles to the north, then it is
advisable to cross the passes to go around Loch Corodale into
Glen Usinish. Another route is to take the track from
Lochskipport which soon peters out, and then head
southeastwards over the rough ground towards the bay of
Mol a'Tuath. There is a track here that leads around the
headland to the lighthouse and natural cave below Beinn
a'Tuath.

Benbecula

The literal translation of the Gaelic name for Benbecula is 'Hill between the Fords', which fits the isle perfectly. The hill, Rueval (124m.), is surrounded by lochs and rough moorland. The description of Benbecula by the 18th-century geologist, James MacCullock, has often been quoted but in its succinctness it can hardly be bettered: 'The sea here is all islands and the land is all lakes. That which is not rock is sand; that which is not mud is bog; that which is not bog is lake; that which is not lake is sea; and the whole is a labyrinth of island peninsulas, promontories, bays and channels.' Indented by countless inlets, the overall oblong mass stretches roughly eight miles wide by four miles in length between the extensive tidal shallows that separated Benbecula from the Uists, North and South. Quicksands, bad visibility and fierce winter storms gave the sands a justly morbid place in local stories before the modern causeways were constructed. Large conical-shaped stone cairns built up across the estuaries are all that remain of these ancient routes.

The main (A865) road that connects the ferry terminals at Lochboisdale in the south to Lochmaddy in the north runs straight through Benbecula. A half-circular B-road curving around the western machair, past the excellent beach at Culla, connects the two main townships. Creagorry is a small, undistinguished place on the shore of the South Ford and whose main attraction for the traveller is the hotel where food and refreshments are available except on Sundays. Balivanich at the northwestern end of the isle is like a cosmopolitan city by comparison, with its airport and daily connection to Stornoway on Lewis, and thence to Aberdeen or Glasgow. It has a large army base with related establishments, a supermarket, garages and other amenities. The rows of council house-type regulated accommodation probably contains the majority of the island's 2,000 inhabitants. In the last decade there has been a population increase of nearly 600 – Lewis is the only other isle in the Outer Hebrides that has seen a similar rise in population, although here most are probably army personnel from outside.

Borve Castle

Visible from the coast road, less than two miles out of Creagorry, is the ruined tower of Borve Castle. Thought to have been built in the 14th century by Amie Mic Ruaridh, who was responsible for many of the churches and priories throughout this part of the Hebrides, the tower was at least three stories high, with walls varying in thickness from five to nine feet with an infill of rubble between the outer and inner casings. Almost 500 yards to the southwest of the castle and supposed at one time to have been connected by a tunnel was the ruined mediaeval monastery dedicated to St. Columba. Teampull Bhuirgh is now covered by blown sand.

There are the remains of three duns built on islets in the middle of lochs that seem to run in a straight line from Borve Castle past the dun near Griminish, to Eilean Iain Dun, and to Dun Buidhe at Knock Rolum. This 'yellow fort' in the 'Loch of Murdoch's dun' seems to have been of considerable size and importance from its massive causeways, the masonry, by the water's edge, and the great mount of rocky debris which measures nearly 80 feet (24.5m.) in width. As already stated, 'Borve' stems from fort or castle, but also seems to signify a fertile and habitable stretch of land which appealed to the Norse raiders and later Viking settlers. Their longships were not built for paddling through a mase of watery inlets, and as the place names here confirm, their concern was with headlands and landmarks along the Atlantic coastlines. From the open sea, Borve in Benbecula, in Harris and in Barra have similar land configurations. The Gaelic term, dun, refers to the same circular forts and this often results in a Hebridean peculiarity, combining both Gaelic and Norse terms, as in Dun Borve, which when transliterated into English compounds this even further as in Borve Castle.

The castle was burnt down by irate members of the

ClanRanald because he (Ranald) would not support the Protestant King George II. This is but one of many sites on Benbecula associated with death and destruction. Just over a mile to the north, a 14th-century nunnery was destroyed after the Reformation and the nuns massacred. Some of them were said to have been left at low tide on a large rock in the middle of Culla Bay and drowned when the tide rose. There is a class of seaweed on it called 'nuns fingers' because the fronds are so shaped as if the hands of these women are still clutching the pitted rock. The masonry from the ruined nunnery was eventually used to build Nunton House (now a farmhouse to the east of the road) which the ClanRanald chief lived in when he returned from France (to where he had escaped from Cromwell's wrath).

In common with many of the great Highland clans, there was a prophecy about the downfall of the MacDonalds of ClanRanald which eventually came to pass. There is also the story of two terrifying green fairy dogs, held together on a gold-studded leash, who burst into the house and then flew off together again with the Sluagh or fairy host. Another very peculiar story concerned the exposed graves in the burial ground at Nunton during the early part of the 19th century. The small bones were thought to have been the skeletons of fairies or even mermaids. Dr. Alexander MacLeod, known throughout the Isles as An Dotair Ban, was called in to investigate and he concluded that they were the bones of small children. Much the same was said about the pigmy bones found at Lubruchan near the Butt of Lewis, which more recently were stated to be those of animals; but on Benbecula, with religious feelings running high, various inferences were made at the time regarding the unholy activity of the nuns. Clearly this had more to do with some deep-seated psychological guilt that may be endemic to the area than historical or scientific fact. There is a little roofless chapel in the overgrown graveyard which according to Muir was built to a simple Celtic design, meaning, I suppose, that it was rectangular in shape with thick rubble walls.

Knoll of the Hooded Crow
On the headland beyond the army installations at Balivanich

there was once a hillock called Cnoc Feannaig, meaning 'Knoll of the Hooded Crow,' associated with St. Torran who is traditionally said to have brought Christianity to this part of the Hebrides. Along with three brothers, he had been sent on a mission to Ireland, which at this point in time had returned to its heathen ways, but the Irish would not listen and packed him off in a coracle to the mercy of God and the waves. This was a time-honoured method of dealing with holy men, criminals and idiots! The boat drifted across the Irish Sea and eventually was washed up in a creek near Baile na Monach, 'Town of the Monks,' from the mediaeval seminary that was disbanded after the Reformation.

Torran was thirsty, so he prayed for water. Immediately a spring gushed from the ground, which he blessed and named Gamhnach, or 'Farrow Cow', for some unaccountable reason. Curiously enough, when we visited the well, known as Tobar Chalum Cille, which formally was a place of healing and pilgrimage, there was an ailing cow lying in a wet puddle beside it. Trying to tell a local farmer about the plight of the animal, I received the only nasty response from an islander during our journeys in the Hebrides. It all seemed part of the bad karma of the place. The saint, too, was rebuffed when he tried to build a chapel on Cnoc Feannaig, close to where he landed. Every morning the people would find their previous day's efforts had been moved to an island in a nearby loch. This continued, so Torran kept watch one night to see if it was the work of demons. However, it turned out to be a host of angels who were moving the stones and so taking the hint, he decided to build his chapel in the loch. Known as Loch Chalum Cille, it is still a very swampy place and the remains of the early chapel are thought to be on a small promontory near the later ruin of the Teampull built by Lady Amie Ruaridh.

The Knoll of the Hooded Crow in fact got its name from a witch who once lived here, and perhaps its pre-Christian association as an ancient ritual centre explains why Torran initially tried to build his chapel on it. The story concerns the evil witch who married a king with 12 beautiful children and her attempts to get rid of them. She brewed a spell in her cauldron which turned them all into seals. When they began

The Cairn of the One Night

flapping around their father, he was understandably annoyed so requested she turn them back again to human form. She, however, refused, saying the curse on the children could not be lifted except for three days in every third month until the ninth generation had passed. The king was furious and raised his hazel wand, turning her into a crow, chanting: 'Carrion you are, on carrion feed; evil you have done, evil be on you; death come to others, life be to you.'

The hoodie is usually to be seen picking in the large high-wire rubbish compound, past the Market Stance on the track that leads to the ruined chambered cairn near Loch nan Clachan south of Rueval. Known as the 'Cairn of the One Night,' this was the scene for the most grisly macabre tale from the whole of the Hebrides. Three men had been working on the moor and decided to spend the night in a shieling hereabouts rather than return in the dark to Nunton. They had hopes that a few milk maids might arrive with food and refreshments. Eventually there was a knock on the door and three young women entered and presented themselves to the men. So two of the men and their new companions retired to the back room leaving the headman alone with the third woman. However, instead of the expected amorous byplay her mouth turned into a large beak and to his consternation he could see blood flowing out from beneath the door from the other room. He quickly made an excuse that he had to go outside to relieve himself but she understandably enough did not want him out of her sight. They eventually compromised that she should hold his cloak, but once outside the shieling he pinned the other end of it to the door with his dirk and ran for his life. When she discovered the ruse she chased him across the moor. As he had his dog with him he shouted to it that if the mutt did not work for him now, it never ever would. The dog kept the bloodthirsty creature at bay so that the man reached his house in safety. He left three pails of milk outside the back door for the dog and immediately went to bed. In the morning, however, he found the animal dead on the doorstep with not a hair left on its body. The other two men were also dead and the shieling was never used again.

There are the remains of a house near one of the dilapidated chambered cairns, which is noticeable for being the only habitation in the vicinity—but whether this was the scene of this ghastly tale depends no doubt on the time of day or night when one happens to be in the vicinity.

Benbecula is such a small flat isle centering around its single hill, Rueval, that, with the above catalogue of stories involving death in the shape of nuns' fingers, witchy crows, wild beaked women and even a loch called Loch nan Meirbh, 'Loch of the Dead,' with small islets known as 'Little Death', where those accused of the evil eye would be staked in a hole and left to die, and 'Big Death' where their remains would be buried, one could be accused of the wrong emphasis. However, the 'Cairn of the Long Night' is now dwarfed by a vast geodesic installation constructed on the very summit of the Reuval, proclaiming that death and destruction is still around on Benbecula, even today.

The North Ford

Prior to submergence making it the extensive tidal estuary it is today, the land here was probably like the low-lying Baleshare Isle off the North Uist coast, which is now a three-mile-long sandbank making both an effective buffer against the Atlantic Ocean and an enclosure at the northwestern end of Oitir Mhor. One result of this is that during storm weather or at heavy spring tides, the gap between Benbecula and North Uist bears no resemblance to the ford its name suggests but becomes an enormous waterway strewn with dozens of large and small isles. The broad geographical divisions from the higher ground in the east to the flat sands of the west apply here among the isles of the North Ford as much as elsewhere in the Uists.

Cairn at Eileanan Glasa

The early archaeological sites in Benbecula such as the recently excavated Bronze Age habitations at Rossinish, the cup-marked standing stone at Haka above the Sound of Flodda, and the two stone circles at Gramsdale, as well as those on Ronay Isle and around Loch Caravat in North Uist, indicate that it was the deeper eastern sea approaches that were important then. The remains of the ecclesiastical centres, however, show that the estuary was basically much as it is today, for they were situated at important landing places that also seemed essential connecting points along the east and west coasts. Balivanich, or 'Town of the Monks,' on the northwest of Benbecula has already been alluded to, but probably the most important religious centre in this area was Teampull na Trionaid at Caranish in North Uist. Sunamul Isle lies roughly equidistant from both, and perhaps the triple circle carving on the block of stone that was found in the sands here, may have indicated a connection between them and St. Michael's Chapel built at the eastern end of Grimsay.

For early sea craft dependent on the tides as well as the winds, the positioning of these Christian communities would have been extremely useful in all weathers. These early teampulls (roofed with stone) and chapels (thatch) were sited with extreme care, usually in green, well-sheltered and watered spots. Another feature is that they lie on prominent landward positions. The three at the entrances to the estuary have already been alluded to; Hougharry and Tighary are close to the extreme westerly point of North Uist; Toehead and Rodel are at both ends of the southwest coastline of Harris. On the east coast of Lewis, at North Tolsta, Eye and the mouth of Loch Erisort, are three ruins dedicated to St. Columba. Howmore and Kilbride (no trace now except in the name) are on the coast, South Uist and Cille Bharra are at the neck of Eoligarry Strand. Of course, nearly all the smaller isles have sites or ruins of chapels.

So as well as being the centres of religion and learning, the temples were probably the main clearing houses for outside commerce as well as having extensive land holdings. It was this inter-connective aspect, controlling the most obviously material, as well as the spiritual, life of the times that helps to explain the vehemence of their destruction after the

Reformation. It is worth remembering that the Hebridean islands as a group are one tiny wing off the main stages of destiny and dependent on others for a few props, a costume or two, with little interest in the finer points of the human drama called 'Western Civilisation'. The momentous social changes that occurred elsewhere were often washed up here like discarded driftwood, and even though the effects on individuals and property were often no less virulent, the time gap between outrages was often a long one. So the churches are sad reminders of the forces active outside the islands. This may help to explain why they are left to rot and why the islanders hold such foreign cultural artifacts in so little regard.

Teampull na Trionaid, Caranish

The mediaeval monastery was said to have been founded by Beathag early in the 13th century and enlarged by Amie nam Ruaridh in the middle of the 14th. Dun Scotus, a famed scholastic in the court of Charles the Bold, Duke of Burgundy, was educated here and it had such a wide-spread reputation as a centre of learning that an Act of Parliament in 1496 ordered 'all barronies and freeholders' to send their children to be educated. However, like most of the Catholic religious houses of Scotland it had probably declined or been corrupted by secular powers and material considerations before its destruction in the Reformation around 1560. Certainly by 1601 it had lost its traditional place of sanctuary, for the MacDonalds of Uist drove a maurading band of the MacLeods of Harris out of the Teampull, and the ferocity of that battle at Caranish was remembered in the name of a nearby hollow called 'the ditch of blood.' The stream which runs through the sands a mile to the south at low tide, is called Sruthan na Comaraig, meaning 'Stream of the Sanctuary,' and if this was in fact its traditional boundary, a glance at the OS map will show clear water completely surrounding the ishmus of Caranish extending it considerably beyond the present land form. The area immediately to the north is so flat that except at high tides it is possible to walk over the estuary to Baleshare itself. It is by far the best way to examine many of the rock cairns, mounds and other fort-like stone structures that proliferate here. One of these was said to have been the

Teampull na Trionaid

site of Crois Moireag, Cross of Little Mary; the diminutive, here, is an island term of endearment, and on Baleshare half-a-mile southwest of the schoolhouse are some foundations of Teampull Chriosd, a dedication which was also found on Kilda.

Teampull Trionaid today consists of two roofless buildings of irregular size. The larger (61 x 21 feet 18 x 6 m.), with its thick rubble infill walling, was connected on the north side by a low semi-circular vaulted passage (now blocked) to the second structure known as Teampull MacVicar (23 x 13 feet 5.5 x 3.6 m.), built on a west to east axis. It was not a chapel but the final burial place of Clan a'Phiocair, the hereditary teachers at the seminary. As well as the books, manuscripts and works of art that were reputedly burnt or thrown into the sea in the 16th century, the stonework of the Teampull was said to have been decorated with carvings and sculpture as ornate as in St. Clements, on Harris: 'Stones in the walls figured with angels, armed men and animals.' Muir's informant also said that there had been a pinnacle or spire upon the east gable with the figure of a giant with three heads on top representing the Trinity. During the 19th century the teampull was restored and the roof thatched with heather, which was the traditional manner but in this case clearly a mistake for the masonry has suffered extensive crumbling due to erosion. The weeds growing inside and around the walls, in contrast to the closely cropped grass of the exterior, show that it needs some human attention as well as the efforts of the sheep.

In this tranquil setting, near the shore to the northeast is a hillock with the remains of a cairn on top that is known as the Knoll of the Angels. It brings to mind the more rounded hill of the same name on Iona, which is mentioned twice in Adamnan's *Life of Columba* as being the spot where the saint regularly communicated with the heavenly beings. On the top of the slope just beyond the west side of the Teampull is a small curved boulder set into the grass, showing two well-preserved cupmarks, that are called slochdanan in Gaelic. They are usually considered by archaeologists as belongings to the Bronze Age and having some unknown but ritual significance. There is in fact no way at present of dating such durable material as stone for the Carbon-14 technique needs some organic substance. In the same manner that the altar stone covering a saint's relics was considered the most holy and vital part of a chapel, so perhaps the holes in the stone on this prominent spot may have been carved for containing or sustaining the earth's energy as some mysterious part of religious observance during the Neolithic era. Yet there is a suspicion that there may well be a profounder connection between early Christianity and these 'cups'. In or near several other chapel ruins, notably by St. Brendan's on Barra and in the floor of St. Columba's at Eye on Lewis, a similar kind of dark gneiss stone has a single hole in it, which later may have been used to contain holy water. On the edge of the promontory past Udal sands in North Uist are some stones with cup-markings beside a spring with a cross carved on the boulder above. Columba and the early Irish missionaries seemed to be familar with the age-old traditions of the Pagan religion they were successfully replacing, and no doubt also knew the practices of its druidic guardians, augers and seers. They were intelligent enough to realise that a radical graft might be rejected out of hand, and, perhaps to prevent

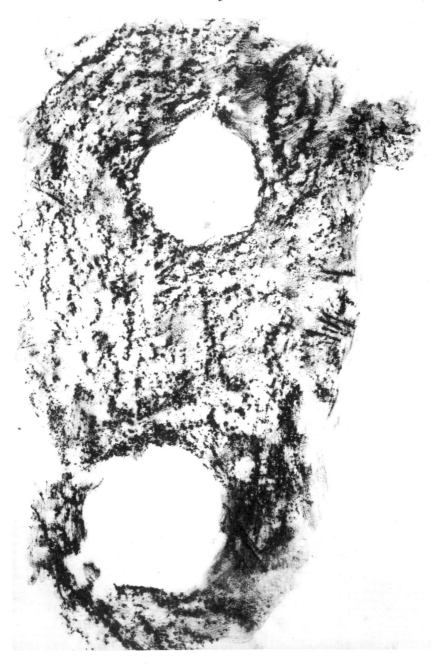

Rubbing of cup-marked stone

people's natural recidivation, many of the older ceremonies and ritual sites were retained, altered slightly and re-incorporated into the new faith.

More than once, one has a feeling after visiting many of these early holy places in short succession that the 'founders' were following a well-trodden and ancient path. Columba was said to have displaced a community of Culdees on Iona, after he had received permission in AD 563 from the Irish King of Dal Riada (now roughly Argyll) to settle on this strategic spot off the coast of Mull. Being himself a royal prince before he had been trained for his mission, he did not encounter any difficulty from the King of the Picts in obtaining his consent to convert the people to Christianity. There is some confusion as to whether the Culdees were a lay brotherhood originating from St. Ninian's, at what is now Whithorn Bay on the shores of the Solway Firth, operating independently of the Iona mission, or an order of anchorites known as Ceile De, the Companions of God, much later in time after the Viking dispoilation of the monasteries had ceased. However, if one takes the traditional view of these matters, there is no reason to reject the idea that communities of learning and religion were part of the normal pattern of life long before the advent of Christianity on these shores. And with the need for solitude and contemplation far from the haunts of mankind, the small isles and rocky eminences were always considered ideal. The Norse had named three Pabays, meaning 'Hermit's Isle', in the Outer Hebrides, showing that the practice of retiring from worldly affairs was well established long before the sudden Viking onslaught in AD 794 so pithily recorded in the Annuals of Ulster, 'All coasts of Britain ravaged by the Gals'. The island monasteries in the Hebrides, along with those off Ireland, were devastated as the islands were used first as summer bases and then later for permanent settlement to be ruled by the jarls, who usually acted independently of Norway, for the next 400 years. However, after Somerled became King of Argyll in 1156 the emphasis in relation to Christianity changed to building. It was Somerled's daughter, Beathag, who founded Teampull Triodaid and Regnall as King was famous as a builder of monasteries rather than ships. He founded St. Mary's on Iona in 1203.

Part of the irreparable devastation wrought by the Viking mauraders was the loss of so much Church art at a period of its highest creativity. From what was hidden, overlooked or taken to safety in monasteries on the Continent, we can get a fair idea of their styles and uses of different materials. Much of the precious metals were melted down but small reliquaries and other sacred objects taken in plunder have been found in Norway and elsewhere. The surviving illuminated Gospels such as the Book of Kells, finished during the first half of the ninth century, show the heights to which this tradition had reached and indicate clearly the important place of the scriptorum in the early monastic settlements. The more durable art of stone carving cannot give even an indication of the richness, colour and depth of symbolism that decorated the cloths and wood panels of the interiors. Yet within the context of those troubled times it is easy to understand how the Irish sculptured High Crosses developed and became prominent aspects of secular expression. Other forms of carving have been identified with particular areas such as Lower Loch Erne in Northern Ireland (White Island Figures), Islay in the Inner Hebrides, and Kilmartain in Argyll. The stone for building the church on Iona and St. Clements Church on Harris came from Mull, and more recently the quarry supplied the masonry blocks for the restoration of Kisimul Castle on Barra.

Strome Sunamul

The few carved stones that have been found in the Outer Hebrides are all extremely fine examples of the art but nothing is known of their carvers or even where they may have originated from. The Pabbay Isle symbol stone, the runic cross stone from Barra, St. Aseph's patterned stone, with spiralled square and plaited knot, found on Berneray and the regular incised cross stone, Clach an Teampull, found on Taransay Isle off Harris, as well as the curious carving found on Sunamul Isle, are the most distinctive.

The carving found in the sand at Strome Sunamul, a small isle directly in line with Benbecula airport, is certainly one of the most unusual that has been discovered in the Hebrides. Shaped in the form of a polygon it measures three feet by two

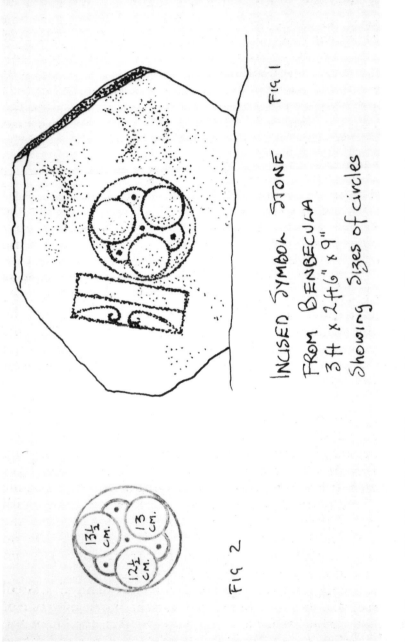

INCISED SYMBOL STONE   FIG 1

FROM BENBECULA

3ft x 2ft 6" x 9"

Showing sizes of circles

FIG 2

13½ CM.

13 CM.

12½ CM.

Stone Carving, Oitir Mhor (National Museum of Antiquities of Scotland, Edinburgh)

feet nine inches thick. There is a double ring incised on one
face with three smaller circles bisected on the inner ring and
lying tangenital to the outer. The original location or setting is
unknown, though it may have been part of a larger pillar or
even an ornamental door post. It was a common practice for
monastic establishments to have their bounds defined,
establishing both ancient rights and sanctuary limits. On the
other hand the three small rings within the larger circle is a
striking design that may be illuminating the mystery of the
Holy Trinity, Father, Son and Holy Ghost as One God. One
can also think of the triple aspects of the eponymous goddess,
Bride, and even the fondness of Celtic peoples for the potent
three-in-one number.

The dimensions of the rings on the polygonal stone are
quite regular. Two of the small ones are $5\frac{1}{4}$ inches in
diameter and the third is 5 inches, superimposed on a 'curving
triangle' that goes through their centre points. The outer ring
is 12 inches (30.5cm.) in diameter. A fragment of a stone
found at the parish church at Kinneller makes an interesting
comparison. Here the dimensions were $4\frac{3}{4}$ inches, $5\frac{1}{4}$
inches, and $13\frac{3}{4}$ inches, while the stone measures 27 x 19
inches.

The rest of the design is a rectangular-shaped 'box' with
curved lines that could denote the tidal waters and thus it may
have been a sign in a prominent position indicating the
proximity of the three chapels within the one establishment in
the estuary of the North Ford.

A replica of the granite block is on display at the National
Museum of Antiquities with other replicas and original
carved stones as well as the runic stone from Barra. Enquiries
last summer as to the actual whereabouts of the Sunamul
carving drew some blank looks with an assurance that it must
be around somewhere in the building.

St. Michael's Chapel, Grimsay

From a half-way point across the causeway road, two side
turnings branch off around this largish isle, allowing one a
pleasant circular drive. The scenery is quite representative
with the rocky inland terrain and frequent lochs found
throughout the Uists, but the swell of the sea and sudden

vistas of the surrounding small isles add to the quiet charms of this thinly populated spot. There are a number of ancient fortifications such as Dun Ban in Loch Hornary, overgrown with shrub and small trees, and covered with blue bells, when we passed it on our way to the extreme eastern edge of Grimsay. All that now stands of St. Michael's Chapel is a crumbling eight-foot high (2.6m.) gable end, but it occupies a very prominent place on the small green plateau which is the highest point of the small promontory jutting out into the sea. It was a small rectangular structure only 23 feet (7m.) long inside that is attributed to Amie Mhic Ruaridh, who it is said was saved from a gale here and as an expression of thanks rebuilt this ancient site as an extension to Teampull na Trionaid. The little harbour at Kallin—which is derived from the Gaelic, Na Ceallan, 'The Cells' (of the monks)—is an unloading point for the local crab and lobster factory. A mile away, a small loch was called 'Loch of the Abbot,' and just off the southern headland are the Isles of the Teampull, all fairly indicative of an early Christian site. On the large rocky uninhabited isle of Ronay opposite, the high points have equally suggestive names; 'Hill of the Priests' and 'Hill of the Druids.' The latter has no real summit as such but more a grand plateau within three grass-covered structures with a fine view to the steep valley below. There are also rather peculiar conical stone stumps covered with deep green grass. There is a wild harsh quality about this steeply undulating volcanic environment that is borne out in its Old Norse name meaning 'Rough-Isle'.

Sithean Rossinish

Directly across the water from the Little Isles of the Teampull on the northeast coast of Benbecula are the sand dunes at Rossinish. Excavations into the extensive midden indicate that they were built up during the Bronze Age, and some of the sheltered inter-isle straits still retain remnants of the 'old machair' that was formed then. Such 'fossil' remains of ancient landforms have also been found in similar environmental conditions at Northton in Harris and at Udal in North Uist.

Between the closed sea-inlet and the 'Fairy Mound' of

Rossinish, which is an extensive area of 400 square metres and up to 17 metres above the sea is the site of a small corbelled stone tomb. It is situated slightly north of the ruined sheilings. In 1964, sand removals for cement revealed the rounded stone dome cover, and two locals from Grimsay opened it and removed the contents which included the remains of a man, two young women, funerary pottery and a pendant. During the excavation that took place nearly a dozen years later it was estimated that the five-foot-high Thalos-type tomb had been sealed for nearly 4,000 years, ever since it had been first covered over. This was a rare find indeed, for in the past such discoveries have not been thoroughly examined let alone excavated. Also the two men had contacted the archaeologist, Iain Crawford, as soon as they discovered the burial and so he was on hand to help and facilitate the investigation.

The report (P S A S, Vol.108) makes fascinating reading as it shows clearly the sequence of events, beginning with the pile slabs that were used to construct the pear-shaped structure to ensure solid foundations in the sand. The human remains with some Beaker-type funerary pots were set inside and it was sealed, covered over with a mound of sand and a large fire then lit. An almost circular ring of flat stones, nearly 3.5 meters in diameter, was laid around the whole thing but slightly off-centre. Outside this circle two smaller stone cists were erected on either side, slightly to the front of it on a north–east axis. The one to the right had an unbroken pot and the other to the left contained fine sand and a giant oyster shell. The adjacent shore area is full of human and animal bones, pottery shards and other ancient refuse. Also a number of the same thalos-type beehives have been reported as well as some flat stone circles, which suggests that the area was either an extensive burial place or a major prehistoric settlement. An eight foot high stone with very distinctive cup markings, that once stood on the knoll above the Sound of Flodda, is situated less than two miles west of Sithean Rossinish.

It is interesting to note that the only comparable type burial suggested by the archaeologist was in North Uist, at Udal sands, and a few miles to the south on the rising ground above the shore at Buaile Risary, is a cup-marked standing stone adjacent to ruined aisled-houses. Such a connection does not hold much weight in archaeological terms, where the main interest lies in isolating each site, unless there seems to be a strong alignment of pottery shards especially of the Beaker-type. The mythical 'incomers' called the Beaker Folk after extensive and distinctive funeral pottery found throughout Britain, usually alongside more cruder ware, were a phenomenon created by archaeologists for other archaeologists. Though there is no doubt that this line of research based on systematic examination of shards has opened-up many other areas of thought, nevertheless even mainstream archaeological researchers have now begun to question this model of a new race of people as largely hypothetical. For the non-academic who merely plods these sands observing and noting comparable structures and methods of building, especially in the almost unchanged traditional use of stone right up to the late 19th century, it is the social bonding in relation to an equally unchanged environment and climatic conditions from the end of the Bronze Age onwards, that appears to be the most cohesive factor in understanding the prehistoric communities of the Hebrides.

Unless you travel by boat, the best way over to Rossinish is from the Market Stance, three miles up the main road through Benbecula, then off on the track around Rueval which Martin mentions as an old road across the island. This is private land now so one should seek permission from the South Uist Estates before wandering around the machair. The standing stone at Hake, situated 400 yards north of Loch an Tairibh, was discovered by A.A. Carmichael in 1868, as part of the roof of a piggery. He noted its nine cupmarks. The dimensions of this well-dressed stone monolith and its situation on the high knoll overlooking the estuary suggests that it originally must have been an imposing landmark. It still inclines at an angle amid the ruins of the pigsty next to the roofless sheiling, with its indentations quite prominent. The largest cup is 2½ inches (6.8cm.) deep.

Stone Circles, Gramsdale

Marked on the OS map as a 'Standing Stone', as there is one five-foot-high pillar covered with lichen and birdshit still

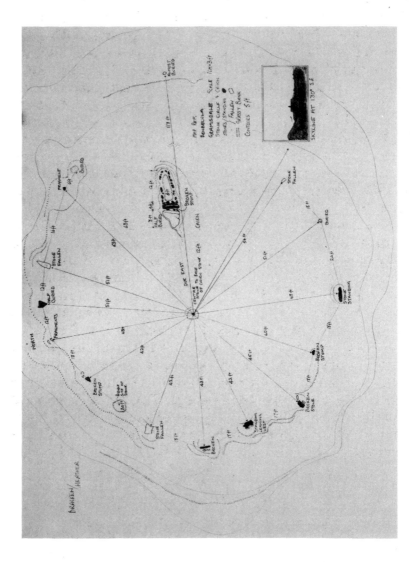

Stone Circle, Snidheachadh Sealg

standing, Suidheachadh Sealg is nevertheless quite an impressive stone circle. It lies a little south of the track to Kyles Flodda. There are some stumps and more than six stones overthrown, making a total of at least ten on the edge of the perimeter forming more than half of the western part of the original circular structure. Its 80-foot (24.5m.) circumferance shows it to be one of the larger stone circles in the Hebrides. There is a small tufted rise with two parallel slabs over five-foot long near the centre. Otherwise it is quite flat, thus ruling out the possibility that the stones may have been part of a chambered cairn. The site stands only 50 feet (15m.) above sea level, but because of the surrounding low terrain it still commands a fine view east to the Cullins on Skye and Beinn nan Druidhneach on Ronay, and north to the Uist hills and the South Harris hills; while on the south horizon there is a large boulder visible on Reuval.

Less than a mile due north and a few hundred yards south of the North Ford is another five-foot-high standing stone with a group of prostrate slabs on the south and west quadrant of a possible stone circle. Roughly 100 feet (31m.) in diameter, there is a six-foot-long (1.8m.) flat stone east of the possible centre point. According to the old crofter who lives here, a small stone about two feet high that once stood on the nearby rocky knoll was known as the Gramsdale Cross. It was overthrown and eventually buried in the ground, possibly during the erection of the telephone pole which now stands in its place on the ten-foot-high mound. The story in the local tourist brochure that it was a ten-foot-high cross, 'now disappeared and slipped into the sea,' seems to be based on a misreading of the Royal Commission Report.

North Uist

This is probably the most popular resort for regular visitors, who return time and again to the excellent trout fishing and bird-watching on the Balranald Nature Reserve. It is also a favourite away-place for the Hebrideans themselves, especially Lewis people who find the climate here relatively mild. As a point of access between the Long Isle in the north and the southern spread of the Uists, business and commercial travellers use the road as a throughway to the car ferry from Lochmaddy, with regular services to both Skye and Harris. When its present road developments are complete and the airlink opened with the new runway on the Isle of Berneray, connecting by small ferry to both Harris and Newtonferry a few miles away, this trend will continue. Like a magnet the main town pulls everything into orbit because there is so little available elsewhere, including petrol.

At Clachan where the circular road divides and turns south, there is a post-office shop, and local bus service connections. The minibus, with a post office 'grill' up front for the driver, is a cheap and interesting way of travelling up to Balranald, for it leaves the main road quite often to deliver mail and parcels to the small houses. At each stop there is usually greetings and chat in Gaelic, as well as the business of opening gates to every croft. It is such an intelligent use of local services that one wonders why the other islandss don't utilise their post vans in like manner. Jackson's of Clachan will post their excellent smoked fish anywhere in the world, and there is a pleasant hotel bar at the nearby Langas Lodge. The Westford Inn is at Bayhead on the west coast. There are a few shops here and there on the swing around the north end to complete the circuit back to Lochmaddy.

Once the haunt of 17th-century pirates, it had its name from either the tall rock stacs—'dogs'—at the mouth of the harbour, or the shell fish that once proliferated around its extensive inlets. There is a solid 'mainland' air about the town now with its imposing courthouse, churches, shopping amenities, garage, cottage hospital, and even a bookshop tucked away among its labyrinthian spread above the loch. The hotel has the comfortable feeling beloved of fishing people who have been out on the lochs all day cramped with their friends in a small boat rowed by the gillie. The brackish waters of Loch Scadaway are ideal for brown trout and although not very large in area it has an extensive shoreline. Even though the number of gillies and boats available has drastically declined since the 19th century, the breed are still much the same and like nothing better than a warm fire and good meal at the end of the day. The excellent food, cheerful service and a good bar are a very welcome respite from the damp weather as any visitor here for more than a few days will soon appreciate. The slight air of gentility that surrounds the hotel with its great stuffed fish, and most of the town itself, is not conducive to the family 'car-loaded' tourists for there are no camping sites here. This is not to say that people are not welcome, there is a tourist information office—North Uist, like all the Hebridean Isles, depends to a large part on the tourist industry for its life blood—but there is an emphasis on working that belies this dependence.

The terrain here and its possible utility is so limited by the geography and climate that it is surprising to find that the farms on the machair, some of the largest single units in the Hebrides, have a well-cared-for appearance unlike the more ragged character of the rest of the Uist. Also it occasions no surprise to find out that tulip bulbs were once seriously considered as a cash-crop around the rich flatlands of the Paible area but were finally abandoned through lack of capital finance. Fish-farming is on the increase, but neither it nor cereals are labour-intensive or help alleviate the plight of the poor crofter. Also it is noticeable that it is mainly outsiders who seem to run their own business with quiet efficiency, adding to the feeling that the hand of good management is on the tiller.

The population of North Uist now numbers around

2,000—although a century-and-a-half ago it was more than double that. The Rev. MacRoe, writing in the *New Statistical Account of Scotland* about the conditions of the people, gave agriculture as their main employment and listed work as male or female servants as another important source of livelihood. He ended his account with a moral rebuke for the poor: 'At present it is notorious that there are no less than 390 families not paying rent but living on small plots of potato ground given them by their neighbours and relations.' The method of potato cultivation then was much as it is now except that today it is grown as a seed crop. The sand was covered with sea wrack which was allowed to rot throughout the winter before the thin grass was turned over into rills. The tubers were small and sweet to the taste. The minister and his kind assured of a fine manse, a good living and a few acres, were for the most part the spiritual spokesmen for the landlords and the gentry. They did not see the plight of the peasants as a result of the collapse of the kelp boom nor the effect of its terrible aftermath, the potato famine, as anything other than ignorance.

Widespread starvation and death reluctantly forced the gentry into some palliative actions such as the building of the Committee Road in 1846, from Claddach to Valley Strand. The road around Grimsay Isle was yet another begun by the Destitution Committee at this time. Lest it should be thought that such short-term solutions to social problems are a thing of last century, the recent closure of the kelp factory at Boisdale in South Uist was 'alleviated' by using the redundant younger members as a labour force to extend and widen the road across the causeway into Benbecula, jointly funded by the military and the Comhairle nam Eilean. Lord MacDonald of Sleat's solution immediately after the famine was to clear the people from the best land and introduce the more profitable and less cantankerous 'Highland Ghosts', as the sheep were known. The people of the North End objected and the militia were brought in to evict them. Ugly pitched battles erupted with those around Sollas in 1849 the bloodiest in the Outer Isles. Afterwards many of the people emigrated to America.

This was also the period when the Presbyterian ministers

seceded from the Established Church to form the Free Church of Scotland, largely in protest against the callous indifference of the ministers to the evictions, forced emigrations and general plight of the poor. However, there had been a great surge of popular Evangelism moving through the Isles since the beginning of the 19th century when a blind fiddler in Skye named Munroe was converted by an illiterate preacher. The blind man broke his fiddle and thereafter spoke out with such zeal renouncing every kind of bodily recreation, that the people threw their pipes and musical instruments and books on public bonfires. The new puritanism swept the Hebrides like a force-ten gale, and with the exception of Catholic Barra and South Uist, carried away much of their traditional poetry, music and ancient custom.

On Lewis, the Free Church, or the 'Wee Frees', is still strong among the community, although elsewhere and outside the Hebrides it is mainly the Kirk or Church of Scotland that is dominant, ever since 1929 when a union between the two was agreed upon.

Due to the final effects of glaciation scouring away the soft cover and leaving behind what amounts to a perforated, slightly concave, granite landform, the island is now filled with water and peat bog while the coastlines are heavily indented. In fact, along the eastern side the extensive sea-lochs have cut so deeply into the interior that a casual glance at a map of North Uist makes it difficult to differentiate between islands littering the water and lochs enclosed by land. It has also given a distinctive character to the main upland areas on the edge of the coast, such as Eaval and south Lee across the narrow straits of Loch Eport, North Lee and the Portain headland enclosing Loch Maddy and the Beinn Mhor area in the northeast below Newtownferry. Their rugged quality and sharp inclines interspersed with long sweeps of heather hillsides and often quite deep narrow lochs, make them a world apart. As well as the soaring gannets and petrels that can usually be seen from the sea cliffs, hovering or swooping predators such as the short-eared owl, merlin and hen harrier, or even the occasional sea eagle, can be glimpsed here. The red deer tend to roam from the Lees around the edges of lochs to the sweep of soft hills that begin around Marrogh in the centre of the island right up to the northwest corner around Ben Scolpay.

It was throughout here on the south-facing slopes that many of the chambered cairns were built, probably before the onset of the peat bog when the weather was warmer than at present. Traversing this range on a long axis from one site to the next may be a monotonous hike with no great view except a myriad of lochs stretching off and merging with the sky above Lochmaddy , but as one moves along the narrow deer trails through the tough heather, the sudden tantalising appearance of a small family of these beautiful animals on the next rise or by a corner of a hill, if the wind is behind them, is almost akin to a spiritual uplift. Watching any animals in the wild is like a gift you learn to appreciate. With their acute hearing, smell and vision, there is little chance of getting close to them, but often by sitting patiently they will come quite close; very gently, other things begin to impress their attention on your wandering consciousness—like the sound of the insects or the movements and colours of the hills as clouds race across the sky.

The other major area of geographical interest is of course the sandy machair that stretches across the North End, with rounded scooped-out bays that can often be crossed at low tide, and then southwards from Hougharry where the Nature Reserve is situated.

The Inn at Caranish is quite a good starting point to continue our south-to-north itinerary. From here to Teampull Trionaid is but a short walk and out on the moor, around Loch Caravat, are a number of ruined chambered cairns. In fact, the easiest way up to the best of them, Dun Bharpa, is from the broken 'circle' of standing stones on either side of the main road half-a-mile prior to Caranish. Most of the 16 remaining stones are either broken or badly tilting, and the largest—eight feet long—is lying prostrate on the extreme east point. There is another dilapidated stone circle on the high ground a few hundred yards above the post office at Clackan. Three of the stones are actually erect, and the tallest is a flat pillar about four feet high. Nearby on the summit of Cringraval hill is a heap of stones that was once thought to be a ruined chambered cairn, because it has some large slabs set on edge, but more recently it is considered to have been a ruined house. The area around Craonaval, on the south side of Loch Eport, is rich in prehistoric remains, but as the bog is extensive and distances are deceptive out on the moor, the following route is recommended for the intrepid walker and should take a few hours with stops for snacks and contemplation of the sea and sky.

Finn's Armful, Craonaval

From the Lochmaddy road turn off onto the B894 towards Locheport, and after a mile stop beyond the Loch Oban na Curra on the right-hand side. Cross the moor, taking care to go back on yourself in a southwest direction for about a quarter of a mile. A hundred and forty yards east of Loch a 'Phobuill is a slightly oval circle of 20 fairly low stones, the largest with a seven-foot girth and four foot high. It measures roughly about 120 feet (36m.) in diameter and is called Sornach Coir Phion, but was known locally as Sornach a Phobuill, 'place of the furnace of the people.'

Continue around the slope of the hill towards the south aspect of Craonaval and you should pass two grass-covered stony mounds, one with a number of slabs protruding from it. Two hundred yards north of Loch Caravat is the 22-foot-long (6.6m.) monolith known as Ultach Fhionn, or 'Finn's Armful', sitting on the side of the hill, its huge girth resting on several small boulders indicating that it had been dressed at the

Finn's Armful

base and waited to be erected in its present position or even
nearer to the summit of the hill. Whatever intervened, it rests
today as it has done for millennia. There is a certain poignancy
in an unfinished great work that always moves one into the
realms of the might-have-been. For instance, from the two
stone circles at Gramsdale there are within a narrow five-mile-
long corridor at least five other stone circles, and in terms of
possible alignments, 'Finn's Armful' would have made a
prominent backsiting marker. Whatever the underlying
intent behind the erection of these circles or their multifarious
ceremonial use over a long period of time, perhaps their
decline came in a short sharp burst, rather like the destruction
of the monasteries after the Reformation, for all of them look
as if they have been knocked about a long time ago. Yet there
is a curious anomaly that keeps reasserting itself throughout
all these isles, and that is that there is usually at least one
megalithic structure of its kind left in good condition. Either a
large standing stone or a chambered cairn, or both, such as
Barpa Langas and Beinn a'Charra here on North Uist. On
Lewis there is a standing stone, Clach an Trushal, which rivals
'Finn's Armful', as it is much the same size and girth but
nowhere throughout the Hebrides is there any structure akin
to the great stone circle and avenue at Callanish. Apart from
the recent vandalism which is usually recorded somewhere,
the wholesale destruction seems far too complete to be either
accidental or due to weather erosion. Monoliths have been
broken in two, rolled off the summits of hills, stone circles
disarrayed, broken or completely laid flat, and of course most
of the great chambered cairn material is usually found
scattered over a wide area. The explanation that it was used
for later building holds true for some cases, but there are many
cairns near the shore that have suffered in much the same
manner. So, taken as a whole, one can sense a violent reaction
to a hitherto dominant religious culture. It could be much the
same story elsewhere but the main difference is that here on
the Hebrides, the surrounding terrain has not been covered
and reutilised by subsequent buildings. The landscape may be
described as an open book but with many empty pages of
undecipherable monuments.

However, the imagination of the people who lived here but

recently was not curtailed by social changes or the weather, or pseudo-scientific asides on possible alignments. They named this stone after their giant hero Finn MacCumbhall's armpit and an indentation in it (30mm. x 10mm.) was called 'Fingal's thumb mark.' On the northwest side of the top of this heather-covered hill is another recumbant dressed stone called 'Slab of the Month-Old One,' which is 12 feet (3.6m.) long. Nearby is a slightly shorter one and both are partly embedded in the peat. Further over to the southeast on the summit of a ridge between lochs Caravat and Oban nam Fiadh is a dilapidated cairn with six uprights marking out the outline of the central chamber. This is marked correctly on the OS map (1:50,000 series) with a cairn symbol, but on the Bartholomew (1:1000,000) map of the Uists, it is listed as a 'stone circle', as is the next mound nearly half-a-mile to the northwest on the return towards the road. Called Loch Gren na Feannog, it is about 50 feet (15m.) long with a short passage opening on the east side with small slabs set on edge. There are also large lintels displaced around the five-foot-high exterior of the cairn and the remains of some shielings on the northwest side. If you now follow the contour line round by the edge of the loch you should come out roughly where you began this little jaunt.

This road continues along the south edge of Loch Eport and ends past Sidinish. Without a boat it is difficult to explore the deserted township and dun around North Lee or by South Lee where there is supposed to be a 'throne' or large stone seat in front a cave facing the turbulent waters of the Little Minch. However, Druim na h-Uahm, 'Ridge of the Cave,' is accessible to the walker. Marked on the OS map, it is to the southeast of Burrival on the high ridge between the two lochs and is 20 feet (6m.) above the ground of a small valley. It is about double that depth inside as the roof narrows into a point. Around the turn of the century Beveridge reported a good spring of water, 18 inches deep inside, but the floor is now covered with bird droppings, small pieces of sharred bones and pottery shards. Prince Edward Charles is reputed to have spent a night here when he was on the run from the Red Coats. On the ledge outside are brambles, stinging nettles and foxgloves, and below on the ground can be seen the foundations of old buildings. This cave is one of the few places where a strong sense of early man actually living and breathing prevails. Sitting on the ledge overlooking the hills and the waters and watching the great face of Eaval change under the drifting clouds, a sense of timelessness and empathy with nature begins to soak through one's bones. Further south on the eastern spur of Eaval is another small cave which we did not visit, for hiking across these gullies and around sharp ledges, with welcome clumps of mountain ash, ivy and juniper, is quite an exhausting business—especially as one has to make the return journey without that exhilerating sense of discovery experienced when first looking for an ancient site.

Chambered Cairn, Barpa Langas

Among the hills of North Uist are the highest concentration of chambered cairns in all the islands—more than all the others put together. It is worth repeating that we do not know anything about their builders or users; nor if the single standing stones and stone circles were erected at the same period as part of an overall design or function in which the durability of the stone material seemed paramount; or much

Stone Circle, Pobuill Fhin

later in time indicating some possible changes of religious and group rituals close to the original holy places. Whatever the ceremonial use to which these megalithic constructions were put, either as group burial chambers or even perhaps playing a role in initiation ceremonies, there is no doubt that they were primarily temples.

Barpa Langas is the only one on North Uist that retains its outer mound of small packing stones intact and with an inner chamber where one can still sit. According to a local man, it was still possible to stand upright inside it when he was young, but it has now filled with debris leaving a gap of about four feet between the jumble of rocks underneath and the jagged uneven stones from the roof of the chamber. The eight-foot-long (2.6m.) supporting lintels and the smooth greenish portal stones of the chamber pressing cold around one's body are impressive reminders of its early funerary purpose. One imagines that the mental distinctions we now make between the spiritual world of the living and the spirit realms of the dead were not so defined then, so perhaps such close contact with the elemental forces of both man and nature was part of the religious energy which helped shape these early forms of monumental architecture. The enclosed ancestral chamber played an important part in shamanastic practice of many cultures, ancient and contemporary. Practices of some Tibetan Tantric schools include the use of lunar energy during the invocation to the wrathful deities, and are often carried out in ancient burial places or the burning grounds of the dead. Such practices force the mind to enter deeper into the 'death' realms of putrefaction and decay, and in so doing, regarding one's own death as an integral part of the life process and thereby bringing about a greater clarity of mind and spiritual awareness.

I must say my own painful experience inside here was a reminder that one should not trifle with the ancient mysteries. On the other side of Ben Langas there is a fine circle of about 20 standing stones known as Pobuill Phinn, 'People of Finn.' I had been helping measure the radiation count here. I had offered to do a three-minute reading with the geiger meter every 100 yards along the four cardinal directions out to a half-mile radius. The chambered cairn is just over that distance,

Interior, Barpa Langass

south, from the Langas Circle. It had been a long soaking-wet day and exceeding my brief but curious to find out what the radiation count would be inside, I took the meter into the chamber. Sitting on a 'ledge' in the semi-darkness beneath the long stones supporting the great mass of the mound and looking at the light filtering through the passage stones, the world gradually receded as the sound of the meter clicking filled the space. After 20 minutes exactly I received a violent 'kick' in the kidneys that sent me flying forward against the rocks. I was lucky to escape minor injuries from the large, protruding stones, but the sudden nervous shock and a sore back for a few days afterwards were more than sufficient to repay me for my morbid curiousity. The radiation reading was no higher than for the outside, but in fact nearly a third lower than in the evening, so I can only guess that at dusk there was a kind of shift in the accumulation of energy inside the stone funnel as often during a change of current within the electricity grid a light bulb will dim for part of a second.

Tighe Cloiche, Uneval
There is a track from the main road, past Langas Lodge, to the

stone circle above the loch called Cearcall Cloice Langass. As an oval it measures 54MY east to west by 36MY north to south. It has a good view of Craonaval as well as the lochs and small isles of the North Ford. To the northwest, a midsummer alignment has been calculated from here towards the ruined cairn known as Tighe Cloiche on the south side of Uneval, so from here the sun would be seen to set on the hill. To understand the importance of these observances for an ancient priest who could be an astronomer, geomancer or engineer, a simplified explanation of the possible steps involved might help some readers. Having decided to erect a stone circle or single monolith in these hills, a line can be demarcated for one of the more obvious astronomical manifestations—say, sunrise on midwinter's day, at a chosen position on site from a prominent notch on the horizon, across any number of geographical features along the ground. Then another astronomical line for the sun setting onto a prominent isle or hill could also be found. If these interact, as often happens, then that single point common to both lines can be permanently fixed by means of a particular standing

Chambered Cairn, standing stone and Iron Age houses, Leachach an Tigh Cloicel

stone within the circle. But a third astronomical line cannot be
made to go through this point unless by pure chance the
natural topography allowed it to happen. Occasionally this
did happen, and was used by the builders showing how acute
their observations were. Alternatively, it could sometimes be
arranged for a distant horizon point to be defined by placing
or rolling a large boulder on it, and this could be then used to
mark the third line from the intersection of the first two. It
should be remembered that in this kind of visual sighting, a
boulder or a notch will stand out more at a far distance,
especially if roughly on the same eye-level, than at close
quarters where there is nothing to differentiate it from the
surrounding rocky terrain. This idea of intersecting points
seems to have been used several times at Tiche Cloiche where
Alexander Thom has shown that at least five such alignments
pass through the site. For him it was the most important
astronomical site on North Uist because so many alignments
passing through it illustrated the capacity of ancient man to
manipulate lines of sight into megalithic construction. For the
original builders and users its importance would probably lie
in the greater frequency of visiting it to take readings and
check coming dates in their ritual calander. This site was
excavated by Lindsay Scott, who pointed out that no peat had
formed below the cairn and its square-shaped siting of slabs
on edge enclosing the structure had never been higher than its
present height of four feet. On plan it is a rough diamond-
shape set out quite accurately in relation to the cardinal points,
so perhaps it may have been purely an observatory. The lines
that Thom postulated from Tighe Cloiche were the
midwinter sunrise on Scurr nan Gillian in Skye,
(approximately southeast); a vernal equinoxical sunset on
Haskier Isle (approximately west–northwest); and its autumn
rise from Uneval, probably to fix the ritual dates of Beltane,
or summer festival, and Samain, or winter rites, at the turning
points of the year. To Ben Tuath on Wiay Isle (approximately
south–southeast) is a major moon standstill rise, and from
South Clettraval to here (approximately southeast) is the
minor moon standstill rise. The midwinter sunset from the
Langas Circle has already been mentioned. However, it must
be emphasised that accurate surveys are needed before these

lines can be proved or disproved.

Since Professor Thom created a different perspective in which to view megalithic structures, their possible multipurpose use in terms of burial rituals, tribal ceremonial gatherings and calendrical indicators is becoming generally recognised. As more researchers are beginning to follow this pioneering path, his surveys and calculations for hundreds of ancient sites have become more accurate as time passes, and are now considered highly precise. Unfortunately for us, his work in the Hebrides was all done in the very early stages of his research and is therefore among the least detailed and possibly least accurate.

The easiest way up to the old cairn on Uneval is by the track that is off the main road at Claddach Kyles and then due east across the moor for a mile. Leachach an Tighe Cloiche is usually translated as 'Place of the Slabs of the Stone House' although Thom calls it the 'House of Stone on the Ridge.' The name probably arose from a stone house built on the northeast corner of the mound from the original material. At this period the inner chamber was unroofed and apparently used as a cooking pit by the inhabitants. We have already referred to its diamond shape of thin outer slabs set on edge but there are also a twin set of recumbrant portals at both the east and west entrances. During the excavation in the late '30s an oval inner chamber of seven stone slabs with a stone floor overlaid with clay was discovered. Against the southwest corner was a pentagonal rock enclosure, five feet by four (1.4 x 1.1m.), built of thin slabs which contained human remains. The middle was filled with dark brown earth and some bones, including part of a skull, had been pushed against one wall. These bones were charred but not cremated, and flints and bits of 'grooved ware' were also found here. Archaeologically, this is considered an example of a square chambered burial cairn, although from Thom's findings it may have had a different use when first constructed. A number of other such squarish low-lying stone enclosures were noted on our travels through the Isles, and all have pronounced bearings on the four main compass directions and as far as one can ascertain strong celestial alignments as well, so perhaps we are dealing with a different class of building, or

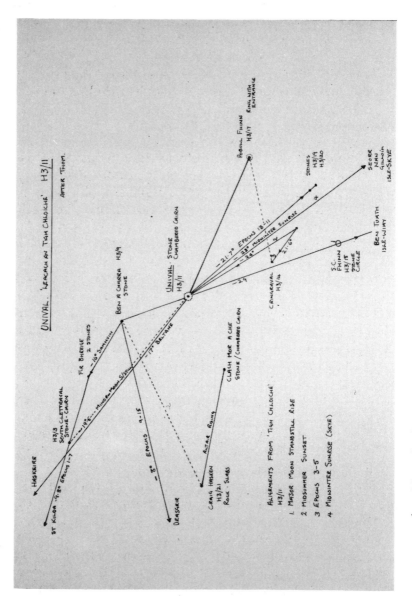

Alignment map centred on Uneval, after Thom

at least one that at some stage in its lifetime had other functions than just ritual burial.

There is an eight-foot-high (2.3m.) standing stone covered with lichen quite near to the northwest of Tighe Cloiche, and between it and the small loch below there are a number of other single stones. On Loch Fada there are the remains of a well-built dun on one of the inlets, and on the lower east slopes of Uneval are some green mounds with the remains of a souterrain.

Clach Mhor a'Che, Claddach Kyles

The literal translation of the name of this standing stone by the shore into 'Great Stone of the World' does not quite live up to the actual size, the stone being a mere eight feet (2.3m.) tall, nor its general situation either. It is close to a dilapidated stone cairn on the edge of a tiny inlet opposite to the low-lying sandbank called Kirkibost Island. Martin Martin, however, recorded a stone that was 12 feet high (3.6m.) set opposite a church on the isle, and to which malefactors were tied during Sunday service. Past the old school there is a natural boulder which was known as the 'witches stone' because a pair of them were burned here; while to the south are the remains of a possible small circle of stones, although there is now no evidence of a church on the island apart from its name.

It is often difficult when reading Martin's book to ascertain if he is recording contemporary observations or age-old fancies. However, it would be silly to dismiss as the latter his mention of a five-foot-high stone called the 'Water Cross', situated near Eilean Trostain, a few miles further north off Ard an Runair. He said that the cross was raised when the natives wanted rain and 'when they had enough laid it flat on the ground.' There is a local adage hereabouts that if you see St. Kilda clearly on the horizon it will rain the following day. Now the Island-group are 40 miles to the west and when we saw them ourselves early in the evening, it always rained the next day, so whatever the ritual or ceremonial background to the 'Water Cross', in general the story told to Martin seems to be based on some observable fact. Beveridge suggested that the 'Great Stone' might refer to Che, one of the seven sons of Cruithne, eponymous ancestor of the Picts, for others gave their name to Caithness and Fife. Today if one was looking for a possible candidate for its name, then in weight, breath and situation, the 'Limpet Stone of Freya' on the slope of Beinn a'Charra would fit the bill. A mile up the Committee Road, which turns off to the right past Claddach Kyles, and 400 yards up on the south slope of the hill, it stands over nine feet high and nearly seven broad. Around the base of it the peat has collapsed making a two-foot-deep rain-filled pool in front. Probing around the pool, the bottom of the stone seems a few feet further down. It looks sturdy enough but even this massive stone could be overtoppled in the hurricane gales that often sweep through here in winter—the pool ought really to be filled in with packing material to prevent such an eventuality. We tend to admire the largely impressive monumental stones but in antiquity it may not have been volume or size that determined importance. We can measure the exterior dimensions, examine the natural qualities, and even get the 'feel' or 'aura', but there is no way now that the mind can encompass the special relationship between the medium of stone, with its own essential qualities, and the ideals of those who erected them. Recent experiments have

Standing stone, Clach Bharnach Bharaodag (Limpet stone of Freya)

shown that individual stones or groups do affect certain patterns of earth energy, but whether in a manner we would consider scientific, is something we shall never know. Perhaps we are too educated in the ways of this material world and have lost the ancient faith of the stone builders and their humility before the mystery of the universe. The assumption that because we are born into the world and it is therefore ours to play around with, has wrought terrible consequences on the delicate balance of nature.

Nature Reserve, Balranald

During late summer when the midges are most active after the heat of the day, the only advice is *don't* go outdoors until the sun has set; but if you feel you have to, then aim for some high ground where there might be a little breeze. In sharp distinction to these minute devil hordes who always seem to attack the corners of the eye and the inside of the wrists, there is a decided lack of bird life among the treeless hills. An occasional cry of the hoodie or whistle of the stone chat is about as much as you can expect, but it is only when straying among the extensive sand dunes of the Nature Reserve that the full extent of this deprivation of natural habitat is brought home. Especially so during the nesting season when the Arctic terns kick up an almighty fuss if you happen to go anywhere near them. There is a keeper's hut maintained by the Royal Society for the Protection of Birds near the old cemetery at Hougharry, where all the regular and unusual winged visitors are logged. The occasional scaup nests here as well as the shellduck shoveler, rednecked phalarope, short-eared owl, hen harrier and corncrackes.

This is also one of the few areas left in Britain where the last-named birds nest, and it was one of the reasons why conservationists and other environmental groups were extremely perturbed when the Western Isles Integrated Development Programme (IDP) was going through Parliament. There was a lively debate in the House of Lords (Hansard report, Vol. 435, No. 142). One of the results of the publicity generated by various pressure groups was a massive influx of bird watchers in North Uist. While we stayed at the Gatliff Trust hostel at Claddach Belshare, near Clachan, for a

few days last summer, many of the younger and vocal bird
enthusiasts seemed to be under the impression that the whole
of the machair was going to be reseeded and turned over to the
tractor and plough. The Bill was made law in 1982 and the
IDP is funded jointly by the EEC and the British government
on a 60/40 basis to the sum of £55.5M. over a period of five
years on agriculture, fisheries and forestry improvement. Just
over £3M. are to be spent on improving the machair lands of
the west coast of the Uists through drainage, herbiciding,
reseeding or inbye land and grass pasture, lowering the water
table to dry out or reduce the size of lochans, and improve the
dry machair way from the shore.

The machair at present supports the highest breeding
densities of wading birds anywhere in Britain and probably
Western Europe, also ringed plovers and dunlins—unique in
that they breed at sea-level—as well as large numbers of
redshank, lapwing and snipe. There are, too, many varieties
of rare wild flowers in the wet pastures and hay meadows, so
there is not much doubt that the changes during the next five
years in particular, and thereafter, will alter some of the
existing flora and wildlife patterns. The R.S.P.B. welcomed
the scheme, for in the main there should be no harmful effect
on nature conservation, and it should benefit the local
community, but it is concerned with the improvement of
machair and inbye land and the fact that no finance for
environmental monitoring or protection is available from
EEC sources, although this may be forthcoming from
government departments.

It is early days yet to try to assess any effects on the local
environment. There is no doubt, either, that because of the
public outcry, any schemes for the improvement of the wet
machair will be carefully screened. The IDP team maintains
that it is essentially a pilot scheme, the first of its type in the
U.K., and that the full potential will only be realised once the
introductory works have been completed. The scale of the
response has been quite daunting with over 3,000 applications
during the first year including over 100 township
improvement schemes. Whether the three key factors isolated
by the team leader, 'more effective land utilisation, high-value
products and improved marketing techniques,' (*Stornoway*

Gazette Supplement, June '83) do integrate in terms of an overall improvement in living conditions, it is clearly on farming and especially crofting rather than fishery or forestry, that the IDP will be finally judged. From journeying up through the Hebrides before and about nine months after it was introduced, the most obvious effect was the new fencing along the main roads, which certainly helps to keep the sheep in, but one wondered if this was given priority because of its eye-catching ability, for apart from on a few well-managed farms the fencing did not extend too far back from the road. The other gripe is a bit more serious and a sad comment on how the islanders are projected without a business sense, almost as geriatrics in the modern world. Most of the tenders for this fencing came from mainland companies who proclaimed quite loudly and to the point that all the crofter would have to do was sign on the dotted line and they would take care of everything, as well as pocketing the profit. A proviso that the work should be done by islanders themselves, as far as possible, would have stopped the influx of the coyboys after easy pickings and kept some of the wealth within the pockets of those who need it rather than always to people with keen business expertise. One might have hoped that, contrary to the way other schemes in the past have been handled by the bureaucratic middle men, at least part of the job would have included enlightening locals on both the explicit and implicit side-effects of capital improvements instead of justifying foreign expectations. In short, it always seems to be the language blockage in the tube, with each side doing the correct gesticulations but talking to themselves in restricted codes and later hurling brickbats at each other when yet another marvellous venture has sunk without a ripple. Certainly the IDP are already accumulating data on the different types of projects, materials and methods which will provide an information pool and perhaps even a land utilisation map based on a realistic assessment of present use which will be needed in the debate on crofting that this scheme will almost certainly generate.

Within the Reserve are many different types of terrain, such as lochs, marsh, sand dunes, and beaches, each with its own peculiar wildlife, not to mention sea cliffs where the white-

tailed sea-eagle can be seen. The Reserve also includes the
rural township of Tigharry, with its well-kept air of good
land management—it retains the old harvesting techniques,
thus enabling the corncrake and corn bunting to thrive in their
natural habitat.

Perched on the summit of a slight hillock 600 yards
southeast of Hougharry is the old kirk-yard which surrounds
the site of an ancient chapel of Mary. All traces of it have long
been obliterated, but the largest tomb of clan Ranald (dated
1768) is thought to have occupied the site. Fulmar nest on top
of the MacDonald family tombs during the late spring and the
sight of these large birds silently hovering above one's head is
an eirie reminder of the early belief in the transference of the
human soul into bird or animal form. These birds live so long,
30 or 40 years, and mate for life as the mute swans do and with
their long narrow grayish wing feathers jutting out from the
top of their plump white bellies, that they would be our
nearest equivalent to the albatross. There is an interesting
collection of broken stone crosses from all ages scattered
about the overgrown kirkyard, including one that may have
looked similar to that at Kilpheder, a few miles to the north.
Beveridge, whose book *Archaeology of North Uist* (1909) is
crammed full of odd side lights and comments from someone
who was a proprietor here with the time and interest to
explore its ancient monuments, narrates a legend to explain
the earlier name of 'Colasaidh' for the area. The initial
intention to build a chapel at Hosta, over a mile to the
northeast, was altered in obedience to a command given by a
voice from the sky. 'Seachainn Hough agus Hosta, agus dinn
Cill-Mhoire an Colasaidh,' which means, 'avoid Hough and
Hosta and build St. Mary's in Colasaidh.' There is another
story about Loch Hosta containing an inundated township,
whose remains have been sometimes seen during drought
years, that may have had some connection with a common
and fairly traditional account of chapel siting. Colasaidh was
also said to have been the stone near the centre of the
churchyard so large that at one time a pair of horses could take
shelter behind it. Blaeu's map of 1656 shows 'Colliner Skye'
as a rock to the west of Ard an Runair, so that when one puts
these accounts together with Martin Martin's stories

alongside the name of Clach Mhor a'Che a few miles south of here, one can hear glimmerings of the extinct oral tradition of storytelling in which the explanations of natural and supernatural events were much more poetic than in our time. The American poet, Robert Duncan, summed this up remarkably well:

> Storytellers must have thought of themselves as makers; they made the story up and they talked about weaving a tale. And it may be that telling stories, being able to weave a tale, not just telling what happened, being able to weave a tale, goes along with being able to weave cloth. And the beginnings may well have [been] their very core, may have been the story you told as you wove the cloth, as the cloth was being woven.*

Megalithic Remains, South Clettraval

Eastwards from Tigharry, the old winding track that once hugged the hill and used for transporting peat has now been transformed into a proper metallic road to service the military installations that dominate the summit, a surrealistic dressed-steel geodesic construction. However, it's an ill wind... for the remains of the Neolithic cairn and Iron Age house are now more accessible for the visitor. In 1934 Lindsay Scott undertook an extensive excavation of this site which is 400 yards (364m.) southeast of the summit and 400 feet (121m.) above sea-level. Many of the structural slabs and most of the cairn material had been removed in antiquity to build the round-house abutting into the west end of the original wedge-shaped cairn. The upright megalithis that formed the 30-foot-long (9m.) passage slightly overlapped leading to the innermost compartment which was over seven feet (2m.) wide. In its southeast corner a number of slabs formed a cist-type structure. No roofing or capstones were found. The floor was paved with slabs and filled with black earth up to two feet deep. Charcoal, pottery shards, bones and other small artifacts were found. Small portions of human and animal bones were discovered in the lowest levels of the

* *Talking Poetics from Naropa Institute*, Vol. I, 1978.

Kilpheder Cross

innermost chamber, indicating the collective burials – about the only known feature of the people who used these cairns for over a millennium. This site is one of the few in North Uist that actually gives one some idea of the internal size and the required amount of stone slabs and smaller material necessary to have covered the sub-structure. However, most of this seemed to have been used to construct the wheel-house, also an enclosing wall to what is thought to have been a farmhouse and other subsidiary buildings, all of which have left traces in the immediate area. Some of the pillars can be seen quite clearly radiating out from the central hearth and are bonded to the circular outer part of the aisled house.

The wheel-house is a rather special form of architecture peculiar to the Hebrides, and there appears to have been two main types of living complex utilised from around the first century BC to about AD 400 though no doubt some of them were occupied later on. The single type of aisled-house which can be traced out of the site at South Clettraval is similar to many others that have been found along the sandy shore, and is roughly circular or oval, with access from the central area to the beehive compartments built up from the radial piers. This could have been roofed with grass or thatch but also left open during warm weather. The other kind of housing was a modular form with several circular areas interconnected, such as was found at Fosigarry. Beveridge seems to have investigated most of the examples that have been recorded on North Uist. It is possible that many more have been covered over during the intervening period and, given the violence of the storms here, these could be uncovered as happened with the stone house at Maes Howe in Orknay.

Directly northeast of Clettraval on the slopes of Ben Risary is a fairly clear example of a round-house with many similar ruined structures adjacent. The general elevation halfway up on the slope overlooking the sandy shore that leads out to Vallay seems to indicate a site of some importance, for most of the other recorded sites would be in clear view from here. In fact, looking up from the main road by the small bridge at Loch nan Clachan, the long green mount stands out clearly below the summit. Below it are the known sites at Fossigarry, Vallay Isle and on the promontory at Udal. From the finely made bone artifacts and other trinklets, as well as the evidence of their prodigious eating capacity from the vast mounds of shell fish they left lying about, they were clearly a wealthy and flourising community. There are also many examples of cup-marked stones close by or in the vicinity of these sites. At Buaile Risary a large embedded eight-foot-long (2.3m.) flat stone with a single squarish depression is at the north side of the complex. On Vallay quite a number of examples have been found and at Middlequarter is a natural boulder, which now seems to have been tipped over, with a great variety of round depressions as well as a deep kidney-shaped one. Outside this area of North Uist the only other cup markings that have been discovered in the Hebrides are on Tiree. The eight-foot-long (2.3m.) stone above the Sound of Flodda in Benbecula is near the ancient remains at Rossinish, and at Borve in Harris is a cup-marked stone which is fairly close to another extensive Bronze Age habitation site at Northton.

The archaeological chronology based on a general use of metal within an area and called the 'Bronze' or 'Iron Age' should not be too readily be applied to the Isles. A small stone axe factory excavated at Eilean an Tighe in Loch nam Geireann, south of Oronsay, was dated as Iron Age because of the pottery found there but it would be misleading to imagine that iron or bronze artifacts were much used there. It was the harder stone material and methods of stone construction that were preferable and used up to the late 19th century. It is generally accepted that the wheel-house people and the broch and dun builders were contemporary. The fact that the chambered cairns on Clettraval and on Unaval were plundered to make aisled-houses might be an indication of an increase in the local population there, either internally or from the outside. From the previous discussion about the duns it would certainly be necessary to have organisational centres within each major area and perhaps many of the masons were based there to prepare, dress, and construct the fortifications from there on down the chain of the Outer Hebrides. Beveridge listed over 100 ruined dun sites in North Uist alone, and with countless others ringing the coastlines perhaps we should consider this extraordinary expansion as the revitilising factor, an early IDP in fact. A society with patterns of living unaltered from an early prehistoric period right up to the Roman threat and even then there is little evidence, from the duns that have been excavated, that it altered much afterwards. Many of the duns themselves were in use spasmodically until the 16th century, and from the comment of Dean Munroe during this period, perhaps even the earth-houses, too, were used: 'Into this north heid of Ywst there is sundrie covis and holes in the earth, coverit with haddir above, quilk fosteris is many reballis in the countrey of the north heid of Ywst.'

If you continue further along the main road from Tigharry, on a hill by Kilpheder is a stone cross, set on an ugly plinth, which looks like a war memorial. It was in fact erected by Alexander MacLeod, or An Doctair Ban, who had his own ideas on how ancient monuments should look. He dismantled a dun in the middle of nearby Loch Scalpaig and replaced it with a folly, a curious octagonal tower topped with battlements and an enclosing wall around the edge of the islet. In the garden of Balelone House, which he had built in 1822, there is a rounded pillar stone with a figure of a swan or a snake in faint relief curving around its natural flow. The present owner thought it represented a woman and that the 39-inch (1m.) round column originally came from Cill Pheadair less than a mile to the northwest, where the stone cross is also supposed to have been found.

On the seaward end of the rather steep-sided Ben Scolpaig, at the very northwestern corner of Uist, are a number of ruined forts, natural arches and the deep bay supposed to have been the final rendezvous of the local pirates. Ancient midden heaps of packed brown sand proliferate along the shoreline. Clearly visible from this vantage point is the eastward sweep of low-lying sandy headlands, promontories and islands that have the most suggestive shapes in the changing light at sundown or under fast-moving clouds. Vallay Isle looks like a stickleback, Udal headland has the shape of a man, whereas the next one along, below Newtownferry, has the vague outline of a bear with open mouth chasing the small triangular morsel of Oronsay.

Some local yarns point to the finding of treasure. Apart from the old pirates meeting at Scolpaig, a hoard of gold and silver ingots were found in 1860 in Oronsay – whose name is suggestive of precious metal – so there is some basis for the islanders' treasure riddles, though probably not the 'seven skinfulls of gold' reiterated by Archie MacDonald in the midst of a delightful evening of endless stories made possible by the hospitality of the proprietor of the island, Lord Granville. Whether the short quatrains are variations on a 'one-tale' or esoteric reference, retained as folk memory, to stages of a hidden teaching which we ourselves favour, is an open question.

For some insight into this method of exploration the riddle printed in Beveridge's book will be used, as this was our first introduction. The only way we made any sense of the numerous ancient sites, ruins and old stones littering the machair was for Keith and myself to follow our intuitive noses from the 'swan' figure at Balelone House through to Vallay Isle and then across to the 'neck' of Udal and finally over to Berneray. This 'receptive line' cuts across ancient springs, chapels, cup-marked and 'witch' stones actually to join up with another alignment on Berneray that goes through a number of standing stones to Clach an t-Sagairt, the Priest's Rock, with an incised cross carved into it, to Crogarry Mor (180m.), one of the highest points in this region. It is also on its slope, just above the junction of the Newtonferry road and the main A865, that the story of the riddle begins.

The Fool's Seat, Crogarry Mor

'Treasure is concealed somewhere on Crogarry Mor at a spot from which can be seen three crofts, three duns and the shadow on the ground of a man ploughing.' Most of the hills have ancient sites on the south-facing slopes but after meandering down from the summit, whose name means 'Great Enclosure', past the fairly level plateau to the 100m. contour line on the northeast slope the place seemed to suggest itself. What had been, moments before, a half-hearted gesture in checking out yet another reference suddenly flickered into meaning as I sat comfortable on a rough quartz rock in the shape of a seat and looked at the wet sands of the estuary set out like a giant picture book. There were certainly more than three crofts visible, but taking it in the older sense of a large contained unit, the three isles of Vallay, Boreray and 'Oransay around the almost figurative shape of the 'man' in the peninsula beyond Sollas seemed a possibility worth following up. Even in the early summer evening the movement of the sun created a heightened contrast on the terrain below between the light-coloured sands and the wet surface of the estuary sand with an imperceptible shift due to loss of direct light. Without putting too fine a point on it, one could visualise the figure of the ploughman with his 'shadow' moving over the sands and lining up to the small surrounding islands. So sitting in the fool's seat, some of the riddle was becoming clear, for the 'shadow' suggested the movement of the sun, either rising or setting, and also the possibility of direction across the land linking two or more ancient places by a set of coordinates dependent on the time of day and the time of year. 'Fool's Gold', of course, goes back much further than the alchemical tradition and the matter of transmuting base metal into gold was an essential part of all inner teaching.

The natural world is normally a closed book to the city dweller. Life in the Hebrides has always been dependent on the people intimate with the cycles of the year and the day-to-day changes in the natural environment, so obviously here the kind of treasure that would be worth seeking would be very much to do with the finer workings of nature. Therefore becoming attuned to one's 'spot' and presumably visiting Crogarry Mor for important sunsets and at the full moon, which up here is often as bright as day but with a defused silver light, while absorbing a range of rudimentary observation about the natural world, the celestial bodies and the 'three R's' of that time, the seeker might suddenly have a flash of illumination that the answer lay beneath his gaze. One must bear in mind that such a form of teaching was an intimate affair between master and pupil, unlike today's impersonal schooling. Learning was more of a craft, the gradual unfolding of knowledge through an almost pragmatic observation of the natural world. The movements of clouds, birds, animals, even men, have a gestural quality, and within this landscape where the sky is ever present, each have a bearing on the others. Noticing such details with the changes in air and pressure, one unconsciously acquires a set of responses allowing one to 'read' the surrounding world.

One possible answer to the riddle is that earth's treasure, the harvest, will only appear after the ground has been turned over, the time when the first blade cut into the earth was very important in ancient Greece with special rites to Demeter. The Romans, too, had their form of propitiation which was much like those in Scotland. The traditional time for first ploughing was after the harvest fesitival of Lammas and probably before Samhain (1st November). On the first morning the farmer's wife would bring out a repast of specially prepared bannocks rubbed with cream cheese and a jar of whisky or beer for her husband. After blessing each other and the work that was to be done, the man would eat some of the cake and then give some to the horses before turning up the earth with that first cut of the plough.

So looking down at the strange shaded landscape of tidal runs, sand dunes and marron grass, the point of turning away from the old year revolves around the 'neck' of the figure. Beyond Udal sands at Ard a–Mhorain is a large smooth natural boulder which has a crude cross inscribed on it above a fresh water spring. A few yards away on an outcrop of rock are seven cup markings in a long line that goes down below the level of the shingle. So following this line towards Vallay, for at low time one may walk across the sand, you might discover the two standing stones there called by the suggestive name, 'Leac nan Cailleachan Dubhe.'

'Flat Stones of the Black Hags,' Vallay Isle

The island is about two miles long and can be reached at low tide, even in a car, across the ford from Claddach-Vallay. It is dominated by the gaunt ruin of Vallay House built by Ewen MacDonald, the factor in 1727, and it was from here that Ernest Beveridge, a retired manufacturer from DunFermline, devoted himself to his antiquarian hobby. He did sterling work on the ancient remains of North Uist, and his book of the same title – of which 300 copies were privately printed in 1911 – classifies and explores the remains of prehistory here. He did a lot of digging and poking in the 19th-century manner among the duns, chambered cairns and, especially, the earth-houses; and even though his methods would be frowned upon by today's professionals with their detailed analysis of every grain of dust, his writings are full of worthwhile information. He had the time to explore the numerous small islets in the lochs that are such a feature of the Uists, and being the proprietor, the locals were more than pleased to tell him the traditional stories associated with each place. He was also interested in cup-marks on rocks. A quarter of a mile west of the house and 200 yards from the shore is a stone with 13 cups on a flat surface low in the ground. Beveridge referred to another stone in the centre of Vallay with at least 40 cups on it; later, in 1931, a Mr. Pike from the Ordnance Survey found an additional 70 on the nearby rocks, but this area now seems to have been inundated with blown sand. On the northeast side of here, at Cean Uachdarach, is a small black stone protruding from the sand. Not far away on a grassy headland are the two stones, roughly six and five feet (5.5 and 4.5m.) high, standing by a small mount, and known as the 'Black Old Women' or 'Black Nuns'. The story, here, concerns two witches who were accused of stealing milk and then buried up to their necks by the gate of a field so that the cattle trampled them to death. The moral is clear. In days gone by, tampering with livestock whether by rustling, stealing their produce or giving them the evil eye to deprive their owner of milk, was considered the worst of crimes. But if we look deeper into the mytho-religious content perhaps we may see a reversal of a former practice of the rite to the goddess. In fact, the figure of the 'ploughman' could very easily be the 'sower' of seed, like the traditional Virgoen elongated figure of the celestial zodiac. The goddess is now accused of stealing the cream from the agrarian husbandman, the new lord of the land, and to prevent any deviation her wise women are trampled to death by 'his' cattle.

Lammas became the important ritual festival of the harvesting and thanksgiving, rather than Beltane, the older Fire rite, represented here by this 'Receptive Line' which in fact goes through the site known as Chapel Mhoire where, according to Martin, the local people offered milk on a thin flat stone called the 'Brownies Stone'.

Mary's Chapel is located by the old burying ground where some crude cross-incised slabs stand against the wall. The site of the aisled-house at Bac Mhic Connain dug out by Beveridge is near the cup marks west of Vallay House, and most of the pottery fragments, arrowheads and other artifacts he collected here are on display at the Museum of Antiquites in Edinburgh. The decorated knife handle carved in Ogham characters has been dated to between AD 600 and 800. The script of horizontal nicks on one edge of a stone, the Latin alphabet, was used extensively in Southern Ireland and seems then to have spread to Wales and into Scotland. The only other example found in the Hebrides is on a stone on Gigha. The Irish 14th-century manuscript, the *Book of Ballymote*, lists over 100 different kinds of cypher-languages, although that on the stone memorials was the most widely used and is now the best known. The 'Tree', 'Plant' and 'Bird' Oghams were the essential part of bardic learning and integrated into the natural lore. For example, using the tree alphabet, one could form a message using a string of different leaves, but unless the recipient knew the key – as in the first three letters, Beth-Luis-Nion, corresponding to Gaelic names for the birch, rowan and ash – the gesture would be undecipherable. It was a useful means of memorising a wide range of poetic and herbal lore.

Ancient Habitation Site, Udal Sands
The land around Sollas is typical of townships that were cleared and then later resettled as crofts with houses sited on each. There are some interesting cup markings to be found hereabouts. At Middlequarter is a single depression in a black outcrop of rock, behind the croft, slightly less than 100 feet from the telephone kiosk. Directly north of the schoolhouse is a large stone that stands out as a slightly elevated outcrop at the end of the croftlands. It measures 4 by 12 by 7 feet (1x3.6x1.9m.), and it is possible that it would have stood upright with its pointed end outwards showing its own cup markings and those on the bedrock underneath. There is a faint cross incised on the face, and the ruins of a house next to it were once called Tigh na Croice. Half-a-mile out from Middlequarter, on the Machair Leathann, is the site of one of the most outstanding wheel-houses yet found around this coastline. The structure comprised 14 radial sections arranged

like spokes of a wheel with an overall diameter of nearly 40
feet (11.9m.). After excavation it was filled in and covered
over by Beveridge.

The safest way to get to the extensive excavations among
the sand dunes at Coileagan on Udhaill is to take the path by
the telephone kiosk at Grenitote, and continue along the sands
(at low tide) until you reach a cutting in the dunes, and then
follow a well-worn track. However, you may actually miss
the site because there is little to be seen. It is an example of total
excavation. Ian Crawford of Cambridge has been clearing this
area since the 1960s, taking each layer to be examined and
minutely recorded. It is part of a long-term research into
settlement, economy and the environment of the ancient
peoples who once lived on this promontory. He has found
evidence of continuous occupation from the later Iron Age to
the 15th century. Four hundred feet (119m.) northwest of the
main settlement a small circle of stone and a broken burial cist
were found, the latter similar to the better-preserved example
excavated by Crawford at Rossinish in Benbecula. Continue
on the track to the cemetery and 200 yards (182m.) to the west
on the shoreline is a well beneath a rock inscribed with a cross.
Near the 'Rock of the Cross' are two parallel ridges of
outcropping with seven cup markings of roughly three and a
half inches (8.9cm.) diameter. Beveridge mentions that the
well was curative and that the cups were used in a local Pascal
pilgrimage to hold boiled eggs. There are other cup-marked
stones nearby, in particular a flat-topped boulder 'around the
corner' on the shingle with a series of cups marked out as a
triangular configuration. This was discovered by Duane
Granville, the proprietress of North Uist, who also
mentioned seeing spiral carvings on some rock faces within

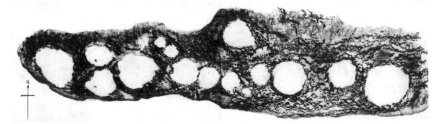

Rubbing of cup-marked stone, Aird a Mhorain

the area years previously but could not remember the exact location. At the tip of this promontory is a small pebbled island (covered with sea cabbage, which is quite tasty to eat) with a large circle of unhewn boulders – whether the results of the action of the sea or of the hand of man, it is impossible to tell.

From this point the mile-long isle of Boreray is quite visible but unless you can persuade someone to take you out in a boat it is inaccessible. It is now used for grazing cattle. Known as the 'Black Women', three long slabs on the northeast headland stand on edge, but look as if they were once the passageway to a chamber as nearby there is a large capstone. There are some cup-marked stones here including a large smooth brown block on the shore with quite a few weathered examples on its upper surface. Further along the southeast shoreline is a five-foot-high (1.5m.) standing stone, and also a most peculiar carving of an H-shape on a flat stone near the high-water mark. Similar to the modern symbol for helicopters landing, perhaps it was used by the kelpies skimming across on flat stones from the main island.

Stone of Judgement, Berneray Isle

At Newtownferry while we waited for the boat to Berneray, a local man told us the story of the stone where an accused would sit and if found guilty, especially of the evil eye, would be taken to the nearby eight-foot-high (2.3m.) standing stone at Cladh Maolrithe for beheading. The heads would be interred in the local graveyard and the bodies buried at Eilean an Dunan on the other side of Loch Borve. This fitted in quite well with the quest of the riddle for if an acolyte had progressed this far by way of sacred sites through the 'neck' at Udal and failing to answer correctly, he might then lose his status as a seeker of knowledge or be sent back to the fool's seat to begin again. There is a very curious legend recounted by Otta Swire (in *Folk Tales of the Outer Hebrides*) that Berneray was once inhabited by a 'sept' (clan) called MacAndy who were 'a house divided against itself,' in that half the people loved the land, its plants and animals, and occupations such as farming, and swore by the sun. The other half loved the sea, its plants, its creatures, and the occupation

Stone of Judgement

of fishing, and swore by the moon, and the light of the stars. One day a witch of the land people put the old druid to sleep, stole his wand of power, and touching all the others turned them into birds of light. The land-lovers cursed by this evil deed done in their name have ever since been grubbing for their living like 'worms of the dust'. This division is still evident today within the 300 people who live on this fertile isle although the only fishing now is for lobsters.

If you follow the road up from the pier at Bays Loch towards Borve you should pass a very curious-shaped conglomeration of earthfast boulders and a four-foot-high (1.2m.) standing stone called the 'Cairn of the Children'. The reason for its name is that children of every generation have played here. West of Borve Hill on the flat plateau which is being turned into an airstip is a circular setting of small stones and to the south of it is the Judgement Stone, shaped like a seat with a curved back. Slightly to the west is a startling white stone and directly opposite is a black one about two feet (0.6m.) high. An earth house was found nearby but the stones were removed for building.

The planned airstrip on Berneray will effectively extend the

inter-isle communications network. It will make the ferry
link between it and North Uist (Newtonferry to Lochmaddy)
and Harris (Leverburgh to Tarbert) more viable, bring in
more people, help the hotels and generally aid the island's
economy. Once completed and in operation it will seem a
beguiling part of an acceptable chain of tourism. Yet each link
has been planned, designed and constructed seemingly in
isolation. A minor consideration in all the planning logistics is
that the special quality (serenity/peace/beauty – call it what
you will) of a small island like Berneray will evaporate under
the noise of the aircraft and all the accompanying pollutants
and general bustle, and that those who have lived there all
their lives will be affected worst of all. Pro or con, the
arguments are circular, but one thing is certain: anyone who
lands here in a plane cannot possibly experience what the isle
was like before the advent of the machine.

There are a number of tales about the ravens who inhabited
this isle. One pair, 2,000 years old, were believed to have been
sent from Noah's Arc prior to the doves finding dry land. All
the ravens found in the way of food were dead carcasses so
they were cursed to live here forever. They were also said to
have been brought here by the Druids and 'that the standing
stone by the church was once part of a stone circle in which the
Druids stood to observe the birds and from their doings to
draw auguries'. There are now no traces of the church, but the
stone was broken in two early last century and the top
patterned section can be seen in the Museum of Antiquities,
Edinburgh. The stump which is now missing was then
surrounded by a heap of small white pebbles, bone pins and
bronze needles offered by the pilgrims to the chapel of St.
Asleph. The pattern on the remaining slab of dark gneiss is a
square divided into eight triangles, each filled with a single
straight-line spiral. The sheaf-like incomplete interlace design
is reminiscent of many of the St. Brighid corn dollies, and the
spiral pattern has been found on other stones at Invergowerie
in Scotland and Tuam in Ireland.

This design may have been a key to the higher grade of the
teaching: namely, megalithic geometry and the conjunction
with celestial bodies. For having survived the riddling and not
lost one's head at the Judgement Stone, one could proceed to

the summit of Beinn Shieible (93m.) and perhaps begin to see the connections between the St. Asleph's Stone and that at Cladh Maolrithe, in the form of a new 'Energy Line' along which one could proceed back across the water to the stones at Port nan Long, known as Crois Mhic Jamain, which have the appearance of nipples protruding from the curves on the mounds. From here to Clach an t-Sagairt, which is a great boulder of solid mass with an inscribed cross and a fresh water spring below it, would indeed be a new beginning, for from this earth stone out to Boreray in St. Kilda is the path of an equinoxical sunset alignment. The final rays of the sun itself, viewed from important sites along a great curve of nearly the length of the Hebrides, fall on Berneray, thereby creating a rudimentary calendrical system known as the Ritual Year, the astronomical background of which, formulated by Professor Thom, is considered in the Harris section of the book.

St. Asaph's, Berneray

Another important factor in attempting to see these monuments as part of an old sacred geography is that the ground geometry, coherently assimilated here, could be a proper basis for the next grade of the teachings on the Isle of Lewis focussed on the dynamic relationship between the stone circles at Callanish, the landscaped figure known as the Sleeping Beauty, and the 19 year cycle of the moon.

Dun Torcuill, Lochportain

On the road from Newtonferry, the remains of a galleried dun can be seen in a shallow tidal loch, half-a-mile south-southeast of Port nan Long. Three well-built causeways extend from the shore, the southern one nearly 200-feet (60m.) long with loose stones on top which may well have been 'clattering stones'. Various interpretations of the name Dun an Sticer have been given such as 'Little Black Fort', 'Fort of the Skulker', and 'Isle of Bad Counsel.' All part of a local tradition of a Hugh MacDonald who laid claim to the island in 1601 but was driven to take refuge in the dun and later imprisoned at Dunvegan Castle in Skye. Some stories say he escaped using beef bones from his dinner and others that he went mad on salt beef and no water.

Further on, at Clachan Sands on an islet in Loch Trumiagarry, another ruin – Dun Aonghais – which was occupied by Angus the Fair early in the 16th century. It was probably built up from an earlier dun site. Certainly the best example of one of these ornate 'castle'-like duns is Dun Torcuill. One hundred yards (91m.) from the turn-off on the minor road to Lochportain is a sign giving some details, but unfortunately there is no track leading to it though it is possible to skirt the edge of the loch to a small islet near the shore. The 'clattering stones' are very much in evidence walking across the causeway which is level with the water. Any sudden noise would have given ample warning of people approaching the fort at low tide. The walls are nearly 14 feet (4.2m.) thick with evidence of internal galleries and stepped lintels. The top of the wall is broken and uneven but gives a clear picture of the structure even though the interior is now filled with brambles and nettles. The central courtyard is nearly elliptical with a small abutment looking out over the loch. Mute swans now nest below on the bedrock. Since the foundation rises abruptly, the fort was built upon it. There are also two walled enclosures on either side, probably used for cattle and garden stock. Complete, it must have been altogether a most elaborate structure which probably belonged to the early castle building phase rather than the late Iron Age dates usually given to this type of broch. There may have been a smaller fort here previously but the style and the grandeur of concept make it akin to the walled keep. The Torcuill associated with the fort probably refers to a MacLeod chieftain. During the 16th century, the MacLeods of Dunvegan and Harris disputed the MacDonald claim to North Uist, and occupation of the fort can reasonably be assigned to this period. There are at least four other dun sites within Loch an Duin, as well as a number of stone slabs and earth houses around the shore. On the land side of the causeway leading to Don Torcuill is a cairn of stones that may have been a memorial. Out on the great headland, half-a-mile south of Lochportain, is a dilapidated soutterain in a rather inaccessible position between the base of a precipice and the edge of Loch Hacklett. A long narrow gallery of dry stone walling is visible in a gap of the roof, but the ends are blocked by falling masonry and look out over the edge of the loch. It has been used by otters. Further south and near Loch Grota are the remains of ruined hut circles at a place called 'Hollow of the Kettle.'

The name for the small standing stones on the northwest slope of Blashaval, Na Fir Bheige, stems from a story of three men from Skye who deserted their wives and were turned into stone by a witch. The name 'False Men' is also applied to the stones on Toroglas as well as at Straith Aird on Skye. Moreover there is a widespread association between megalithis and people turned to stone. In Cornwall it is the 'Blind Fiddlers' and the 'Merry Maidens' while in Oxfordshire it was the 'King' and the 'Whispering Knight' and his 'men' who became the Rollrights because he angered a local witch. The Callanish Stone circle was said to have originally 'been' the wise men of the district, who refused to build a chapel for a Christian saint.

Two miles from Lochmaddy, almost opposite the

telephone box on the main road, is a turning that leads to the narrows between Minnish Isle and Collestone. Access across the stepping stones at low tide leads to the foundations of a chapel on Eileann an Teampull. Fifteen yards north of the ruin is a broken standing stone with the stump still in the ground. There is also a very interesting example of a dead-eye mounted on a plinth. This is a round flattish wooden block that was set in a rope or iron band passing round it, and pierced with three holes for a lanyard. Minish Isle is merely one of a vast number if islands in the tidal reaches of Loch Maddy.

All the isles in the Sound of Harris are now uninhabited except Berneray, which has a regular ferry service with Leverburgh. This is probably the best place to make enquiries if you want to explore any of the others for you will be told quickly enough who is likely to be going out for some fishing, when and from where. These isles are usually leased for grazing so one should first of all ask permission before attempting to hire a passage across.

Ensay

At the northwest end of this small fertile isle is an important archaeological site now registered by the Scottish Survey as an Ancient Monument and therefore protected. It is not a 'dig' as such but rather a recording of each level as it is exposed by natural erosion. In 1960 storm winds broke through the grass cover and the sand blowing away at a rate of three to four feet per year gradually revealed human burials of progressively earlier periods. These have been carefully rescued each summer and studied to determine the age, height, physical condition and much else about the islanders of earlier times. The present level is probably 15th century with a possible 12th-century chapel which had been covered by blown sand. This chapel may have been built on pre-Christian midden as pottery shards seem to indicate.

One hundred yards north of Ensay House, a building was restored as a chapel in 1900, having been formally used as a stable. The present altar and small recess probably date from then. Beside the entrance is a drum of granite in which a small font has been wrought. There is also a little quartz stone basin and a five-inch (12.7cm.) communion bowl. At Cnoc a Caistel is an irregular-shaped stone slab, five feet (1.5m.) high, set on edge with a considerable slant to the west.

Killegray

On the northwest promontory, Rubh an t-Soithich, are the grass-covered foundations of an old chapel measuring 21 feet by 12 (6.3 x 3.6m.). It is situated 30 feet (9m.) above the shoreline and aligned due east/west. To the south is a fine spring of water. Chapel and spring are probably the Teampull na h'Annait and Tobar na 'Annait mentioned in the Statistical Register of Scotland, Vol. 5. The term 'annat' is considered to have been applied to the earliest Christian settlement in any island community. At Shadar on Lewis the word was used in its plural form to mean the stretch of pastureland extending inland for a few hundred yards from the shore by Teampull Pheadair.

On a rocky tidal islet near the southwest shore are the remains of a circular fort, Dunan Ruadh, which is located on a grass-covered plateau and surrounded by a small wall. Further south there is the site of a second dun.

Pabbay

The mound on which Teampull Mhoire was originally built seems to have grown up around and inside the chapel with grave slabs occupying the inner recess, which is open to the sky as the east wall has disappeared. Early in the 19th century Muir mentions the ruin, measuring it as 40 feet by 20 (12x6m.), and with two windows. One in the north wall has completely disappeared now and a whole section of the remaining south wall is bowing out and will no doubt soon collapse. The masonry over the door is also beginning to sag, and beyond the doorway is a six foot by five foot (1.8 x 1.5m.) section of a four-foot-wide (1.2m.) wall that may have been part of a second chapel.

Near the centre of this round isle at Creag Huristan is a natural rock which stands out as quite a landmark here, with a cave-like cavity receeding downwards for about ten feet (3m.). From the strong smell, it is certainly used by the small herd of red deer as a rump-rubbing and sheltering den. The atmosphere is cool with the same feeling as inside the stone chamber of a burial cairn. Name graffiti have been scratched on one overhead soft rock and a few simple 'drawings' of deer can also be seen. Up to the 19th century Pabbay had a population of over 300 people, but it was cleared in 1858 for, it was said, illicit whisky distilling, so the graffiti must have been done prior to that date.

The remains of a circular cairn lie west of Bailenacille, 'Town of the Chapel,' which now has one house occupied by a new owner part of the year. There are many ruined shielings and enclosures in the immediate vicinity so this was probably the main township of Pabbay. There are oval-shaped curb settings of overgrown stones on the hillslope, that may have been used as wind-breaks by the shepherds, and they are remarkably similar to the structures on the west slopes of Mingulay, south of Barra. Twenty yards (18m.) below the summit of Beinn a' Charnain (196m.) is a nine-foot-long (3.6m.) dressed stone that may have once been standing but is now lying backwards against the slope.

Ruins of Teampull Mhoire

Mapping the Long Isle

Stone and Hag, S. Harris

South Harris

The collection of stone-built houses clustered on the sides of the road down to the pier at Tarbert do little to dispel the accumulative impression of deserted rock-strewn hills prevalent throughout Harris. Even the long-established ferry services to Uig in Skye and Lochmaddy in North Uist have not generated anything memorable hereabouts. If arriving by road from Stornoway for the first time (regular bus services are available), you might expect the gateway to Harris to contain more than a few grocery shops and a woolen-tweed store with its own dash of island character being no more than a glorified tin shed. There is a 26-bedroom hotel here, and the Tourist Information office during the holiday season will advise you on other accommodation and any local events. This portacabin was blown over into the ditch during the winter gales of a year or two ago. Coming in from the sea through the long sweep of East Loch Tarbert, past its low-lying islets and grey headlands, the short wooden pier and sudden halt to the engines is always a bit of a surprise. Within minutes the boat is tied up and passangers and cars are being unloaded with such speed and efficiency that, very often complete with a mountain of baggage and wobbly 'sea-legs', the transition to terra firma has an air of fearful unreality about it. Especially if the drizzle that formally was making such delightful patterns on the surface of the sea is nothing less than a downpour with the wind behind it, and you belong to the breed of travellers, like myself, who rarely make any prior arrangements in order to sustain the full primitive spontaneity of meeting the isles on their own terms.

However, to avoid being reduced to such unpleasantness a 'phone call in advance to the Tourist Information will elicit the available accommodation within your price range, and there is usually a local taxi though you may have to wait your turn for it or share with others going in the same direction. If, however, you plan to tour South Harris, then you should stock up on supplies since there will be even less amenities elsewhere on the isle than in Tarbert. This may sound a rather ordinary introduction but the usual Hebridean village shop-cum-post office offers little more than cheese, biscuits, tin food, chocolate and white sliced bread – if you are lucky enough to remember the times of the ferry when the vans deliver. So it is as well to have that something extra with you to top off a day spent on some of the more strikingly beautiful beaches in Europe that would be full of bare bodies if on a more southerly latitude than 58° north of the Equator.

The Scarista House Hotel situated along the western coastline, serves an excellent set dinner which has received the only entry in the *Good Food Guide* for the whole of the Hebrides. The rosette for the 1984 good breakfast has also been added to its highly recommended wholesome food, excellent sauces and fresh green vegetables that are such a rarity up here. There is also a small hotel and homely public bar at Rodel, which was once the 'brew-house' alongside the MacLeod residence until the end of the 17th century. A plaque over the front door commemorates the Queen's innaugural visit after the Coronation in 1956. Hunting up a morning coffee, the staff usually seem surprised to see anyone else afoot and they also have that elastic notion of time which turns the most placid visitor to the Hebrides into a raving zenophophic extolling the virtues of the clock and other blandishments of the civilisation just across the water which previously was so eagerly eschewed.

On the way south there are a number of minor roads on the east side which lead down to the rocky shoreline and which form a series of short circular loops through the minute habitations of Grosebay, Kyles Stockinish to Ardwey, on the road down to Rodel where the A859 along the west coast meets up with this even larger loop around the mountainous interior. Harris was never crowded but the present population of a few thousand people is roughly half that of a century ago. Even without natural soil, this area was settled after the people had been cleared from the rich pasturelands of the machair, much as we have seen elsewhere, and by extensive cultivation of lazy beds supplemented by fishing they managed to sustain a living. This was the period when the Napier Commission, set up by Gladstone to look into the conditions of the people, toured the Isles and was largely instrumental in the creation of the Crofting Acts of 1886. Security of tenure probably gave these bays and inlets a new lease of life, for it coincided with the steamships opening up the Hebrides to the ordinary traveller; hitherto, the isles had been the preserve of the gentry or the nouveau riche sporting and yachting crowd. The combination of cheap rail and steam tickets with three-day or weekly excursions from Edinburgh and Glasgow created a unique mode of travel, which enabled visitors to tour the islands at something approaching their own pace, stopping at small piers like Rodel to pick up mail and passengers. 'Boats like Lochiel, Lochearn, Lochdunvegan, Clyeside, Lochbroom, Hebrides and Clansman became an almost permanent part of island life. Their arrival and departure was often the focal point of the week in a remote community. In the summer months they brought visitors and relatives but all year round they were carrying cargo, cattle and sheep, often in weather which would have daunted a skipper unused to such wild seas.' (*Road to the Isles*, Derek Cooper, 1979). It was World War One which largely put an end to this form of travel, and since the last War not only has the inter-isle excursion become a thing of the past but also the self-sufficiency of the small communites that existed on its delicate infra-structure for survival.

The Old Burial Route
Unless you can hire a boat, the car traveller of today (and islander, too) is deprived of the ancient vantage point of the sea from which the Hebrides have always been approached. And unless you have a particular love of walking or mountaineering, the interior of Harris is also a closed book. Yet there are valleys across the island that repay the slow minute observation of the natural terrain and compensate for the vast panoramic overview of hills, lochs and seascape visible from the inside of a car. At the head of Loch Stockinish is the beginning of an ancient route across South Harris from

east to west, over the pass known as Bealach Eorabhat. It is a dark and atmospheric boulder-strewn place where changes of light on the Stocklett range (from the Old Norse, meaning 'a head cast-up') reflect the mournful memories of the traditional coffin-carrying journeys to the burial ground at Luskentyre. As you walk away from the bridge, and follow along the river towards the west, the profile of the hills above begins to take on the shrivelled aspect of an old crone. At a mile from the Pass, the track lifts and bends above the swampy plain and the first flat-topped resting stone (a boulder eight foot long, three feet wide and six feet high/ 2.4x1x1.8m.) is visible below the full profile of the dark mountain. On the southern slope of the hill beneath West Stocklett is a circle of 13 varied-shaped unhewn boulders set in a crude ring 60 feet (18m.) in diameter. It is looking back, due east from this circle, through the narrow tunnel of vision, which shows the mountain as a figure of a woman against the long sweep of the valley down to the sea, with the distant peaks of the Cuillin visible on Skye. Beyond the Pass, beneath the slopes of Clett na Duach (Gaelic, meaning 'Rock of the Ugly'), is a small flat area beside the path with eight cairns built on it as well as a three-foot-high (0.9m.) standing stone. The path drops down past a small loch with a pair of resident swans and finally moves into the open valley with a marvelous view of Traigh Luskentyre. Below its great headland are wonderful beaches, and beyond Taransay, on a clear day, the twin humps of Hirta and Boreray are minutely visible 40 miles out on the horizon. The traditional manner of transporting the dead across such paths and resting the coffin on flat-topped cairns has of course become a thing of the past but it is the male relatives who still carry the deceased into the burial ground, while the women wait outside or more usually at their cottage doors as the cortege passes. It is only after the dead have been buried that the women visit and tend the graves.

Moving slowly down the east coast towards Rodel, we were trying to contact some outsiders from England, friends of a mutual friend, who with their small children were trying to make a go of it somewhere near Manish. We eventually received directions from a passing postman who was also selling cartons of long-life milk; he told us we should continue down the road until we came to a turning with a large Co-op van lying on its side. The only thing I knew about Pete and Sharon was their mobile shop selling health foods, brown rice and homemade bread, but clearly this venture had not been successful. At the end of the uneven track we would have to walk until we reached the shore. It sounded idyllic and it seemed so in the sunlight. Their house was just above the rocks on a stretch of green sward in the lee of the hill amid the constant beat of the waves. After exchanging news over a cup of tea, we arranged to meet later in the bar at Rodel. Pete, like many of the young men from the area, was learning to weave, for apart from fishing it was now the only trade with active government support and subsidy. The clackity-clack of the looms and the blare of Radio One from their corrugated shacks on Lewis is common enough as the weavers spend long solitary hours at their painstaking work. In fact this is the only cottage-based aspect of a manufacturing industry. In 1976 the weavers voted overwhelmingly against a proposal to use larger power-driven looms rather than the Hattersley domestic one with its foot-operated treadles, first introduced here by Lord Leverhulme. At the time the vote was generally condemned as a restrictive practice and a perfect example of Hebridean shortsightedness, but with the uncertainties of world markets due to the recession and other factors, their move is now seen in retrospect as a wise one. During the pre-War days it usually took months to make a country gent's outfit, whereas now the modern cloth is tailored to suit the demands of London and American fashion markets. The fleece is clipped, scoured in warm water, dried and then dyed in large vats followed by various machined stages to turn it into yarn, to be passed over to the weavers in large hanks with the warp running lengthwise as well as the necessary amount of waft to weave the actual cloth. The bundles of their finished 'greasy' webs are left outside the post office awaiting collection and delivery to the factory in Stornoway. Afterwards it is finished and marketed under the familiar trade mark of the orb and Maltese cross, coat of arms of Lord Dunmore (who bought Harris in 1834 for £60,000). It was Catherine Dunmore, the proprietor's wife, who first took the tweed to the mainland for sale during the famine of 1845; and to popularise it, had it made up for her gillies and keepers to wear, based on the traditional hacking garb of the gentry.

St. Clements Church, Rodel

It is said that Lady Dunmore had one of these same gillies loose off a shotgun at one of the carvings on the outside of St. Clements Church tower but this may be an apocryphal story as she had the church repaired in 1884, 1887, and again in 1893. Sheela-na-gig carvings—male and female figures of lust— were common features on many of the Romanesque churches in Ireland, England and on the Continent. The only other example found in the Hebrides is at the nunnery on Iona. Iona certainly influenced the builders of St. Clements in some of its structural features and the use of the same freestone dressing as was used on the Abbey Church of Iona and brought from a quarry at Carsaig on Mull.

Dated early 16th century and possibly erected on the site of an earlier building, it accommodated the irregular-shaped underlying rock so as to slope snugly into the hillside above the northwest shores of Loch Rodel. Built to a cruciform plan, measuring 85 by 21 feet (25.8 x 6m.) externally, it comprises a nave, choir and two cross aisles beneath a continuous roof, although the aisles are slightly lower and the tower on the western side rises to nearly 60 feet (18m.). This elegant church is one of the best-preserved and outstanding examples of ecclesiastical architecture in the Isles and must have been a prominent landmark within the deep sheltered bay. Inside the church a block of Lewesian black gneiss sparkling with quartize was carved into the arch of the north transept. There are also a number of ornate tombs, the largest and most elaborately carved, that of Alaistair Crotach MacLeod was built into the south wall. The earliest reference to the church was by Dean Munroe, who wrote in 1549: 'within the south part of this isle lynns are monesteary with one steipill, quhilh was founded and biggis by McCloyd of Berneray Horrey calit Roodill'. As well as the MacLeods of Bernera, it was also the burial place of the MacLeods of MacLeod (of Dunvegan and Harris). Donald MacLeod, known as 'old Trojan', is buried in the grounds. In a very troubled era he managed to live to a ripe

Rubbing of Angel, from the tomb of Alaistair Crotach Macleod

old age, marrying three times, the last at 75 to a girl of 16 who then had nine children. At his funeral it was said that his eldest son was over 80 and the youngest not yet ten. Clearly a ladies' man, it was for him that the bardess Mary MacLeod, Mairi Nighean Alastair Ruaidh, produced some of her best poems. It is said she was buried face downwards here. The Clement to whom the church was dedicated was not the Bishop of Rome but a more humble Dominican Bishop of Dunblane (d.1258) who is shown on the great tomb inside with mitre and crook holding a skull in his right hand.

An old man locally remembers that when he was a boy, the tower was roofed with turf and hit by a thunderbolt. When they repaired the roof to its present pyramidal shape, a copper lightning conductor was installed from the pinnacle to the base level and while digging a large hole in the floor, which is 11 feet above that of the rest of the structure, the bones of many bodies were found. These were reburied in the graveyard outside. Around the outer walls of the tower are a number of panels with stone carvings of animals and people. As one strolls through the trees and fuchsia bushes or among the family tombs—largest is that of Sir Norman MacLeod of

Looking due west over church, Rodil

Bernera (1614–1709) who purchased Harris for the sum of £15,000—the green turf is like a gentle oasis after the grey windswept hills of the rest of Harris. Compared to it, Rodel is like a soft green heart pulsating with unearthiness and traces of ancient sanctity. This gentle aspect has an unsettling effect that is common to nearly all the early ecclesiastical sites throughout the Isles.

Martin mentions two stone circles here, one he saw himself to the east of Rodel Bay within eight yards of the shore. 'It is about three fathoms [18 feet/5.4m.] underwater, and about two stories high; it is in form broader above than below. I saw it perfectly on one side but the season being windy, hindered me from a full view of it.' The islanders reported to him that there was a second such circle in the waters on the other side of the bay. The sea hereabouts is quite deep and the cliffs are continually sliding away. There is a local tradition of an entire village falling into the sea, and it may have been part of this that Martin saw at a neap tide. Otta Swire reports a belief in a small stone circle called the 'The Stones of the Sun' and wonders if the stones were used in the building of the church tower. Outside by the marshy ground there is now a large ring of boulders, originally quarried from the bedrock of the knoll to the south of the tower, that have been placed around it as a boundary wall or enclosure. On the bottom edge of one of the boulders is a carving of a sunwheel, only half of the rayed symbol being visible above the ground. This may have been a cross that had been placed in a prominent position before this knoll was blasted. The rayed motif, developed from 'Chi-Rho' encircled crosses, is found carved on stones in Irish monasteries, especially at Clonmachnois.

Not much is left to see of the two ancient forts built on either end of this knoll. A mass of grassy stones rises about six feet (1.8m.) above the foundations of a dun on the summit of the highest point locally, roughly 100 feet above sealevel. It was said that Donald MacLeod had a castle here but there is now only a well-built stone cairn. Dun Stuaidh was built at the rocky end of a slip of land that juts out into Loch Rodel. Stuaidh is the name of the shingle isthmus itself, barely a foot above water at ordinary tides. The remains of a seven-foot stone rampart with a two-foot-wide wall can still be seen, obviously adding to the naturally defensive nature of the small rocky peninsula. The edifice is now a green-covered mound. However, it aligns due west with the church tower and the cairn on the hill, along the Spring equinox line.

Leverburgh

The A859 from Rodel along the rocky southwestern coastline passes through some evocative place-names from local history, though their present-day surroundings hardly merit attention. Leverburgh, once the epitome of an ageing soap magnate's dream to drag the Hebridean Islands into the 20th century, still has a small ferry service to Berneray and Newtonferry in North Uist. When he became disenchanted with the reaction of some of the Lewis folk to his good works and good intentions, he moved to Borve Lodge, about five miles north of Leverburgh, which he had decided should become a major fishing port, and accordingly changed its name—Obbe—to make it a fitting reflection of his own. The project was abandoned after Leverhulme's death two years later in 1925 and the buildings and installations were sold off or demolished. A few managers' homes and the schoolhouse, originally Hulme Recreation Hall, are all that remain today. Above the schoolhouse at the edge of a tiny island, the top of a standing stone stands clear of Loch Steisevat (marked on the 1865 six-inch map), and on the opposite shore are three standing stones in a line, the largest four foot long by seven foot (1.2 x 2m.) wide.

Imbued with the notion of service to others, entrepreneurial altruism is rather like a new faith that sweeps in on a spring tide, creates an eddy and disappears again after its own fashion. When Leverhulme bought the Isles of Lewis, Harris and Kilda after the Great War, his energy, personal magnetism, wealth, and general flamboyant attitude in doing what was normally considered impossible, put the Hebrides on the news map of the civilised world for a few short years. Yet he, in common with many outside groups and individuals before and since, treated the islanders paternally, like a family of unruly children rather than as people whose knowledge and acceptance of the obdurate nature of the islands is often the very thing that exemplifies their 'backwardness' to outsiders.

However, his grandiose insensibility in incorporating that most sacrosanct of titles in local history, 'Lord of the Isles,' as his own after he had been knighted, did not endear him to a people whose natural reserve and politeness towards others is one of their most noticeable charactcristics. When the Lewis ex-servicemen returned home demanding land to live on rather than paid employment, as labour for him, he took this as a personal affront and moved south to Harris. Even here his foolishness outdid him for he tried to set up Leverburgh when he was financially unsound. In fact, it is not for such grandiose schemes that he is probably best remembered but for his acute business sense, as when he put up the investment for the Hattersleylooms, and for helping local fishing by creating outlets on the mainland with the MacFisheries chain of stores, in which ways he was encouraging a work pattern that was an intrinsic part of the life here.

Similarly, Lady Dunmore, too, had encouraged the application of the weaving skills, and it was at Strond, less than a mile from Rodil, that the first web of tweed was sold by the 'Paisley Sisters' in 1846. The wearing of the tartan had been outlawed a century earlier, and when the Scottish parliament forced the people to weave and wear the accursed grey, known in Gaelic as 'riochd-mallaichte', a decline began in the age-old use of natural coloured dyes. According to George Buchanan, the natives then often slept out in the snow, wrapped in their huge purple and blue plaids, and indoors they lay down for the night on some ferns or heather strewn on the floor. The colours in the cloth indicated rank and privilege. One for servants, two for farmers, three for officers, five for chiefs, six for the bards and seven for kings and queens. It was the women who dyed and spun the fleece. Occasionally one can still come across their large iron pots set beside a small stream in which they boiled the water for the dyeing, infusing herbs and lichen in it to produce a particular colour: bright blue from bilberry mixed with alum and the paler shade from elder, or broom; ling heather pulled before flowering produced green as did iris, broom and furze bark; the yellow lichen on rocks called crotal turned wool dark brown and the plant known as corcer produced purple or crimson.

The words of the weavers' songs were often improvised or without much meaning, merely there to pace the rhythm as the women worked together but there are many that almost illustrate the process itself. The 'Sett' from Benbecula is a good example (*Poems of the Western Highlands*, G.R.D. McLean, p.318):

The black go by the white thread.
The white go by the black led,
The green go in between red,
The red between the black thread.

The black go in between red,
The red between the white thread,
The white between the green led,
The green between the white thread.

The white between the blue thread,
The blue between the bright red,
The blue, the scarlet-hue wed,
The scarlet true the due thread.

The scarlet to the blue thread.
The blue to scarlet-hue wed,
The scarlet to the black led,
The black onto the bright red.

A thread one to the threads two
Of colours two, good and true,
The two threads of black due,
The one the thread of white through.

Seven threads to five be,
And five be unto three,
Three to two, two to one,
In every border done.

The lichen on the rocks, as well as the colours of the birds on the foreshore and the summer flowers on the machair, were all incorporated into the outer appearances of these people. There was never any clash between inner and outer

harmonies. They mirrored the land they walked on in a way we shall never know about, and used whatever it or the seas produced with thanks and joy. They utilised the flowering elements of nature without distorting the ecological chain. Even their blackhouses were tucked away unobtrusively out of the wind as much as possible, merging into the rocky ground itself.

Rubh'an Teampull, Toehead

There is a turning off to the left through the pleasant little township of Northton to the great rocky headland, just before the extensive sands of Traig Scarista come into view from the main road. An old earth house was recently uncovered, east of the last croft at Northon, as sewerage pipes were being installed—but the site was subsequently covered over again. This 'house' had been originally reported in the RCAHM inventory '1929' but even then it could not be located with accuracy. There are a number of midden heaps on the shoreline near here from which cockle, limpet shells and bits of pottery are continually being uncovered as the sea erodes the neck of the sandy isthmus connecting Toehead with the rest of Harris. In recent years this area has been extensively excavated and the earliest pottery, of a Neolithic type, was found in the few feet of blown sand that had accumulated on the old land surface of glacial till. There were also bone tools, sea shells and animal bones, as well as the stone burial cist of a child. Among the upper levels of midden was some low stone walling, some of it built in an oval boat shape. The extensive occupation from earliest times to the arrival of the Norse, confirmed by pottery resembling that made at Eilean na Tighe in North Uist, seems to suggest a strong connection with other sites at Udal and Rosinish, where similar artifacts and midden refuse have been found. The surrounding sealevels are thought to have been low during the Neolithic period, when cockle gathering on the tidal sands was an important food source. Weatherwise there had been a warm period throughout Northern Europe between the fifth and third millennia. It then became progressively colder so that by the first millennium BC a completely different weather pattern had established itself, and this may correspond to the period when the seas rose, perhaps turning Toehead into an island, and limpet-gathering became predominent. These weather cycles, with their accumulative influence on fish and the lives of people dependent on the sea, have continued right up to modern times, when cod and herring moved south with the cold during the 16th and 17th centuries but subsequently moved north again as our weather became warmer.

The track continues around the headland to a small chapel which was dedicated to St. Maelrudha. It is in much better condition that many others around the Isles and seems built to a standard Celtic rectangular pattern, its length just over 20 feet (7m.) and oriented east to west. It was built on the broad foundations of a ruined broch for it sits on an upturned dish of a slightly raised rocky platform with the steps cut into it up to the door of the chapel. Under the east window is a stone platform that may have been an altar. Nearby is an old graveyard. Directly north among the windswept sand dunes are round heaps of stones resembling cairns and hut circles. A stone cist formed by small slabs was uncovered many years ago containing human remains with small piles of stones at either end of the body.

A walk up the steep spine of the headland should not be

missed for, the view from the top is breathtaking. It is also interesting to note that the quartz bands that encircle it like white ribbons are actually great veins over six feet (2m.) deep when clambering up the rugged terrain. The northeastern stretch of beach between here and Luskentyre contains a number of ancient remains of chambered cairns, impressive standing stones, and duns; as well as more recent buildings such as Borve Lodge with its walled garden and maze. Down the road from the Scarista House Hotel is a more modest eating place, a wholefood café that is open daily including Sunday mornings. This is actually a room in the cottage of a local landscape painter and his wife. She provides tasty bacon sandwiches and coffee. Unfortunately we cannot compare our recommendation here with the *Good Food Guide's* in the nearby Georgian Manse for after clambering over hills and sandy beaches the thought of actually having to wash and look like respectable researchers rather than two weatherbeaten stone freaks was not worth the effort at the time.

Before you get to Borve there is a six-foot-high (2m.) standing stone above the shore and nearly a half-a-mile inland on the highest group of rocky knolls are the remains of Dun Borve. It was once quite a sizable fort from the low thick green-covered walls. Situated 200 feet above sealevel, there is a fine view all round, including the Isle of Taransay to the north. There are many stories about the Dun Borves in different parts of the Hebrides and numerous versions of the magic stone that will not stop working until the correct command is given. The green mound here, it is said, once belonged to the fairies, and a sailor resting on it pulled out an iron blade that had been stuck in the earth. The little people inside had been making a terrific din for quite a long time because they could not leave, but once the iron was removed they rushed out and invited the sailor in. As he was leaving they gave him a quern stone and the magic word to start it and one to stop it. As salt was a precious and expensive commodity, and the captain a greedy man, he eventually threw the sailor overboard. However, he forgot to ask how to stop the stone grinding out its salt, so it and the boat sunk under the weight. The stone is still at the bottom of the ocean grinding away, which is why the sea is so salty today.

Clach Mhic Leoid, Horgabost

A mile past Borve and less than a quarter from the main road, this ten-foot-high (3m.) monolith stands out quite grandly above the Sound of Taransay. It is white gneiss with marked quartz bands running across its lichen-covered face, and although a fair girth at the bottom it narrows towards the top with a cut like a fishtail making a 120° notch. A number of small boulders seem to spread out from its base in a westerly and southwesterly direction. Unfortunately, one of these stones is now broken, with its stump still protruding. Eastwards, two earthfast stones lie side by side about 50 yards (45m.) up on the sloping area of flat rock which is known as 'Fhionn's Cauldron'. There is a surprising amount of white quartzite showing in the solid rock. The standing stone itself points towards the southern tip of Taransay but it may have indicated Boreray before it leaned and twisted. If so, Alexander Thom considered this stone to be an important backsight indicating the sunset there on the equinoxes. However, for the isle to be visible one would have to stand either on Clach Mhic Leoid itself or on the platform behind it.

The other standing stones that Thom considered as important calendar alignments on Boreray were An Charra in South Uist, a stone near Rueval in Benbecula, and Clach an t-Sagairt in North Uist. In his first book he gave a rather cursory examination of the Ritual Calendar and it is unfortunate that he never found time to return for a more detailed study. However, other researchers since have confirmed these alignments and I am most indebted to Ron Curtis of Edinburgh for his figures and clarification in this matter.

The publication of *Megalithic Sites in Britain* in 1967 provided a key by which Thom's understanding of the engineering principles underlying megalithic structures could be examined and verified by other researchers. From his detailed and statistical analysis of hundreds of sites throughout Britain, he advanced a number of startling theories which subsequently received much scrutiny and a measure of acceptance by the archaeological establishment. He set out a basic unit of length measurement equal to 2.72 feet or 0.829 metres, which he called a megalithic yard, and

Standing Stone, Clach Mhic Leoid

2.5 MYs equal a megalithic rod. These, he claimed, were used to construct the stone circles whose geometry fell into certain specific shapes such as the invented 'true circle', the 'flattened circle' and other variations or types. Enough research has been undertaken by others since to verify that some defined units of measurement were in use; however, Thom's claim that the megalithic yard was general in Britain is not entirely accepted. It has been suggested that the 'Body Measure', or pacing by foot, which like the hand and thumb was in common use until the 19th century, may have been more likely; and, indeed, it would help to explain the extreme variation, local and otherwise, in measurement. The main area of his work concerned megalithic astronomy. He maintained that single menhirs or pillar stones as outliers to the circles could have been used as 'backsights' with distant mountain notches or other prominent features for lunar observation. In fact, the greater distance between them, the more accurate the observation. For a proper understanding of his work and that of other astro-archaeologists currently continuing and elaborating on his often rudimentary analysis of sites—due to lack of time and proper supportive back-up for in-depth surveys—one needs a fair amount of mathematical and astronomical knowhow.

The accepted norms of scientific measurement that underlie our notions of time and the calendar do not readily apply when extrapolating from the rudiments of megalithic engineering. As the majority of stone structures were elegant in both positioning and siting, their infrastructure was probably the geomantic landscape as with the Chinese traditional approach. To determine the proper position for a temple building a celestial relationship to both wind and water was essential: the contours of the hills and their internal capacity for storing or releasing water. One must beware of any glib analogy between the two ancient cultures, for in Chinese geomancy it is not the ground itself that was important but the superimposition on it of a venerable system of kinship to satisfy a set of harmonious principles. All these factors are largely missing when we look at what is left to us from the megalithic period and one cannot even be sure if what we see standing before us now is what was *there* then or how the ancients perceived it. However, then as now the sun's motion creates the circle of the year in its regular settings and risings on the horizon, and the division into four quarters can be considered by noting where the sun sets on midwinter, the spring equinox, midsummer, and the autumn equinox. There are of course only three such 'points' on the horizon as both the equinoxes coincide. Reversing the procedure and establishing one important point on the horizon, as with the 1,200-foot-high stac of Bororay nearly 50 miles out in the Atlantic, a series of separate positions can be determined along the length of the Long Isle from which to view the sun setting out there. This, apparently, is what Thom did. Having established that Clack Mhic Loeid could be used as a backsight in this manner, he then found a number of significantly astronomical alignments further south. Looking at the diagram, there seems to be a movement from the stone at Harris on the spring equinox to the midsummer sunset from Dun Trossary in South Uist; the latter is an enormous structure, with a nine-foot-high (2.7m.) standing stone that was partly dismantled and knocked about in the building of a modern sheep fank. The viewer then returns north again for the autumn equinox on Harris. Whether this constitutes a 16-part ritual calendar as Thom maintains is an open question. As it concentrates on the summer sunsets, it could be a primitive but effective device, rather like a cyclic sun dial, for regulating the planting and harvesting of different crops, or even the collection of shell fish, as in the old saying: 'Any month without an R, don't for mussles go.' However, each of these sites needs accurate and repeated surveying by theodolite on the spot at the right time, an exercise yet to be undertaken.

Isle of Taransay

Permission should first be sought at the garage in Horgabost in order to visit this large uninhabited isle. Of course, you have to take a tent and all you need, but there is plenty to see and the silence is sublime. It abounds with ancient sites, natural beauty and a profusion of wildlife. On the west side is a tremendous arc of rock which the sea has hollowed out. Guillimots, shags, fulmar and razorbills all find shelter within the huge and cragged face. There are small herds of cattle, sheep and deer that wander between the isle's two distinct parts. The latter are divided by a narrow isthmus, and it is here that a six-foot-high (1.8m.) standing stone, with an incised Latin cross, stands out clear on the smooth green dunes.

The abandoned village of Paible on the eastern spur has a naturally protected harbour and a fine fertile valley running back into the hills. Down through here are a series of connected lochs and rivers from Loch an Duin, with a number of ruined grain mills. The lazy beds that snake to the top of the hills and the Norse mills in this northern part indicate that the isle did more than support its people, for from its situation and the lack of other mills in the area, it probably milled and exported flour to communities elsewhere. The traditional quarry where the large mill stones came from was said to have been on the Haskier Isles about eight miles out south-southwest.

At Paible a wall with a gateway to the south encloses two distinct chapel ruins, each with its own graveyard separated by a small dry riverbed. Martin recounts a local superstition to the effect that if the women were buried in the graveyard of St. Keith's, the eastern chapel, and men in St. Tarran's on the western side, their bodies would be found above the ground the following day. He had a dead man buried in the latter and was quite pleased with himself to report that, 'contrary to the ancient custom and tradition of this place, but his corps is still in the grave from whence it is not like to rise until the general Resurrection'. Such righteousness to 'undeceive the credulous vulgar,' places Martin as a writer of his class and period but also makes his book so entertaining and informative. Captain Thomas, RN, who explored the Hebrides during the mid-19th century and wrote about the beehives and other ancient structures, suggests that St. Tarran, whom we have already come across in the legend of the angels rebuilding the church at Bailivanish in Benbecula, was a bishop of Lismore in southern Ireland. In fact Lismore itself, founded by St. Carthach in the fifth century, was an important centre of culture and learning with wide contacts in Spain and France, and it was probably this stream of influence that generated the Irish Peregrination (spiritual wandering or pilgrimage away from home and country). This is also part of the Benbecula tradition associated with St. Tarran, but in a wider sense it was the main impetus for the numerous anchorites building small cells or chapels on little islands far removed from general commerce. It was probably through such singular example done for the love of God rather than any missionary promulgation that Christianity took such a firm hold among the Irish and Picts.

St. Kilda

In 1930 the last families of Hirta were taken off at their own request. For close on 50 years a visit to 'lone St. Kilda' 50 miles west of Harris, was part of the regular summer excursions around the Hebrides. But even before then the declining population due to emigration, frequent boat and rock-fall disasters, which depleted the fowlers and fishermen, and high infant death rate because of the 'eight-days' sickness or tetanus infantus, had wrought drastic changes in this age-old community with its close interdependence on a harsh environment.

The islands are now in the care of the National Trust for Scotland, with a resident warden and an army presence roughly equal the 72 people counted at the last census in 1921. The Trust organize fortnightly excursions during the summer season (approximately £100 per week) and visitors are generally expected to help in the rebuilding of the Old Village, a row of 16 cottages erected in 1863. Keith Payne spent two weeks here last summer drawing and exploring the ancient sites, courtesy of the Royal Air Force Diving Expedition, and the following vignette is composed from his notes and conversation.

St. Kilda is staggering. You begin to feel the majesty and power of the place as you approach it after hours on the seas that can whittle down even the most hardened sailors. The horizon spins and the winds roar and the great jagged antlers of rock thrust out as they have done to every other traveller before you. To reach Hirta you must cross the tempestuous surface of a cauldron that was once the core of an extinct volcano. The rim, untouched by the glacial epochs, has been smashed by the ocean to form a ragged circle of mountains above and beneath the sea. These are the islands of the St.

Kilda group, a magnet for migrating birds and fish almost since time itself.

Hirta is the main island, 1,575 acres of cold rock for the most part surrounded by sheer cliffs 1,000 feet high, but with one protected anchorage on the east side at Loch Hirta. Also known as Village Bay, it is here that the tiny culture of Hirta began, evolving through at least 3,000 years to be finally swept away, not by wind and weather, but by 'modern progress'. The aboriginal dwellers were hunters of cliff-face and sea-shore, the migrating bird colonies providing the staple diet with fish, seal, whalemeat and seawreck as supplement. The earliest inhabitants may well have walked here as there is a myth relating to a land bridge similar to that between North Uist and the Monachs which was reputedly visible at low tides during the 16th century. Slowly a culture developed. Its sociological structure and religious behaviour blended to stabilise population at a manageable level, which seems to have been about 90 adult women, 60 adult men, with their offspring and aged folk. To keep this balance, a complex ritual of initiation, betrothal and marriage evolved around certain high crags in order to prove a man fit to support a family by 'cragging'.

The dwellings of the early inhabitants show an evolutionary pattern too. From above and behind the Old Village is the place to view the changing attitudes to island life. The earliest structures, the 'boat-shaped' enclosures on An Lag Bh'on-Tuath, are tucked away on a high plateau. Lower down beneath the scree slopes, the souterrains developed next, underground with dark seaward doors hidden by grassy banks. Slowly the roof pushed up into the corbelled beehives that were turfed and difficult to see against the mountains. After these camouflaged dwellings came the defensive 'dun' makers at the mouth of the bay, and the first exposed shelters were built, enclosed with defensive walls for keeping stock in and invaders out. But among those who came were the Norse and the Culdee monks. Soay sheep were introduced from Norway and small parcels of land were cultivated on the valley floor for grains and root crops. As the land became delineated, chapels were built with clusters of dwellings around them, and the old communal 'cleaten', small beehive storage houses which cover the island, became owned. Finally, the sense of unity between the island and the islanders was further eroded by the building of the 'Street', a line of black house dwellings in a row facing the sea. Houses for ghosts and museum pieces sit side by side with the new energy of Kilda, the diesel generator. It keeps the army alive while they watch the missile practice from Benbecula on the radar, as nearly £2½M.'s worth of ballistic junk drops into the Atlantic Ocean every day. The army has scarred the island with great ribbons of concrete, masses of 'gerry-built' dwellings, and their space-invader domes and dishes on the summit of Mullach Geal. They seem to have little regard for ancient dwellings, especially on the west side in Gleana Bay where their debris has rolled down the 1,000-foot slope and destroyed many of the 'horned dwellings', unique in the whole of the British Isles. If there was more co-operation between the National Trust and the squaddies, perhaps a restoration programme could be organised.

Gleann Mor is the most secret and remote valley in the Outer Isles. It is here that a people long dead left a curious monument of their culture and religion. The travellers of the past spoke of the 'Amazon Woman's House,' a beautiful beehive structure that stood out among 20 others in the valley. She is the myth of Hirta. The great hunting woman who coursed her dogs to Skye and back chasing the fine stags. Stretching along the valley floor, the form of the Huntress is built up from dry-stone dykes and beehive houses. Seen clearly on a June evening in the setting sun, this figure is clearly delineated and breathtaking. Beyond the valley is the Cambir, a headland with the terrible Soay Straits beneath and the isle of Soay with its druidesses' altar and souterrains from where the whole of the 'Woman of Hirta' was visible. Sightlines between such altars seemed to have great significance. All are interconnected. But none is as important as the viewing platform at Clash na Bearnaich in the great fault (and magnetic anomaly) on the face of Mullach Sgar. Visible from the village, just above the great boulder, a narrow path runs southeast to a viewing platform that gives a sightline through the 'Gap' and the distant view of Boreray. With the eagle eye of the druid, one could maybe see the 'circle of the sun' there on the high plateau at Sunadal. This is the ultimate and sublime Neolithic statement. The most magnificent and mysterious stone structure in Gaeldom. The last standing stone of the last stone circle in the eye of the sun. Here were the measured sunsets over Boreray seen from the calendar stones that stand erect from South Uist to the hills of Harris. A few people have recorded it previously but it is the most impressive standing stone that I have ever seen. Not because of its size or its part in the now broken circle, but solely for its siting and wonderful sense of untouched mystery.

Nearby, on the very tip of a 250-foot-high cliff, literally three feet from the chasm, is a four-foot-high once inscribed stone in the saddle between Mullach an Tuamail and Mullach an Eilean. Its sharp edge points southwest over the Outer Isles to Skye, visible 100 miles away. Below is the Stack Lee, an iceberg of gannets. To the right are the pinnacles of Glagon na Rusgachan. In front, to the southwest, are the misty isles of Soay, Hirta itself and Dun. Behind is black water to the frozen north. The stone stands timeless against the sky, a last proof of the incredible achievements of ancient builders, astronomers and mystics. God knows what it said!

Soay, St. Kilda

North Harris

The road into Tarbert dips and curves and from above the bay, the town looks as if it is sliding into the sea. The name is Old Norse and indicates a short cut across a peninsula to avoid the longer journey by sea. The half-mile neck of land that separates West and East Loch Tarbert makes more of a division between South and North Harris than between Harris as a whole and Lewis. Even though one land entity, the fact that both places have always been named as separate islands because of the political and social differences, usually confuses people who do not know the Hebrides. The vast blanket of peat bog covering Lewis and the high mountains of Harris also show a superficial difference because both are composed of Lewesian Gneiss. It is one of the few areas in Europe where the old Pre-Cambrian formation is actually exposed, elsewhere being covered over by subsequent geological upheavals. East Loch Tarbert is now the centre of the fishing industry and there is a good protected harbour on Scalpay, the small isle at its mouth, as well as at Rodel and up Loch Seafort at Maaruig, now a popular yachting centre. There are no good harbours on the west coast.

Scalpay
For its size, this isle (population 400 plus) has a thriving fishing fleet that is run on a co-operative basis by a large number of the local men who actually earn a living from the sea. The harbour is on the lee side and is surrounded by pleasant white-washed houses. To get there take the minor road due east from Tarbert to Kyles Scalpay (buses Tuesday and Friday); there is a frequent car-ferry service across the Sound. The land is typically poor, and after it was 'crofted' during the middle of the 19th century (some of the Pabbay people moved here)

the population rose steadily, declining again during the past few decades so that the present energetic community holds out some hope that, with the right mix between optimum numbers of people and employment outside the croft, the Hebrides could be revitalised—especially as more young people return due to the downturn in the general economy. The lighthouse on Eilean Glas is one of the four originally commissioned in 1789, and William Daniell produced a fine etching of this scene in 1819. He also did Rodel and Stornoway as part of the illustrations for the five-volume tour of the coasts of England, Wales and Scotland, sketching the landward aspects from the sea. Over a century earlier that other intrepid traveller, Martin Martin, referred to a hole or cave on Eilean Glas in which a 'lunar-stone', whatever that may be, advanced and retreated according to the state of the moon.

Rhenigadale

At a curve in the Tarbert road, as it crosses the neck of Loch Laxdale enroute to the Scalpay ferry, there is an unmarked path that rises gradually and unobtrusively into a most exhilerating walk. A two-hour trek by those fit enough to appreciate the serene beauty of the hills will get one to the small Gatliffe Trust hostel at Rhenigadale. The well-kept path curves up and down from nearly 800 feet (240m.) to the sea loch below in a series of hairpins that suddenly reveal the picturesque valley almost beneath one's feet, for on the narrow uneven bends and dips it feels as if a high wind would dash you down the vertical slope. Sliding along the steep path over the rough-cut rocky inclines is almost worse than the puff upwards, for the back of the legs begin to ache from lack of exercise. Minor grumbles are quickly forgotten when one is confronted with the brown beaten curving track that looks as if it had come straight from the Andes, and is reminiscent of those marvellous photographs in the *American Geographical* magazine. Just as we were beginning to doubt if any human habitation existed anywhere near the red triangle marked on the map, we suddenly met a young shepherd with his girlfriend rounding a bend, who assured us gaily that there was a village ahead. He had a ruddy face and a fine lilting voice but it was the manner in which he carried a crook that indicated his calling. She had a bag of meal to feed a mothering ewe. When we asked if she ever walked to Tarbert, thinking of our own trek so far as well as the four miles by car, she said, 'Och no, there's the boat.' On that thought we eventually reached the village and met her mother who had just returned on foot from there with some shopping.

Until recently when the electricity poles were erected, Rhenigadale was indeed a village that time forgot. As the head of the valley, enclosed between the hills and the sea, we were confronted with the sight of a warm but dishevelled communal habitation that has almost vanished now from the Hebrides. Half-a-dozen thatched houses perched in the glade above the shore with makeshift fencing enclosing small raised beds; surrounded by byres, peatstacks and outhouses for chickens; and threaded by a rough path over which bleating sheep wandered at will. We had a letter for a villager from our friend, saying that it was all right for the bearer to stay at his house further round the point. She seemed very surprised at the necessity for this gesture. She said she had never been there in her life but the way was easy, just follow the telegraph poles over the hill and up the next valley along the path, and the house would be in front of us. We were given a cup of tea and a sandwich by this grey-haired bustling lady and told that the village was beginning to pick up now that the school teacher had had a young child and would open the schoolhouse again. As she chatted on about their life, she made it sound curiously ordinary when to us it seemed that here, so isolated from shops and other amenities bound up with modern living and the tribulations of our times, was a kind of lost world. An arcadia of human endeavour and companionship that so impressed travellers to the Hebrides as late as the last century. There was a sadness here, too, for her man, the 'postie' for 20 years, had died recently. We had actually sat by his cairn on the top of one of the hills where he himself had so often rested. Her family were all in England now except for the thin wiry daughter we had met coming up the path.

After walking around the point and along the line of poles to the cottage, it was fairly obvious why Andy lost heart after putting so much work into the rebuilding. He had constructed a winch to haul all the necessary materials up a 50-foot incline from the loch to the headland, in front of which was littered the remnants of his labours. He had done an amazing job, largely on his own. The walls were pointed, a new slate roof, doors and windows were in, new flooring and roofing timbers were inside as well as a complete plumbing and electricity system. A heavy polythene pipe ran down the hill bringing in water but the poles had bypassed his house because he refused to pay the connecting charges. The shell was complete, beautifully done, but the living in it would have to wait for another creative period in his life to finish the task he had set himself away from his business in London. The letter he gave asserted his right to this spot and all he could survey, the hills/clouds/water/sky and rock. It is impossible to put into words the sense of isolation that overpowered one, sitting that evening on the timber stack outside the cottage. I suppose in part it was the absolute difference between the cosy feeling of well-being that emanated from the village humming with life around the headland that looked out to the Little Minch, and this most difficult spot that an outsider could choose to live in. There was also the very real sense of drear pressure from the towering reddish-brown cliffs of Caiteshal opposite on the far side of the water.

It was near the mouth of Loch Seaforth, probably one of the longest sea lochs jutting up into the heart of Lewis, and in winter with high tides and winds this narrow funnel of rock would be almost a raging inferno. Also on the other side but further to the northwest, the rounded summit of Beinn Mhor was clearly visible. In this almost inaccessible region of the Pairc Estates a hand-glider or gyrocopter would be certainly useful to travel these higher regions without the necessary slog of clambering through bogs and over rocks, wet and exhausted or hot and uncomfortable. Really to explore the countless small isles and long narrow lochs that usually lead to such interesting hilltops, a boat is a necessity and one must not forget the pleasure in not having to hump large amounts of necessary protective gear around. We certainly wanted to climb Beinn Mhor in order to see what the 'Sleeping Beauty' of the hills directly north would actually look like from the summit.

Having stayed the one night in Andy's cottage, we said goodbye to the woman and her daughter as we went through and began to walk up the hill with a completely different rhythm and lightness of heart from the way we had first stumbled in to the village. Yet there was a sense of loss as we reached the top and plunged down towards the next valley. The life glimpsed here was on the wane. The postman dead, the school closed (at least, temporarily) and one of their small houses turned into a hostel to accommodate tourists. There may never be a road across this headland, but electricity, television and the telephone have had a taming effect on even the most backward communities. Not on the place itself but on the people here whose forebears had struggled so fiercely and tenaciously to survive on this rocky waste between the mountains and the sea, planting tiny raised-beds of seawrack after being cleared away from the rich machair lands of the west coast. Now even this was crumbling away. An unashamedly romantic view of the life here, but as outsiders it was what we had come 700 miles to find, a few threads to link us with a past that had almost vanished. There was also the sense of embarrassment for intruding on their privacy, stumbling into their timeless oasis with the brash and unfeeling arrogance that typifies our time and, worse too perhaps, for adding the final nail into the coffin by writing about it.

Shiants
the basking islands. the rocks
like sails or fins or teeth.

high wings of black blades
as the barnaclegeese pass*

One unrealised dream was to get out to the Shiants, the 'charmed' and 'hallowed' isles east of Scalpay and about ten miles as the birds fly. They certainly look like eagles hovering over the sea and were supposed to be the pair that would live for ever after God in his mercy had transformed Adam and Eve to escape the eternal burden of their guilt on the human

* Ian Stephan, *Malin, Hebrides, Minches* (Dangaroo Press, Mundlestrup, Denmark, 1983?).

race. The smaller of the two, Eilean Mhoire, apparently had a chapel on top with a rough and dangerous hewn path up to it, similar in name and in kind to the anchorite chapel off North Tolsta in Lewis. In the old days fishermen in their small boats avoided the tideway between the Shiants and the coast, calling it Sruth nam Fear Gorma, the 'Stream of the Blue Men' (i.e., the Storm Kelpies or some of the fallen angels who had to keep the waters churning). If a skipper failed to answer correctly the riddles of the Blue Men it usually meant a watery encounter in the deep. The oft-quoted description of the glassy blue 'coats' of their bodies riding high in the waves and with grey bearded faces sounds remarkably like some of the accounts of the monsters in Loch Ness and elsewhere.

There is a story of a Harris boy who met the King of the Undersea Kingdom, actually ate of the food of oblivion, and still lived to tell the tale as well as rescue his lady love from the ogre's castle. The imprisoned maiden had to spin nettle fibres to make clothes for the giant, and she knew her life was short indeed once she had finished the task. The lad found an eagle to fly him inside when the giant was away, and the over-sized wife agreed to let her go if he returned with a string of pearls before she had finished the clothes. The otter who took him down to the Undersea Kingdom turned out to be the king's son, and the eldest sister—enamoured with the human— agreed to give him the pearls. She offered him first a drink from a rose-pink seashell rimmed with gold, and not wanting to appear ungrateful he drank a draught and was unmindful to everything but her beauty and that of the palace, which was full of colour and translucent green light shining over pink marble houses and wonderful-looking flowers. The maiden in the castle, growing anxious, consulted a passing salmon that agreed to help her and take a piece of nettle thread in its mouth down to the deep. The wedding feast was ready and the lad about to marry the eldest daughter when the salmon dropped the thread into his lap and immediately brought him back to his task. The wonderful world about him paled into insignificance, as when one tries to pick up the bright jewels from a rock pool into the light of day. He clung to the salmon's back and returned to the castle with the pearls to free the maiden.

Scarp

Above West Loch Tarbert the road winds around the formidable mountainous upthrust that contains a number of peaks with climbing possibilities, such as Gillaval Glas (471m.) and Sgaoth Aird (559m.). However, it is west of Clisham (799m.), the highest point in North Harris, that offers a challenge to the serious climber. Ever since Charles Weld made the first recorded ascent of Sgurr na Stri in 1859, the Cullin pinnacles in Skye have attracted most attention, and although not in the same class, Tomnaval (562m.), and Ullaval (659m.) with its towering 700-foot headland of Strone Ulladale, are, I am assured by others, worthy of respect. There are tracks leading into this hinterland from the B887 that turns off the main Tarbert-to-Stornway road. It continues along the edge of the sea to the fine beach at Husinish and the pier where the ferry to Scarp was available before it became depopulated.

Almost immediately after the turning the road passes an old whaling station at Bunavoneadar which was originally built by Norwegians. It was purchased by Leverhulme, who thought to use the oil extract for making soap in his enormous factory at Port Sunlight and the whale blubber for sausages for the natives of West Africa where he also had business interests. Amhuinnsuidhe Castle (pronounced 'Avin-suey') the grand residence of the Dunmores, is further along the road. The large estate is now privately owned and the river here, along with the Grimersta in Lewis, is the best-known salmon run in the Long Isle. During the season (June to October) the salmon may be seen leaping up a line of small falls that run along by the side of the house to the sea. The road ends at a marvellous swatch of fine sand opposite the three-mile-long rocky isle.

Scarp was the scene for yet another example of the enterprising lunacy that periodically infects outsiders trying to cope with the impossible. Like the single entry for the Hebrides in the GFG at Scarista in South Harris, Scarp holds a special niche in the paper world of the philatalist. A rocket inventor by the name of Herr Zucker attempted to pioneer air-powered mail delivery from here to Harris. A special stamp was produced for the occasion, 28 July 1934, with a picture of an enormous rocket next to the logo 'Western Isles Rocket Post.' However, the thing exploded prematurely and a second attempt from Harris to here had no great success either. Zucker went on to more serious work on his V-rockets in Germany during World War Two. The ordinary mail continued to be delivered by boat until 1971, when the last families left here after being settled since 1810.

Waterlilies near St. Columba's Church on Eilean Chalium Chille in Loch Erisort, Lewis

Lewis

The A589 north to Stornoway hugs the edge of Loch Seaforth, a deep serpentine cleft that stretches for miles into the heart of the Long Isle. The change from Harris to Lewis is imperceptible, though I believe the border is somewhere near Ardvourlie where the road dips down to waterlevel. Houses tuck into the rugged folds of an endless grey rockscape. Wandering sheep and small peat workings are often the only signs that people do try to eke out a living from this monotonous harsh environment. Perhaps after days of wet squalls and a grey overcast one begins to wonder what perverse streak of humanity enables people to endure such a life. Yet as the sun shines on the loch below, sparkling its surface, the land becomes transformed with a range of deep-toned browns, and green heathers of unbelievable subtlety gleaming among the lichen-covered boulders. Slowly, one can appreciate the bonding between this island and its people, and why after generations of exile the songs of the Hebrides never fail to evoke in the native that pristine memory of place. These harsh treeless isles may be an acquired taste as far as the summer visitor is concerned, but it is definitely the sunshine that gives them their palatable bouquet.

Amid the rounded hilltops it is quite possible to miss altogether the comely shaped creature on the opposite heights above the head of the loch. Even when you are aware of what to look out for, the first sighting from the road between Arivuaich and Balallan is hard to grasp in terms of essentials. Like any mountain being, it is often shrouded in mist or cloud but occasionally the absolute clarity of the bared mountainous body created by the summits of three interlocking hills, Mor Mhonadh, Guainemol and Sidhean an Airgid, is breathtaking. The enigmas posed by this proud feminine configuration with her sphinx-shaped head add to its mysterious serenity, shaped over millennia from water action beneath the ice cover to its denudation by the ravaging retreating glaciers and constant glazing ever since by elemental erosion. The head of this figure has its equivalents in the work of certain modern sculptors who rediscovered simple contours dictated by the materials rather than preconceived thought or resemblance to human form. And of course the artists have had to return to primitive or prehistoric sources for inspiration, keenly aware that such direct perception of nature cuts across their acquired conceptions of form and design. Perhaps it was just such a tangible and mysterious congruity that spoke to the ancient peoples who venerated this visible personification of mother earth. To talk of the head, neck, breasts, belly, vulva and knees, is to impart an unnecessary anthropomorphic burden, for its dynamic concordance of parts to whole is rarely evident except from certain well-defined directions, although in good light her profile is visible in a wide arc from the Eye Peninsula to Callanish on the west coast. In fact, the best way to 'see' the figure is by physical touch, walking and clambering along its curvacious length from Seaforth Head to Sidhean an Airgid. However, this is a private estate and permission should be obtained in advance from Eishkin Lodge.

Once you isolate this figure it becomes the centre-piece of the southern horizon with the rounded peak of Beinn Mhor in the background, quite often giving her a pregnant look, and the summit of Clisham to the right with the hills of North Harris fading into the distance. It also enables one to reconsider some of the early myths as an expression of topographical rendition, and may even be a key to the complexity of the Neolithic stone structures situated in the northern half of Lewis but particularly around Callanish on East Loch Roag.

Lewis and Harris, known collectively as the Long Isle, are over half-a-million acres in extent and by far the biggest of the Hebridean group. Lewis itself is mainly one large moor of blanket peat with numerous lochs and small water courses, although over in Uig to the west the ground is hilly with sand dunes and a few good stretches of beach. Tree stumps are fairly common in the peat workings and around the main circle at Callanish five feet of peat was cleared in the middle of the 19th century, indicating that this cover is fairly recent and that the island was once quite wooded. One should take care when traipsing around these rolling moors, for even in dry weather it is very easy to slip in waist deep on some delicate-looking green patches. It is a bit like pitch in consistency, sticking everywhere, and it stinks to high heaven until it dries out. The terrain determines the human habitation, which is mainly on the northwest coastal strip and on the east coast around Stornway. In fact, over 5,000 people, which is a quarter of the total population, live in the main town. Located here are local government, public services, shopping and other amenities; tweed mills, oil service industry, fishing; as well as entertainments. The car ferry plies from Ullapool and the airport has regular inter-isle flights to Glasgow and Inverness. Stornoway looks like a spider's web with roads jutting out in all directions including a few that cross over to the west coast, with regular bus services. So for islanders and visitors alike the town is really the centre of the island, and a pleasant-enough magnet it is with so little light relief from the endless vistas of unrelieved moorland.

Prehistoric tree stumps, Loch Beag

Stornoway

The site of the old castle is by the quay where the Caledonian MacBrayne ferry docks. In the war against Holland, Cromwell used the town's long association with the Dutch herring fleets as an excuse to impose a naval blockade in 1653, and when the garrison left they dismantled the castle. A half-century previously James IV had tried to colonise Lewis by parcelling it out to a group of Lowland entrepreneurs and their mercenaries who were known as the Fife Adventurers. Fierce opposition by Neil MacLeod and the men of Lewis forced them to abandon the castle and leave after four years. This is one of the more glorious chapters in local history but the immediate effect was the outlawing of the MacLeod clan in 1610 when James granted the island to MacKenzie of Kintail. A more beneficial effect which could not be foreseen at the time was the degree of religious tolerance that is now enjoyed by all religious denominations throughout the Hebrides. The outcome might well have been different, for it was these same Lowlanders sent over to Ulster who 'planted' the land of the Ulaid to create 300 years of extreme bigotry and intolerance, not to mention all the blood spilled over the past decade or so. The decisive actions by Neil MacLeod also meant that the language remained intact. From earliest time one form or other or Gaelic was used, and after the recovery of the Isles by Scotland in the 13th century it supplanted Old Norse completely. In Latin it was called the Lingua Scotica (Language of the Scots/Irish), but was changed to 'Erse' in the Lowland tongue, which had become the national language by the 1500s. However, English gradually took over from Latin as the literary and written language. By the 18th century it had also replaced Scots in everyday usage. The Gaelic tongue fared better. Throughout the 19th century revivals, Gaelic prose and verse blossomed. An Comumn Gaidhealach was set up to help preserve and encourage the use of the old language. During the recent census nearly half the population of Stornoway were Gaelic-speakers, and in the Outer Isles as a whole the average is about ninety percent. The street signs are in Gaelic and there is a welcome bias towards it in education and from the Comhairle nan Eilean, the Isles Council. Nevertheless, the overt persuasion of mainland culture is very much in evidence throughout the town among the young, the old who nearly all watch television, and the middle-income classes in the legal, commercial and industrial spheres who ensure that Gaelic retains its lower status.

The foundation stone of the present castle was laid early in the 19th century, and it was after the Seaforths were forced to sell Lewis to Sir James Matheson, a retired opium and shipping magnate in 1843, that the plantation of mixed deciduous trees was started. Unique in the barren peat bog, it is now ecologically interesting and attracts well-known species of woodland birds as well as having a large rookery. Matheson encouraged the expansion of the town and particularly the extensive quay area which later formed part of Leverhulme's plans to make Stornoway into the fishing centre of the Minches, with processing factories and other commerce, as well as a railway link with Breasclete on the west coast. This is the Pentland Road which had been originally laid down by local labour in 1882 as a typical measure to relieve poverty. It was during this period that riots broke out on Lewis because of the insecurity of tenure and appalling living conditions, when a sheep or deer had more value than human life. The riots spread elsewhere but it was the Battle of the Braes in Skye that finally forced some national recognition of rack-renting and other injustices. The hundreds of ex-servicemen, who returned home after four years' fighting in the trenches, demanding land to live and work, forced Leverhulme to renounce all his good plans after only two short years, but before departing for Harris he offered the Isle of Lewis to the people. Stornoway in 1924 became a Trust, which now owns the landward area surrounding it, though the rest of the Long Isle was bought by private estates. The unpaved Pentland road makes for a picturesque though bumpy drive to the west coast, with its motley collection of early-20th-century makeshift junk-houses used by the islanders during the peat cutting season, when the whole family mucks in with the stacking, drying, humping and collection of turf. On average, the process takes about a week's work per family, from the first cutting to the final stacking on the croft of enough fuel to last through the winter. At the end of this track is another memorial to the island's industrial hopes: once part of Leverhulme's scheme, the frozen fish factory at Breasclete and a newly built pier were acclaimed nearly 60 years later as a feather in the cap of the Highlands and Islands Development Board's policy. However, it did not last long for two years ago the factory was placed in the hands of the Receiver, and no doubt the millions of pounds spent on this one venture would make Leverhulme's total losses seem like peanuts indeed.

The major decisions to date by the Stornoway Trust have been to turn the castle into a Technical Trades College, to rent a large area of Arnish for offshore oil development, and—in 1961—to lease the airfield to the Ministry of Defence. At present the latter looks likely to be extended and to be turned into a major NATO base; the Western Isles Council originally voted against, but in May 1984 they voted in favour of the second phase of the plan. It is disturbing enough to see nuclear submarines in the deep harbour, but to have this lovely town go the same way as Balinvanich in Benbecula, a social and service spill-over from the army base, would indeed be a shame.

The Tourist Information is on South Beach Street and the facilities of the New Nicolson Lewis Sports Centre are available to all for a modest entrance fee. For the casual visitor here, the round of hotel lounges and tasteless 'milk-bars' can be interrupted with some cheap forms of entertainment. The best is sitting by the inner quayside watching the bustle of fishing boats in the off-season, as the crew members scrub, paint and polish their craft. Most of the time a small family of grey seals who live in the harbour bob about among the reflections of masts, wires, aerials and gulls rippling in the calm waters. The other pastime is a walk through the castle grounds, now known as Lady Lever Park. From the Porter's Lodge off Bayhead Street a well-marked nature trail will take one to the top of Gallow's Hill, Cnoc na Croich, for a panoramic vista of the town and the Eye Peninsula forming part of Broad Bay. At sunset after a day-long drive there is no better way to soothe the nerves than a walk through these beautiful woods. And for anyone with an interest in the literature or the history of the Hebrides, a visit to the Reference Library is a welcome respite on a wet afternoon.

Everything that has ever been printed about the Isles is collected together in one room, and for the purposes of this book my time spent in there was invaluable for I should have had to spend months in any other library merely checking out the source material. It is a pity that the same zeal in preserving the heritage does not extend further. Not only has the single Archaeological Officer for the Isles been made redundant but when the Comhairle were offered a set of the 500 Ordnance Survey cards listing and detailing all the known information on the ancient monuments, they could not afford to spend a few hundred pounds. Perhaps when the new museum is built some of the artifacts now in Edinburgh and elsewhere might be returned, for the amount that has survived is pitifully small.

Yet 'finds' are regularly discovered on the moors, especially now when the islanders realise that museums pay good money for them. A 12-year-old Balallan boy recently came across a hoard of five stone axes near Loch Airigh nan Caerdaich. Out on a fishing trip with his uncle, he first thought they were bits of old weathered wood. When examined by the British Museum they were found to be highly polished with flat cutting edges, about six inches long. Three were made from gneiss and the others were of a more closely grained sandy coloured stone. One of the six stone balls found in the Hebrides also came from the moor near here. These strange spherical carvings roughly the size of a tennis ball certainly merit the term 'ritual object' that is usually applied to them. Small knobs seem the most decorative feature, though many have spirals, concentric lines and cross-hatching. Just under half of the 400 that have been recorded to date, mainly found in the northeast of the Scottish mainland, have six knobs protruding from the surface and the three found on Lewis were of this kind. The material used varies from the hardest granite, and most difficult to work, to sandstone. They are not often found in the vicinity of archaeological sites, so not being classified as grave-goods or household stuff makes them anomalies as far as the textbooks are concerned. They may have been personal or tribal power objects, radiating energy like the Charingas of old Australia or the small baked tablets of North American Indians. Keith

Critchlow sees them not so much as the embodiment of ritual power or divination, but more as forms of solid geometry (*Time Stands Still*, 1979). He maintains that they reinforce Alexander Thom's theories about the Neolithic people who erected the stone circles; the makers were surely aware of three-dimensional co-ordinates and symetries represented by the Platonic spheres, and with these stone balls left behind a clear and precise statement, beyond any verbal or written form, of their ability.

Traigh Mor, Tolsta

The road to this marvellous beach about nine miles (14.5km.) north of Stornoway passes a number of ancient sites, from chambered cairns and standing stones to early ecclesiastical ruins. At a place called the Priest's Glen above New Valley, a mile from the main road at Laxdale, is the remains of a stone circle. The track goes through what's left of it, namely two five-foot-high (1.5m.) stones on the south side and another fallen one to the north. The stone ball that is now in the school museum of the Nicolson Institute of Further Education, Stornoway, was found locally. To the west of Newmarket, below Grianan, are a line of four small stones curving in an east/west direction; and then further along the peat track, beyond the left fork, is a five-foot-high (1.5m.) stone in the shape of a seat, not unlike the one on Berneray in the Sound of Harris. Up to Newmarket the road is fairly built up, but it branches off through Tong (B895) before finally petering out at Tolsta. Out on the moor at Coll and Gress are the tattered remains of chambered cairns; the latter, called Carn a'Mharc, is a jumble of large stones displaced around the mound with a ring of small ones on the southwestern edge. The walls and gables of St. Aula's Chapel by the side of the road at Gress are still intact, though the lintal over the door has fallen in. On the rise to the northeast, lying among the close-cropped grass, is a broken stone cross of delicate proportions. Further around the bay, on the right-hand side of the road and now beneath the lawn at Gress Lodge, is an 'earth-house'. It was discovered during the 19th century and its description of three, nine-foot (2.7m.) circular beehive chambers, connected by long narrow stone passageways, reads like a souterrain. The farmer dug down for 15 feet below the third chamber and found a large set of antlers and a stone quern. The site has since become covered over by blown sand.

Near the school in North Tolsta is a track that leads to the burial ground which, according to Martin, once contained the Church of St. Michael. At the north end, past the fence, is a sandy gully that drops down to a tiny waterfall. The grotto beneath it is fresh, green and silent. It is like an entry to the heart of Lewis. Beyond the pool, out on the sands of the bay, lies a 40-foot-high (12m.) volcanic boulder called Cleite Dubh, the 'Black Rock', which is indeed its colour, with deep-Reddish tones running around it. This, in fact, is the beginning of a summer solstice alignment that joins up to St. Michael's beyond the pool. Dedications to the Archangel and dragon slayer always seem to occur on nodes that symbolise an alteration from darkness to light, from lunar earth energy to solar heat. The line continues past St. Aula's; through a small standing stone at Tong; over Gallow's Hill at Stornoway; between Laxby cemetery and a nearby knoll; to a small stone circle at Fangs on the shore of Loch Seaforth; to connect up finally with the head of the Sleeping Beauty

Grove, St Michael's, Tolsta

opposite on Sithean an Airgid. So from the 'brow' here (1,250 feet/378m. above sealevel), at an azimuth of 36° 30′ to the horizon on the east coast, one could witness the mid-summer dawn emerging from the sea. It could have been interpreted as a marriage of the sun with the goddess. A legend of the Cailleach, the 'old hag of the hills,' tells of her retiring to a miraculous well on the Isle of Youth. At the first glimmer of dawn she drinks from the waters that bubble out of the rocks and even before the birds sing, emerges as a beautiful new goddess whose magic wand has turned the grass green and brought out the summer flowers.

It is extremely rare for a line of sight, not only to align so closely with an astronomically significant one, but also to be so elegantly placed between two landscape features with such vivid onomastic byplay. At one end is the 'Black Stone' that absorbs the first rays of the sun as it emerges from the sea, visible from a vantage point 20 miles away, with such an odd mixture of names: 'Silver Fairy Mound'—Sithean an Airgid— or, more locally, Thormaid Airgid, which is said to mean 'Moon Maiden of the Hammer of Thor.' A possible myth of solar fire is all that remains now of an ancient religion, which personified the water, stone, fire of the mountain, and the world of nature in general as primaeval aspects from an older time. During the long ages after the sacred cosmology was turned into story and the geometry that laid out the earth had become a myth, perhaps it was only the veneration of the moon as lunar offspring periodically rising from the darkness, that continued in these secret and unsung places of the Isles.

At the end of the Tolsta Road, beyond the parking place, a track leads to the next beach, Garry Sands. Five *stacs* (a geological term in common use in the Isles) or pinnacles of rock stand out like sentinels, though at high tide they are surrounded by the sea. However, before reaching the beach, the foundations of a chapel dedicated to St. Columba can be found on a slightly raised promontory close to a loop in the path. The ruins of a stone cell and sheiling are visible in a large enclosure that contained the 30 foot by ten foot (10 x 3m.) chapel set out on an east/west axis. There are old lazy beds here and stepping stones over a small stream. The stacs below look very picturesque against the broad lines of white-topped waves rolling in from the Northern Seas. The largest and the tallest stac is named Caisteal a'Morair and thoroughly splashed with the droppings of the nesting gulls and fulmer. Sea pinks nestle in the cracks and it has a small natural arch underneath. The remains of a stone rectangular structure occupy the summit. As it name implied, it was possibly an anchorite's retreat whose only access was a stiff climb around the curve of the rock. Apparently a similar kind of structure, also dedicated to Mary, sits on top of the smaller of the Shiant Isles off Harris. The coastal path continues beyond Port Geiraha to another stac called Dun Othail. It can be viewed from the high precipice opposite, and on a narrow shelf beneath in the cliff face are the foundations of a small building that may once have been a chapel.

If you are feeling energetic and wish to see one of the few remaining examples of the beehive houses that once were very common throughout Lewis, Bilascleiter is three miles further north, beyond Cellar Head. The dun on the head here was rebuilt as a folly during the last century. Half-a-mile on, one can pick up the path leading to the track, that becomes the B8015 to Lional and the Port of Ness.

St. Columba's Chapel, Eye Peninsula

Due east of Stornoway beyond the causeway bridge, Eye ('U' in Gaelic) is roughly six miles long by four miles wide, and resembles a single crab's claw enclosing Broad Bay. The main road leads all the way over to Tiumpan Head lighthouse and there are minor roads off to the ancient monuments. Eye has been fairly heavily populated since the 19th century clearances from the west coast, and the peat cover has been much reduced through constant domestic burning. It is also not so wet as most of the main island and with sufficient financial incentive, this area could be turned into decent arable land, without necessarily spoiling its soft character.

The most interesting Neolithic site is at Garrabost, which has been described as a squared chambered cairn. What is to be seen are a number of small evenly placed standing stones, indicating that the structure was built on the cardinal points. The west stone (four foot 1.2m. high) is 57 feet (17m.) from the south (42 inches—just over a metre—high), and from there to the east stone (also 42 inches high) it is 54 feet (16m.). The north stone seems to have been obliterated but there are a number on the northeast side. There is a large triangular stone on an east/west axis in the centre which seems to be indicative of a more than thoughtful approach to its construction. There is a complete absence of cairn material, and as has been pointed out elsewhere in connection with other squared stone structures, such cairns may merit more attention than just being designed as yet another example of a dilapidated chambered cairn. Coming from the main road beyond Garrabost Church, and gingerly driving on the track across the moor to Cnoc nan Dursainean, gives one no idea whatsoever of the marvellous view obtainable on all sides from this site, except towards the northeast corner by the Butt: the hills of Uig and North Harris; the Sleeping Beauty, which stands out clearly; and, to complete the sweep, the Cullins on the eastern horizon.

This structure seems to be roughly in the middle of a line-of-sight alignment from the side of Bayable Hill (88m.) through Clach Stein, 500 yards (455m.) northwest of Lower Bayable. Traditionally said to be cast down by a local man in search of treasure, a ten-foot-high (3m.) marker on the ridge. Clach Stein, points to Cnoc an Dursainean in Garrabost and on to a nearby five-foot-square (1.5m.) sparkling white stone block which stands in a hollow at the western end of a large mound. The line then extends to Cnoc Chailian at Shulisadar, finally ending at the scattered heap of stones known as Caisteal Mhic Croscail, by the sea shore at Portnaguran. This

Stone Enclosure

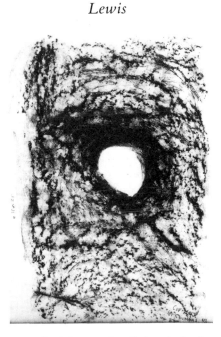

Cup-marked Stone, St. Columba's chapel

is listed as a chambered cairn for there are the remains of a passage of erect stones with a broken capstone by a five foot (1.5m.) circular chamber.

There are a number of dun sites on the coast, but the most striking is Dun Mor to the northwest of Garrabost. There are faint remains of the thick walling around the plateau of what is now almost a great column jutting into the sea. Unfortunately there was a belligerent crow nesting there so it was impossible to get the grand view from the top. Below it, in a steep declivity almost above the shore, in St. Cowston's Well. Water pours out from the rocks and it has the reputation of never going dry, winter or summer. The site of this ancient chapel dedicated to the Saint is on the croft above. The clay along this entire coastline seems to be sliding into the sea and so full of charbayade springs that the hillsides are rutted with rivulets.

Situated on a knobly green sward above a sandy beach, St. Columba's chapel overlooks Broad Bay, in what is now the district of Aignish. The roofless building is in two parts, built of gneiss with a mingling of coarse reddish sandstone, divided by a wall and arched doorway between the eastern part (62 feet by 17/19m. x 5) and the western (23 feet by 16/7m. x 4.5). According to Muir they look like 'a nave with a well-proportioned chancel at the wrong end. Both were constructed at different periods, but which is the older is a matter of uncertainty.' He also states that the chapel had a slate roof and that the burying ground outside was covered in nettles and rubbish. It is rather the reverse now, with the outside well-cared-for and the inside unkempt. The walls are now covered with yellow lichen, and tufts of grass peep through the cracks and down from the tops. In the centre of the floor is a long close-grained slab with a single hollow cup 1½ inches (3.8cm.) in diameter. The single cup-mark is a feature of other Christian sites in the Hebrides. To the right of the chancel is the weathered stone effigy of one of the MacLeod chiefs dressed in full warrior kit of the period with sword and halberd—probably Roderick II, father of Torquill IV. To the left is an engraved stone set into the wall with an inscription below to Margaret, his daughter and mother of John, the last Abbot of Iona. Her date of death is noted as 1503, and since the western part was added about this time perhaps it was conceived as a memorial chapel. The site is said to have been first occupied by St. Catan, a seventh century missionary from Iona. In the graveyard are some interesting grave slabs with mediaeval carvings of skull, cross-bones, coffin, bell and hour-glass—universal symbols of death to remind people of their brief life span on this earth.

Murdo MacFarlane lived across the causeway at Melbost, and, talking to the poet, we had no idea that in a few short months he too would be gone forever. Throughout that summer afternoon the nerve-shattering noise of the Phantom jets taking off at the airfield next door and sweeping up overhead, obliterated all conversation almost at regular 15-minute intervals. The row of bungalows and crofts which backed onto Stornoway Aerodrome began to have a rather surreal aspect as if they were merely temporary shelters or even dummy houses set in bright sunshine waiting for the bomb to drop. Murdo's constant refrain, 'better to be going than coming,' added a macabre touch, for beneath such decibel stress people must either go bananas in a mad docile

way or become vehement about their rights to live in peace.
Murdo had opted for the latter course. The bardie mantle and
the flamboyant passion in his small wiry frame would have
naturally drawn him into the limelight on the side of
humanity against an oppressor; but with the possibility of a
NATO base next to his house, it was understandable that he
should be a welcome speaker at meetings protesting against
the extension of the runway to carry bigger craft with more
awesome weapons of destruction.

He was fond of contrasting the preacher and the bard. 'The
preacher says life is bad, a visitation from on high but it's what
you deserve. The bard on the other hand says if life is evil,
fight the devil and his work.' During the last of his 81 years he
was gladdened when the Lewis Presbytery voted to maintain
the opposition of the Free Church against the planned
extension of the airfield. He withdrew his threat to stop
paying sustentation fees, by which the members maintain the
church, after a lifetime's adherence to his chosen religion. I
wonder if it is right to talk of the recent dead, and as an
outsider to refer to a brief meeting with the man as
representing the iconoclasm of island culture. Much of what
he said would be familiar to those who knew and listened to
him, but for others Murdo was probably the nearest
Stornoway will ever come to having an elder statesman.
Listening to him talk of his childhood and the poverty of those
around him; his hopes when he was a clerk for Leverhulme; in
migrating to Canada with many hundreds of fellow islanders
during the 1920s; and finally the eventual return home; it all
seemed to embody the quintessence of the Hebridean story.
And yet his was of a different quality for he took up the
challenge of the present rather than live in the past, at an age
when few of his contemporaries would even bother to raise a
voice. Exposed to the hardships of life and the fevers of a
socialism of every man according to his needs, his poetry was
not an establishment panegyric. Even though he had cast
himself in the traditional light of the bard, one wondered what
stage of the seven-branched bardic tree he might have reached
had he lived whilst the Clans ruled the Isles. In 1609 the so-
called 'Statutes of Iona' banished the bards of the heroic mould
and decreed that the sons of the Chiefs were to be educated in

the Lowlands. This was part of a pattern of intrusion into Island life that had begun with the collapse of the semi-independent Lordship of the Isles. After the Reformation there was a definite separation from tradition until the Act of Union of 1707 and the suppression of the Clans in 1748 completed the process. The Abolition of the Heritable Jurisdictions Act obliged Highland 'proprietors' to dispense with their retinue of armed followers and assume possession of land to which they had no right, including that held by the bards and musicians, and in so doing they relinquished the panoply, colour and music of the old ways.

North Lochs

The third main area fairly close to Stornoway that is worth exploring is, at the name implies, rather a wet place full of small lochs and bogs. From Leurbost, about seven miles (11km.) to the south, just off the A859, there is a circular road that goes through the rather dreary townships around the headland of the sea loch and back up through Arnish Moor. A fish farm managed by a local co-operative was originally financed by the HIDB, part of a pattern of semi-industrial self-help that appears to be fairly successful throughout the Hebrides. The needs and resources of each community generally dictate the outlet. For instance, on Barra there is a retail shop specialising in hardware, clothing and the like. In the best sense these co-operatives are an extension of the close communal life that has always been a necessary part of island existence. Another unique aspect of this quality is the large furniture store of James MacKenzie in Stornoway, which in fact is a trust whose profits are used to help the aged and infirm of the town.

Perhaps one of the most unusual discoveries in North Lochs was reported in *The Times* of March 1856. This was the appearance of a large animal in Loch Leurbost, a sea-serpent or the hitherto mythological water-kelpie, that was variously described as the size of a large peat stack or a six-oared boat, and shaped like a giant eel nearly 40 foot long. The creature was seen by crowds of people during the previous fortnight and was reported to have swallowed a blanket inadvertently left on the bank of the loch by a young girl who was herding cattle when it made its first appearance. A correspondent in the *Inverness Courier* affirmed that he had seen a similar creature in the loch for several hours but had failed to get a shot at it. He stated that a Mr. Mackenzie from Stornoway, with whom he had dined that evening, told him of something resembling a huge conger eel that had been captured in the very same loch 70 years previously and it had required a farm cart to transport it into the town. Nothing has been seen here since. The sea loch is a deep cleft over two miles long and connected by rivers to many of the surrounding inland lochs and, according to an expert on these matters (Peter Costello, *In Search of Lake Monsters*, 1974), this area should be a classic habitat for a Nessie. Many miles away to the northwest, two local anglers in 1961 reported seeing a triple humped-backed-beast with a short head swimming like a dolphin in Loch Uruval, which is halfway between Achmore and the Pentland Road.

Stone Circle, Achmore

A single upright stone projecting about three feet (1m.) above the moor was known locally as Creag na Biorcreil, or 'Stone of the Hat,' presumably because of its shape. Over the years a few other fallen slabs were gradually revealed by peat cutting. During 1981 the site was partially excavated by Margaret Ponting, and this revealed a hitherto unknown broken circle with about 20 smashed and recumbent stones. They are all fairly thin slabs, the largest nearly seven foot (2m.) long. It is situated 200 yards from the road just prior to Achmore junction where the slip road joins the A580 with the A856.

The appearance of this site belies its importance. Situated roughly midway between Stornoway and Callanish, the elevation above the 100m. contour line gives a good sidelong view of the 'Sleeping Beauty' figure, with its 'pregnant' look created by the conical summit of Beinn Mhor directly behind it. From the head of Sithean an Airghid there are some important alignments running through Achmore to the Cleite Dubh on the east coast, as we have already seen, but also to Clach Stei Lin at Shadar on the west coast. Thirdly Achmore is the first of a number of high points alongside the present route to the Callanish stones from which it may have been possible to view the drama of the full moon, 'emerging from the mountain mother' at the major standstill. In fairness to those who have never set foot on Lewis, each of these points demands some explanation in order to make some sense, but it was their accumulative assimilation over a number of years that finally gave us the extraordinary notion of the 'moondance' on the night when the 19-year cycle begins its physical regeneration with the moon visibly close to the earth.

In the Celtic Ritual Calendar, the celebration of the old year and the beginning of the new was at Samhain, or the 'feast of the dead,' later known as All Hollows Eve but now shortened to our familiar Hallow'en. Martin mentions a tradition in Lewis that was carried out as late as the middle of the 17th century, whereby the people of Ness made libations to a sea deity called 'Shony' on this night, followed by a vigil in the chapel and feasting outside until dawn. Another important festival was St. Brighid's Day at the beginning of February. 'On the day of Bride of the white hills the noble queen will emerge from the knoll,' is taken from one of the prayers intoned on that morning to melt the snows. The tradition of the May-Eve 'needfire' at Callanish has been recorded: all the fires in the area were extinguished on that night to be relit from the Beltane bonfire. The fourth fire festival was at Lammas at the beginning of August, with thanksgiving for the harvest and the cattle run through the heat of the twin fires to prevent murrain disease. These and many other rites were part of ancient celebrations that defined the turnings of the year and which in later Scottish traditions were held on the Quarter Days. There is a phrase in Gaelic, 'Between the two Maydays,' that originally may have signified a complete cycle of the year, but it came to mean the sowing and planting best done during the fortnight between the old and new dates of Mayday. Ten days were removed from the calendar in 1582, when it was adjusted to take account of Easter—which is why it is rare today to see the hawthorn or May blossom on the current date, for the old festival was actually held two weeks later. Such festivals marking the beginning and ending of the seasons are the tip of a traditional mode of behaviour whose very beginnings are lost in the mists of time. Yet it is possible to gain some understanding from these traditional cycles by viewing them as part of a complex response integrating natural lore with social ritual and celestial movements.

The old stories often contain some nuggets from this accumulative wisdom, especially those that seem to show a strong connection between water and the Cailleach, or 'old Hag Goddess.' On the headland beyond the Callanish main circle at Chaolais, a beautiful cow appeared to a woman by the sea shore, desperate because of a local famine. The cow had red ears and spoke to her in Gaelic, telling her to go home and get her neighbours together at the Callanish Stones, where they would have fresh milk. The people were sceptical that this one cow could provide all of them with milk, but nevertheless they went there and all received a pail of milk full to overflowing. They came every evening and throughout the long winter each person received a pail of milk per day. However, a witch decided that she should have two, instead of one, but the cow refused her the milk. Pretending that she was sorry she then brought along a bucket with a hole in the bottom of it and proceeded to milk the cow dry. After that it was never seen again. Across the water on Bernera at the harvest feast a straw figure of the Cailleach was set at the head of the table and toasted with each dram saying 'Here's to the one which helped us with the harvest.' One of the lads then danced with her or if the night was good they would go marching around with her on someone's back. On the road up to Bernera Bridge there is a hamlet called Lunsdale which is reminiscent of Lunasdal, a less common term for Lammas, with its connection between the moon and the thanksgiving festival. At midsummer, the 'Shining or Pure One' was said to have walked down the main Callanish stone avenue into the circle heralded by a cuckoo call or whistling noise as the sun rose. The cuckoo, or druid bird, is usually associated with Beltane and said to be a good omen if first heard around the stones. However, it is usually a blackbird that seems to sing on the centre stone now, but the whistling phenomenon up the avenue just prior to the midsummer dawn can still be heard.

Another story here concerns two girls who were both in love with the same lad. One of them went to the local witch for a love potion, and was handed a small parcel to give to her friend as a gift. However, warned not to wear it herself, she was consumed with curiosity to know what was inside and when she opened the parcel found a marvellous jewelled belt. In a quandary as she did not wish to harm her friend, she took it to the stones. However, as soon as she tied the belt around a stone pillar, the pillar was engulfed in flames and with a loud scream broke in two pieces—leaving scorch marks where the belt had been. Another legend recounts how the stones were first brought to Callanish by a great priest with a company of black men who erected them and then were buried underneath. The priest had robes of bird feathers made from the mallard duck and always had wrens flying about his head. This bird garb is mentioned in some Irish stories as special Druidic costume. When Martin, who did the first published sketch of 'Ye Heathen Temple,' asked the natives if they had any traditions concerning the stones, he was told that during the times of ancient worship a priest or chief Druid stood near the big stone in the centre and addressed the people. In a sense these stories have all been remaindered from the distant past and are often the only extent indication of mythical or ritual importance associated with a particular place now marked by a circle or standing stone; a tumulus or fairy mound; an old chapel site or healing well.

Between Achmore and the shores of East Loch Roag are a series of mounds and high points on either side of the road from which one can get a good elevation on the Sleeping Beauty. In fact the road itself in part follows an alignment that runs from the circle at Achmore to the circle at Cnoc Fillibhir Bheag (C/3), just beyond the north edge of the Callanish main circle, to cross the water at Chaolais and reappear on Great Bernera by the broken stone, Airigh Mhaoldonuich, on the shore of Loch Baraglom, and then to a dun site in Loch Baravat. It is not exactly an east–west line for the grid bearing is 110.5° (azimuth 106.5°) and 290.5° (azimuth 286.5°), nor as it astronomically significant but it may have had an important bearing on the megalithic geometry of the area as a whole. It is only three degrees from being at right angles to the major moon standstill line that runs from Beinn Mhor, across the 'stomach' at Mor Mhonadh, to the circle at Fangs on Loch Seaforth; then through the Achmore Circle and up through

Lewis to the megalithic complex at Steincleit with the five-foot-tall (1.5m.) stone, Clach Stei Lin, to emerge at the sea less than half a mile away by Five Penny Borve.

The midsummer sunrise line is the other major alignment which runs from the head of the Sleeping Beauty for almost a similar distance, but it diverges at Achmore to end up at Cleite Dubh on the east coast. The full significance of these and other long alignments that run through stone circles, sacred mounds and other ancient sites throughout the Hebrides, is impossible to guage. Some have astronomical importance in terms of a ritual calendar, others seem to be expressions of geological faulting that runs beneath the surface in straight lines. There are a number of major fault lines across Lewis and it is possible to see this on the surface in the Valtos Valley in Uig. These magnetic and water-energised 'lines' are susceptible to dowsing or divining, but connections also become apparent through mapping out the ground geometry.

Beyond Achmore are the twin summits of Eitshal, the largest hill on the route; the Trig point is on the lower one (206m.), for there is now a gaunt military structure on the other that looks like a replica of the Eiffel Tower. It was clearly an important site in ancient times with its nearby 'Stone of Prophecy' where the seer Coinneach Odhar referred to a battle that would be fought and much blood spilled. The mast's twinkling red aircraft lights are visible at night across the moor but it is part of the 'Early-Warning System' which is a very different kind of alignment from the ones above but nevertheless still connected by lasar-radar on direct line-of-sight through the British Telecom Tower in London, up mainland Britain, out to St. Kilda, and on around the earth. This is but one of the more obvious military lines of electronic communication that have been installed worldwide in recent years. So perhaps we should not dismiss as glib the notion that in their day, ancient structures elaborated their own form of technical drive and overt functioning that were more important than the structural and formal considerations that archaeologists deem so important.

Nearly a mile to the west is Tom Rostel. Visible from the road, this symmetrical mound rises from the flat moor to 104m. OD, and on closer inspection has a decided artificial or

man–made quality, being packed with small stones beneath its
green covering. A mile west is Clach Ghlas, a stone now
hidden in the tree plantation but almost due north of Beinn
Mhor. Further on is another mound called Tom (75m. OD).
So a walk from Callanish to Achmore, which is roughly six
miles, can be done using these six high points to keep the
Sleeping Beauty in clear view, for unlike the present boggy
terrain the ground during the prehistoric period probably had
paths running through the vegetation and low–lying tree
cover.

To get some idea of the importance of the lunar cycle in
relation to both the mountainous figure on the southern
horizon and the above possible viewing positions, it is
necessary to go step by step through the visible physical
changes that those participating in this 'drama of one night'
might have experienced. It was a tableau in which the full
moon would be seen to emerge and set simultaneously from
each of the aspects of her body beginning with the belly,
breasts, neck, head, and finally the brow itself. This
seemingly impossible situation was hinted at by the Greek
historian, Diodorus, writing in 55 BC of a winged and
spherical temple of the Hypoboreans in the Isles of the North.
These islands, as with the Isles of the Blessed to the Celts, may
have been mythical or based on observations from travellers,
but the site of the stone temple has had many claimants. In
terms of its actual shape and other considerations, many
believe that it was the Callanish Stones that he was referring
to: 'Here the moon was but a short distance from the earth and
every 19 years the god dances continuously from the vernal
equinox to the rise of the Plaiedes.' Alexander Thom and
Gerald Hawkins have both shown that the phenomenon
known as 'the major standstill' occurs every 18.61 years and
that at Callanish the full moon would be seen to skim the
southern horizon in a short arc of less than two degrees while
maintaining its slight wobble or 'standstill' effect for over two
hours. After 9.3 years the effect is known as 'the minor
standstill', when it is at its highest position in the sky. Astro-
archaeological data of lunar co-ordinates relative to siting
position and azimuth are often confusing when assuming a
passive role in relation to the moon moving through the night

sky. But if one postulates a reversal of this for a more dynamic procedure in which the movement of people along a well-defined path of highs and lows at a period when the full moon was close to the profile of the supine goddess figure, then the orb begins to engage in a special dance scenario. This hypothesis was actually tested out at the full moon following the midsummer of 1983 by Ron Curtis and a number of enthusiastic helpers, for on that night it was only eight degrees of arc above the horizon and the nearest it would be to the Sleeping Beauty until the actual major standstill of 1987. According to his data, the 'moon-dance' does actually work. This try-out also showed that elaborate prepreparations by the astronomer priests would almost certainly have occurred before the night of the drama. For just as a full moon is preceeded and followed by a night progression in its size and shape so the months before and after the standstill would be equally useful for observations and calculations. So for an imaginative reenactment: beginning with the festive gathering around East Loch Roag, and from here the full figure of the Sleeping Beauty with Beinn Mhor next to the head would indeed be waiting as people watched the moon every night getting fuller and closer to its standstill. It takes roughly half-an-hour for the orb to move up and over the profile and stop on top of Beinn Mhor. It is at this moment that the ritual walk or dance could commence, for as one moves eastwards so the mountain appears to move westwards with the moon on top of it, across the supine body of the goddess. The up and down traverse of the landscape creates the optical effect of the heavenly body dancing to cosmic music. So having kept the emerging moon on top of the mountain for two hours until Achmore was reached, one then allows the moon to roll down the side of the pregnant stomach to disappear into the body of the Sleeping Beauty. It would then be seen to emerge as a momentary flashpoint at the 'brow' as the goddess gave birth. On this one night every generation, the natural laws that held the cosmos in twain went into abeyance while the great drama unfolded through the action of the people themselves. Their ritual dance bound the moon to the mountain, for the land to become one with the Goddess.

The lunar standstill is observable throughout the northern hemisphere, though not on a latitude to the north of Callanish for the moon would not actually set on that night, so it is possible that similar rituals may have been enacted elsewhere at other sacred sites. Michael Dames in his exposition of Silbury Hill as a goddess figure on the Wiltshire Downs, has indicated the complex and exacting requirements the builders had to satisfy in order that the mound should represent the proper conjunction of moon and earth at the time of lammas festival. The goddess here played out the central role of a ritual drama in which the new moon would be seen to rise out of the 130-foot-high chalk mound and its surrounding water-filled ditch, to reflect the actual body of the universal mother. So throughout the night of the harvest full moon, the assembled people could actually watch the silver head rising out of the spring at its base and move up and around the pot-bellied configuration of the pregnant mother. 'The Silbury goddess is seen on her side, yet the Maltese figurines and temples express a preference for a frontal view of the deity' (*The Silbury Treasure*). In this respect the Sleeping Beauty of Lewis conforms to the generally preferred expression of the Great Mother in labour.

If, as has been suggested, the annual rebirth of the moon was of such importance to the lives of the Neolithic peoples in Southern England, then the 18.61-yearly cycle of the goddess would indeed be vital. The cosmology is certainly interpretative but the facts behind it are based on astronomical alignments. One such factor is that eclipses of the moon only occur when it is full. They are also known to occur in patterns, time-wise, yet at any time of the year. However, in the year of a major or minor standstill they happen (if at all) at the full moon nearest the spring or autumn equinoxes. Researchers into megalithic science have all commented on the importance of the eclipse as the central part of their ground geometry. In the scenario outlined above, knowledge of the time when the sun eclipsed the moon was real power and probably the highest and most secret accolade of the priesthood. An eclipse occurring on the night of Samhain would certainly bode evil for the rest of that year, but a full eclipse of the moon on the night of a major standstill might well be the end of an epoch.

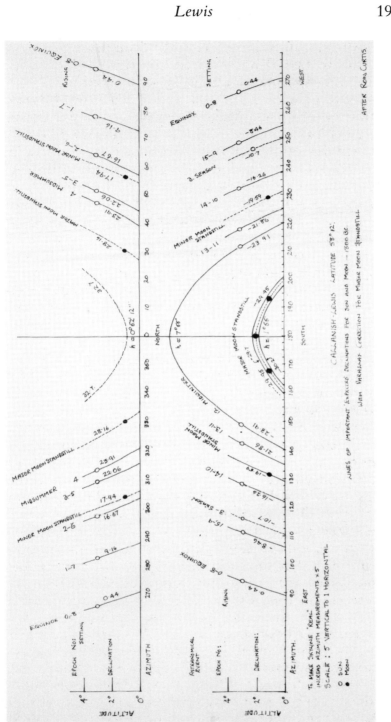

Map of Expected Declination, after Ron Curtis

It would be interesting to know if the moon had ever eclipsed on a major standstill. If so, perhaps it was like the Incas who, after seeing the portents and signs from heaven, knew their time was at hand and waited 17 years for the conquistador to arrive and take over the physical visible remains of their defunct social order. If a stillbirth and its after effects on the matriarchal priesthood appears too fatalistic an outcome, there is the other possibility with equally dire results that the Druids of the incomers with their own solar religion had access to this secret knowledge and challenged the priests of the goddess on the night of an eclipse. Even though such magic contests are common in Irish legend, a recorded historical event and its subsequent implications might be worthwhile in this context as it was the fulcrum by which the Picts could be converted to Christianity. When Columba arrived at the gates of the fort of Bruide, King of the Picts, he was not admitted. So he retired and waited. The chief Druid inside was obviously working at his magic against the Saint at the gate but somehow his own energy turned against him and he grew physically sick and appeared as if he would die. Then the King asked for help to save his Druid. Colmcille picked up a white pebble from the shore and told the messenger to take it to Bruide, saying if it floated in water the Druid would live. The object of the exercise was to confound your opponent publicly, make him admit defeat and accept that the 'new' magic worked better than the 'old'. It did float, thereby upsetting one of the natural laws, so the Irishman was allowed to continue his conversion of Pictland unimpeded.

The Standing Stones of Callanish

If Lewis were indeed the sacred isle that generated this complex monument in stone, it would also be a learning centre of the secret and most arcane knowledge. Young priests of their own volition or encouraged by ambitious chieftains, bright administrators and the intellectuals slowly moving up the ladder of recognition, rich pilgrims and those who had been given a sign in dream or vision: all would eventually find their way here, dedicating themselves to the service of the Goddess. For others it would be enough to know intimately the bedazzling body of liberation and contemplate the sleeping figure awaiting her time of rejuvenation. The advent of the standing stones, so obviously set for those not familiar with the mountain body, may have foreshadowed the end.

Standing eerily on a curved promontory above East Loch Roag the tall grey monoliths look ribbed and as weathered as old driftwood. An overwhelming impression is often of a sepulchral quality as if each stone had been picked for a special kind of commemoration. The Gaelic designation, 'False Men', for these stones is instantly understandable in the often uncertain light from the North Atlantic playing on the rounded shapes with their uneven and misshaped tops. A closed feeling from that closely packed circle likely to be experienced on a wet day recalls the local name, Tursachan, meaning 'a place of mourning or pilgrimage'. However, it would be wrong to emphasise this aspect too much for the sun can instantly pick out the minute white and pink quartize crystals within the natural formation of the gneiss, their myriad variations making strange patterns on some of the inner surfaces like gesticulating or dancing figures that seem to beckon towards the broad centre stone. The structure then appears to hum with an exhilarating energy. Book descriptions of measurements, angles and azimuths tend to be forgotten when alone inside the circle at such moments.

On a summer evening, lean against the broad comforting presence of the centre stone bathed in a golden light watching the sun spread over the still waters of the loch. Enveloping greyness over water, stones; houses tucked into the sides of the opposite hills fold in on themselves without that daytime colour and definition. Often in total darkness the circle becomes overpoweringly present. With the illumination from passing cars rattling over the cattle grid at the edge of the village or the light from a weak moon scudding through clouds, the stones seem to move. Moments of heartbeat. A pure terror manifests when the centre becomes immense and exudes a little of that darkness from within itself. It is not an anthropomorphic change but more a revelation of timelessness. Stripping back the veils we impose on time with the reminder that its primal state is stone. In dowsing too, this quality sometimes comes across as if the ground on which one stands opens to reveal its radiating energy pulses like veins on a heart. A dimension we very often tend to forget when looking at them as if they were merely a group of upright stones. If one could feel that moment of pull as the moon rises on the sun going down below the far horizon, and lock into stone held by magnetic gravitation to a physical earth body spanning 25,000 miles across its axis, one would indeed peer into the blackness of the void. It is not merely their sense of remoteness in time or the physical distance from our usual environment which is disquieting, but the almost sculptural containment. Theirs is a beauty that is essentially ahuman and when measured against our known sensibilities imparts a special quality to the Callanish stone that old churches usually reserve for themselves as if protected against the encroaching changes of the world. There is a deep stillness here. The black heart of an ancient crystal vision.

The archaeological imperative to explore the largest conglomeration of megalithic remains in the Outer Hebrides has been spasmodic and until recent years lacking in direction.

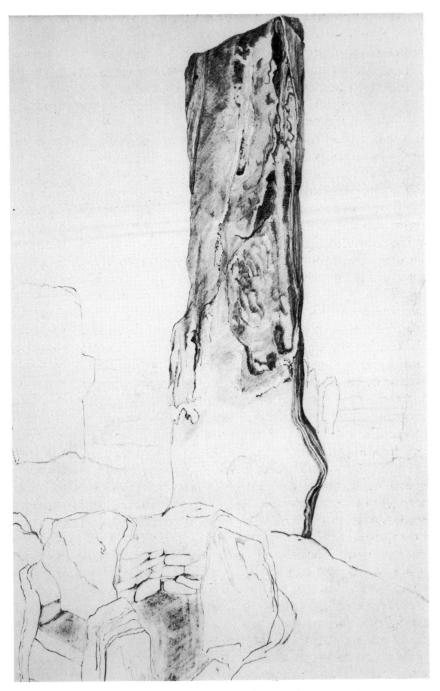

Centre Stone and Cairn, Callanish

Archaeologists building up a comprehensive picture of prehistoric life from the scattered remnants of the past usually ignore why megalithic structures were built and sited at particular locations. The science has not equipped itself to answer such problems, except in the most rudimentary manner, yet this is what ordinary people want to know. If we knew why these stone circles were erected then we might begin to see beyond the stereotyped image of our primitive aboriginal ancestors created by a storybook archaeology to a more enlightened viewpoint of a society with a technical drive that could cut, dress and transport over the most difficult terrain stones weighing anything from two to twenty tons, with an engineering skill to place them precisely and elegantly throughout the length and breadth of Britain and Western Europe. In the mish-mash of dating chronologies and terms like the Neolithic, Old and New Stone, and Bronze Ages, it is quite easy to overlook the fact that some of the most spectacular monuments like the Avebury Circles, Silbury Hill, the chambered mount at Newgrange, the Ring of Brogar and the stone circle and avenue at Callanish, may pre-date the first Egyptian pyramid.

As far back as 60 years ago MacKenzie in his *Book of the Lews*, writing of the prehistoric period, said that the solutions that these remains present are necessarily vague and suggestive. 'The shapes and sizes of the standing stones are fully recorded, the angles given with mathematical precision, their measurements are stated to a fraction of an inch. These are the dry bones of archaeology.' The open surgery method of site research which evolved from pick and shovel mania for grave finds, artifacts and museum treasures, has been refined – but it still remains a first article of faith and principle method of training. However, modern researchers are much more cautious, both in approach and in conclusions, than their predecessors. They can now rely on a range of subsidiary studies such as calibrated carbon dating; pollen counts and microscopic analysis of ancient flora and fauna; aerial and infra-red photography; statistical analysis; and data from prehistoric astronomy. The 'dry bones' may seem to have a bit more meat and colour about them but these skills with their own meta-languages, and in the case of astro-archaeology almost a sub-cult, have become so specialised that few outsiders can fully evaluate their findings. In regards to Callanish it is fairly safe to say that the watershed of current orthodoxy can be defined as being between those who concentrate on outward forms and comparative site stratification and the more mathematical approach of those who believe their fledgling science combining astronomy and archaeology can elucidate a more coherent and cogent picture of the past.

Peat cutting by the local people had gradually revealed the true depth of the stones, and in 1858 Sir James Matheson – proprietor of Lewis – ordered the clearing of the five-foot-high turf that had grown around them. A small unroofed chambered cairn between the centre stone and the eastern edge of the circle was found to contain some black unctious substance which turned out to be a mixture of peat and animal matter. The cairn is thought to have been rebuilt and its rounded drystone walling was a distinctive feature of the site, but over the years with the increasing influx of visitors began to collapse. It was recently repaired by the SDD(AM). The peat around the circle at Cnoc Ceanan a Gharaidh (C/2) was dug out to a depth of seven feet to disclose some small inner 'altars' paved with rounded stones containing charcoal. 'Several of the stones of the outer circle were lying prostrate upon the paved floor. These must have fallen before the moss began to grow'. Cnoc Fillibhir nam Beag (C/3) was originally reported by MacKenzie in 1792 to be mostly buried in earth; Captain Thomas in 1862 added, 'nothing but a few grey blocks protruding two or three feet above the bog would have been seen.' McCulloch (1819) produced a fairly detailed plan of the main site and the most authoritative archaeological records during the 19th century were done by Sharbau of the Royal Commission on Ancient Monuments with a series of drawings of C/1, C/2, C/3, C/5 and Airidh nam Biderean at Garynahine. Pitt-Rivers, first Inspector of Ancient Monuments, visited the area in 1885 accompanied by his assistant Tomkins, who was an accomplished artist. He completed drawings of all the stones at the main site and of C/3, which are at present in the Public Records Office in London. Boyle Somerville's survey and site plan of 1912 were

Callanish, stone avenue leading to main circle

the most accurate until the Geography Department of the University of Glasgow carried out their extensive survey, using up-to-date methods and equipment, of the main site as well as 11 others in the immediate vicinity of East Loch Roag, in 1974.

The excavations at the main circle during 1980/81 has revealed some of the long prehistory of the site.

Preliminary results show that it was farmland before the circle and monoliths were erected, and before that again at least one large ditch existed. Smaller curved ditches lay open in the stone circle for a time, cut through the ploughsoil. They filled up and grassed over, and then the chambered cairn was built probably with a kerb of small horizontally laid slabs. Beaker people buried their dead in its chamber. Then, perhaps in the later second millennium BC, the cairn was broken open and the chamber emptied. The area round it was ploughed. The capstones may have been re-used at this time as the massive kerbstones at the southeast of the cairn. Early in the first millennium BC mosses and other peat began to grow.

Mr. Ashmore, who carried out the excavation, emphasised the multi-period nature of the site:

The farming I referred to could be of either the late fourth millennium BC or the middle third – study of the pollen and plant remains from the site may allow us to be more precise. At least it does seem likely that the circle was not erected by beaker people, but by earlier peoples and the cairn may have been built then too for there are plenty of examples of re-use of cairns by beaker users.

His findings counteract the long-held belief that it was the Bronze Age incomers, users of a destinctive beaker pottery, who were responsible for the large stone circles, and he suggests that it was likely that all the larger circles in Scotland were built during the Neolithic period.

The three main circles at Callanish are intervisible within half-a-mile of each other on slightly rising ground at the edge of East Loch Roag. Their different structure, design, orientation and general appearance add to the acknowledged difficulty of interpretation. The main circle has an elegance and symmetry lacking not only in the other two but in all the rings of standing stones throughout the Hebrides. C/2 is a large open semicircle or ellipse-shaped ring with a diameter of 65 feet (24m.). It has five stones standing, the largest nearly eleven by six feet (3.3x1.8m.). C/3 is small, clustered and rather diffident in definition. It has been variously described as a twin or concentric circle, but the outer ring is a slightly flattened circle of 53 feet (16m.) diameter.

Stone Circle Avenue (C/1)

The slightly flattened circle of 13 standing stones, diameter of 37 feet (15m.) or 15.5 MY, encloses 15 foot 7 inches (5m.) monolith which is over 6 feet (1.8m.) wide at its base and faces E/W. This is the tallest stone of the group and the others range from 9 feet, to 11 feet 5 inches (2.7 – 3.6m.). The overall setting incorporates short arms of four, six and five broad stones, respectively, pointing almost to the cardinal points of W, S and E. The 270 foot long by 27 foot wide (18x8m.) avenue of 19 stones is at 11° azimuth. This cruciform shape, unique among megalithic monuments, terminates at a rocky outcrop called Cnoc an Tursa, which is at 100 feet above sealevel and overlooks the southern end. It may have been originally used as a ceremonial platform.

Between the centre stone and the eastern edge of the circle is a small chambered cairn bounded at the SE by large kerbstones. From Matheson's account of the first excavations in 1858, when five feet of peat was cleared from the circle, it is clear that the cairn had been previously opened and left unroofed. Recent excavations during 1980/81 show that some of its structural features were damaged then: parts of the chamber and cairn were rebuilt, a drain put in, and the chamber bottom scraped clean. The chamber is now refurbished in its Victorian state, concealing the first chamber plan in which the back of the chamber by the monolith was rounded off rather than squared.

In 1912 Boyle Somerville produced a detailed plan of all the stones in the circle and avenue, and the numbering system is still in use today. Sixty years later a very accurate survey of this and 11 other sites in the immediate vicinity of East Loch Roag was carried out by the Department of Geography at the University of Glasgow. Professor Thom's numbers for the sites (HI/1 etc.) were used by the university and are generally accepted for convenience sake when trying to cope with the many variations of Gaelic place-names used by different archaeologists and the Ordnance Survey over the years. Here his numbering is used but with the substitution of C for Callanish as in C/1 etc.

Stone Circle (C/2), Cnoc Ceann a Gheraidh

Within sight of the main circle on a plateau 100 yards (91m.) from the shore, there are five erect stones known locally as Tursachan. Set in a line of circumference (75 MY) they are in the eastern arc of an ellipse-shaped ring whose major diameter is 65 feet (20m.) or 26 MY. The stones measure from 6 foot 6 inches to 10 foot 9 inches (1.9 to 3m.) in height and from 3 foot to 5 foot 10 inches (0.9 to 1.8m.) in width and there are also three broad prostrate slabs (largest 9 foot 11 inches by 5 foot 8 inches (3x1.7m.)) on the western perimeter. During the 19th century excavation it was reported that the peat moss was dug out to a depth of 7 feet (2m.) to reveal a cairn of small stones containing four or five altars whose bottoms were paved with smooth round seashore pebbles.

Stone Circle (C/3), Cnoc Fillibhir Bheag

Nearly three-quarters of a mile E by S of C/1 and 400 yards (364m.) W of the road by the cattle grid is one of the more complex of the local sites. Its shape and possible function in relation to lunar alignments have been variously described. The outer ring, a flattened Type A circle of nine erect stones, varying in height from 3 foot 5 inches to 5 foot 10 inches, and six prostrate, has a diameter of 53 feet (16m.) or 20 MY. The inner four stones (7 feet; 4 feet 7 inches; 5 feet 9 inches and 6 feet high) now stand in a kind of horseshoe shape or lozenge facing the NW. The most prominent stone is eight feet (2.4m.) tall and white, pink and black crystalline lines running through it and it tilts to the east. Its opposite number is a solid five-foot-high (1.5m.) pillar stone of pinkish gneiss while the other two facing east/west are of smaller stature. Curiously there seems to be an outsider in the ring, a three-foot (1m.) stone of broken grey granite with a jagged top notched from it. The remainder have the ribbed quality of the main circle, which is due as much to the diligence of the SDD(AM)'s cleaning department as to the gneiss itself. Their experts claim that the lichen eats the stone beneath, but whether such exposure to the fierce island weather with its frequent fluctuations of temperature will result in a faster rate of erosion is debatable. To add to the variety of sites in the area there are the group of recumbent stones at Na Dromannan (C/10) further to the east on the moor; those slightly south of Garynahine (C/4, C/5, C/7); and the three stones at Bernera Bridge (C/8); as well as many smaller sites and single stones that have not been verified archaeologically.

We have no racial, linguistic or social knowledge of the original builders, much less what thoughts or beliefs gave them this singular building impetus; nevertheless, speculation knows no boundaries—as any library on the subject quickly makes clear. The little that *is* known, and especially the fact that some stones had fallen or were overturned before the onset of the peat growing, can lead to a number of conclusions. The most simplistic is that the main circle, which is now without any doubt the most architecturally satisfying, was the first and best, while the others were of less consequence. The second follows on from that, that the

'Sleeping Beauty Carving,' Shadar, Lewis

subsequent users, as opposed to the original builders, sometime between 3,000 and 2,000 BC, were more concerned with using the main circle and may have added the stone avenue. Perhaps for ceremonial purposes and to emphasise its monumental character, they displaced the other prominent structures on the skyline. Time and lack of care would have taken its toll on the rest. Then there is the possibility that they were all built at different times by different groups, not necessarily from the immediate area around East Loch Roag, but as ancestor/status markers perhaps in the manner that family tombs gradually fill up a graveyard. Finally, that they were structured to a definite set of principles and the purpose behind them demanded that the material, size and shapes were carefully chosen and specifically sited. It is at this point that the notions of megalithic engineering and geometry begin to enter the discussion. However, it is well to remember that a different set of paradigms applied with equal vigour or determination and based on magnetic field theory, crystalline sonic structures or aesthetic reductionism, might not produce a different set of conclusions but would certainly add more information about the purpose behind them.

Stone Row (C/5), Airidh nam Bideran, Garynahine

Somerville first suggested that ancient astronomers may have used complex moon configurations at Callanish but it was Gerald Hawkins with the publication of *Stonehenge Decoded* (1965) who brought the matter to the attention of a larger public. He claimed that the monument was used like a primitive computer to predict eclipses and that it was built at a particularly significant latitude of the sun. Needing verification from a comparative site because of the criticism his theories raised, he chose Callanish partly because of its size and setting but also because it had been sited near a unique latitude of the moon. He subjected the data on the lunar alignments to a similar statistical analysis and asserted, without having visited the site, that an observer looking along the south row of stones from the main circle in 1500 BC would see the moon's maxima at its extreme delineation skimming the horizon every 18.61 years. Professor Thom, however, stated that a similar observer looking south/southwest from the north-northeast avenue would have seen the moon's maxima setting along the slopes of Mount Clisham in Harris, 16 miles distant. Both assertions were as it turned out quite inaccurate because the knoll, Cnoc an Tursa, would block any such viewing. In his later work Thom modified his views on the observer's position, stating that it was from C/5 that visible alignments were possible.

One mile south of Garynahine on the road to Uig, four small stones spread down the hill below Cnoc Dubh. They vary in height from 30 inches to 42 inches. Near the third one is a flat stone that if standing would have made them all equidistant giving the fifty-foot-long (15m.) stone row an extraordinary elegance. Directly across the road (B8011) and clearly visible on the hill towards the loch is a small stone circle of five standing stones, called Ceann Hulavig (C/4). This is the only one in the area still covered with lichen or what the locals call 'goat's beard'. Its soft green texture blends wonderfully with the moor, giving some indication of what the other circles looked like before the regular cleaning by the SDD(AM).

For Thom, the midwinter moonset would be north, over Cnoc Ceann a Gheraidh (C/2); and south for the midsummer moonrise over the Pairc range of hills. The moon would be seen to rise from the side of Mor Mhonadh, up and over Sidhean an Airgid, to set behind Clisham. This is the so-called 'wobble' effect with nine minutes of arc rising from the 'knees of the Sleeping Beauty' along her body and setting behind the highest peak on the island. The idea that the whole of the Callanish area, with its circles and stones amid the surrounding hills, was in fact a huge 'drawing-board' set out in the landscape to test such theories, has gained acceptance – although there are only three or four researchers who have tried to sort out the 'moon' in relation to Callanish.

If this were so then it might seem that many of the ruined circles never needed completing and others such as Na Dromanann (C/10) on top of the moor were deliberately scattered when their preliminary function was no longer needed. It is when one considers the long-term logistics in the planning, engineering, astronomy and countless other back-up skills and disciplines needed for any such construction of megalithics over a large area of difficult terrain, that the encrustation of 19th-century prejudice shrouding the achievements of ancient man begins to fall away. Another significant region of research and discovery by Thom and others has been at Carnac in Brittany where the modus operandi was set out in long parallel rows, using thousands of stones of many different shapes and sizes. However, it was at Stonehenge where the ultimate achievements and most elegant of solutions seem to have been reached. The lunar risings and settings would be more accurate on the flat Salisbury Plain using the outer-rimmed 56 Aubrey holes, a multiple by three of the 18·61 yearly metonic journey of the moon.

Other people in the Callanish area have been working on the hypothesis of the major moon standstill as the linchpin of ancient astronomy. Gerald and Margaret Ponting, who uncovered the stone circle at Achmore, maintain that 'the better-known ring sites do *not* include accurate indications, but appear to incorporate symbolical alignments to solar and lunar extremes in their basic geometry'. Ron Curtis, a chartered civil engineer from Edinburgh who has been working here every summer for the past decade testing and elaborating Thom's ideas, is of the opinion that the ideal circle from which to view the lunar standstill is Cnoc Fillibhir Bheag (C/3). From here the moon would appear to rise from the 'brow of the Sleeping Beauty' and set behind Clisham; then two hours later skim the northern horizon of the promontory beyond the main circle. The Pontings seem to echo this in saying that from the north end of the avenue an observer in 1987, from the same spot as one in 1500 BC, 'will be able to see (clear skies permitting) the full moon setting through the stones of the circle, although the moon's final disappearance will occur between the stones of the west row'. Here indeed would be a vindication of the oft-quoted Greek tale to the effect that at the winged temple of the Hyperboreans every 19 years the god dances continuously the night through from the vernal equinox to the rise of the Pleiades – which is now usually in November. So in effect for six months the phenomenon might be visible.

Previous major moon standstills occurred in 1913, 1932, 1950 and 1969 – and will again, 18.61 years later, towards the end of 1987. For most of us, the idea of being able to verify by visual observation such intricate data and also be present at the moment of a new cycle would be worth at least a note in our holiday diary; but for the astro-archaeologist this is a non-event. They are extrapolating by geometric models for a set of co-ordinates that would have been valid for dates during the mid-period of the second millennium BC. This also answers some of the confusion a non-specialist might feel at the almost irrational definition and exactitude of each viewing point in relation to a general effect of the moon through the landscape. Nevertheless one may be forgiven for pointing out that if these or some similar set of principles underlay the formation of the megalithic stone structures, they would surely have been erected for a more fundamental reason than chasing a moonbeam every 18 years. Or would they? We cannot know what thought exercised the minds of the builders, though that has not prevented the mountain of written speculation since Stukeley's day from growing ever higher.

From Uig to the Butt of Lewis

Beehive Houses, Morsgail
It was Murdo MacLeod who led us gently into the secrets of the Morsgail Forest. His endless tales of the deer and salmon, the loss of birds and the cycles of wild life throttled by mink and human shortsightedness, were a familiar refrain, but one that we had not previously heard so clearly in our journeys through the Isles. For a man who had spent all his working life on the moor as a poacher, his ability to describe the byplay of nature was astounding. To an outsider, this is yet another vast tract of bogland – but for him it was as familiar as the palm of his hand. Like the great auk, last century, the eagle and the pine marten are becoming extinct now. The auk' was known as a ghost bird, probably because after tending its young it would moult completely, looking like a plucked goose with a razonbill and short wings, before flying off until the following spring. The last specimen was captured on St. Kilda during the 1930s. The eagles, on the other hand, are said to have arrived here in greater numbers after myxomatosis was introduced on the mainland of Scotland. They came in search of prey, and being territorial birds nesting in lower and more accessible places than formally, the crofters were able to locate and firebomb their nests. According to Murdo, the last nest in Great Bernera was lit the season before we arrived, so yet another cog in the great cycle of nature breaks down. The loss of the salmon is too well known to recount but there are attempts being made at present to revive some of the rivers. Reared in fish farms the smoults are taken out to the open sea beyond the line of predators and then allowed to begin their

Standing Stones at Bernera Bridge, Lewis

long journey. They then return to the same waters where they were reared to spawn, and in some cases nearly a 50 percent success rate has been recorded in North Uist. We first met Murdo one day as Keith was drawing a stone on the next croft above East Loch Roag. He was unusual in that he actually came over to see what we were up to, unlike the Hebrideans who are a most reticent people. It was not long before he was leaning against the rock and regaling us with an endless fund of tales. The only note of bitterness that crept into his voice was when he talked of the present and the predators who kill without need, 'without rhyme or reason'. He was as harsh on the wild mink, that have cleared all the ground nesting birds and small animals from this area of Uig, as he is on the 'boys from Glasgow and Greenoch' who will clean out a whole river with dynamite. He loved his fish and animals with an unfeigned physical joy. Clearly, during his time as a poacher, the stalking was as much a challenge to the game as it was for him, honing all his craft and guile in a life contest between man and beast. Now in his early 70s, the hunger that drove him out on a dark November night and the long trek home over the wet bog carrying a stag on his back to feed his young family after his wife had died, is long gone, but when he talks one can see in his eyes the yearning for the cycles of return that had the same pull for him as for the salmon and the rest of nature.

The track through the Morsgail Estate is off the B8011 as it curves round the head of Little Loch Roag. A memorial stone cairn, tightly packed into a tall cone, stands on a hillock at the base of Caultrasel Beag just prior to the turning, one of a number hereabouts from the days of the bloodfeuds between the Macauleys of Uig and the Morrisons of Ness. To reach the cluster of beehive houses is close on a three-mile walk across the moor past the lodge and the welcome cover of oak trees, around the small loch and across the weir to a small path that is often waterlogged if it has been raining. On the OS map the path is well-marked, but unfortunately when you come to the fork at the ruined shieling you have to follow not only your instincts but also the stream that leads up to the water shed (150m.) below Scalaval Sandig. Of the five complete beehive houses, described by Captain Thomas RN during the 1850s,

Interior of beehive house

only one still has its grass-topped conical roof in fair
condition. However, the tightly packed group on the rise
above a small stream does have that African 'kraal' appearance
familiar from his sketches.

The intact house is made entirely of dry stone walling,
roughly eight feet (2.5m.) in diameter, with two entrances
close to the ground about two feet high and two feet wide.
Once through these short tunnels, formed by a single stone·
lintal, the inside is surprisingly spacious with a beaten earth
floor and over six-feet (1.8m.) high in the middle. There are a
few small recessed 'storage cupboards' that were termed
'cuiltrean', from 'cuil' meaning a nook, and also a larger
sleeping area formed from thin slabs. The smoke hole in the
roof was termed a 'farlos' and some of the flat stones on the
roof could be shifted to allow the smoke to rise. On every side
of the low roof corbelling, flat stones could be taken out
depending on wind direction and the need for ventilation.
Once inside with a few rugs or mats, an open-fire in the centre
with an iron pot, a bag of meal and some tins and jars to hold
the milk, the house would have been quite cosy no matter
what the weather outside. A third tunnel, now blocked, led to

the next house and probably there were tunnels connecting all the beehives that naturally formed a few small stock enclosures. There was the stream nearby with sufficient pasture, which made these stone clusters ideal fair-weather dwellings for the young maids who looked after the cattle during the summer grazing and made cheese and butter with the milk. They were used as late as the middle of the last century according to Thomas, and 'all the natives agree that no one knows who built them for they were not made by the fathers or grandfathers of persons now living'.

Prior to the Ordnance Survey maps with site references and symbols marking the locations of ruins and ancient monuments, which even now often take some finding due to poor weather conditions, a local guide was a necessity. This is still the best way, for no matter how precise a book may be with directions it is the incidental information that often makes the journey really interesting. We were fortunate to meet a keen student of the ancient dwellings of Lewis, and as she had had the black-house near the Callanish Stones rebuilt in its original manner as a small cafe, she was familiar with the form and structural aspects of the beehives. She has visited nearly all the 'shielings' and old name references from the map of Lewis, and it seems that from the large number of roofless bothies (from 'bo' and its plural 'boths', meaning temporary dwellings) still to be found on the moors, the intact beehive at Morsgail is a very rare example indeed. She also told us about the 'postman's path' which was a regular route on the moor and one for which the postman after a lifelong service was decorated by the Queen during her inaugural visit. Two miles to the east around the north edge of Loch Resort to Creag an Fhithich, 'Giants Stone', and then across the Aird Peninsula, where there is another beehive cluster at Bothan Gearraidh by Loch nan Uidhean, to Aird Sleithenish. Apparently there is a small circle of standing stones on this tiny peninsula. Across the sea loch, Tamanavay, and half-a-mile up by the bank of the river, is another cluster at Gearraidh Sgaladal. Still the only land route down through the Harris hills from Morsgail is from Kinloch Resort south to connect with the track from Glen Meavaig and West Loch Tarbert; or eastwards by Glen Stuladale to Ardvourlie on Loch Seafort.

Suainaval, Uig

The landscape above the road to Uig and along the shores of
Little Loch Roag has a strange quality of its own quite
different from the relatively sheltered area around Callanish
and the flat windswept coastal plateau up to the Butt of Lewis.
On a dull day the melancholic slag-like hills bring to mind an
earlier primaeval era. Climb 50 feet up the damp slopes to the
small stone cairns on the skyline for a change of interest or a
wider view than a car window, and the landscape of volcanic
debris covered in gorse and bog pools remains as uninviting
and unimpressive as it was from the road. A pipeline runs
down by the Gisla river from the dam on Loch Coirgavat,
high on the moor, to feed a small hydro-electric power station
by the shore of Little Loch Roag. At low tide the grey waters
may reveal the black boulder known as Clach na Cruigaigh –
literally 'stone of the hair' or 'mermaid's rock', after the
creature seen combing her tresses at sunrise. Tradition has it
that she married a man who lived by the shore but after
bearing him two children felt compelled to return to her
element. However, during a severe winter she was concerned
at the fate of her human offspring and sang asking that they be
kept well-wrapped and fed. By the time the man hurried
down to the rock to find his lost love, she had disappeared
again. There is also the story of Lord Seaforth's gilly who
came across a waterhorse standing on a hill one evening. The
Bean Uisne or Kelpies, as they were known on the mainland,
were usually considered helpful and docile, and often
amorously inclined towards young maids alone at the
summer shielings, but this particular one was annoyed by the
barking dogs. The gilly took to his heels with the phantom
horse thundering after him and his dogs in hot pursuit of it.
He finally reached his croft at Gisla and immediately fell into a
deep and exhausted sleep. Next morning he found his hounds
on the moor cold and stiff. Such tales of merwives and
waterhorses, as well as of brownies or uruisg (wee corpulent
men with large eyes and a shock of hair), glaistig (a sort of
banshee), the bean nighs ('a washer-woman of the ford, who
made a noise like clapping hands in water), gruagach (who
presided over cattle), and the sluag or 'Fairy Host', who were
likely to shoot elf-shot or neolithic arrow heads at people or

transport them long distances if they repeated their airy song, once formed part of the staple ingredient of traditional lore by the Gaelic storyteller. A century ago a threatened species but now almost extinct. Prior to the introduction of electricity and especially television, the fabric of entertainment in these remote isles throughout the long winters was woven inside the tigh ceilidh. Translated as 'gossip house', the term aptly describes the general hubbub of shared local news and stories. However, by the turn of the century the term ceilidh had come to mean a more organised entertainment in a public place. For outsiders without the intimate link of language it is only from translations of Gaelic songs, stories and poetry that one can get an idea of the simplicity of expression or the depth of feeling, and especially their almost spiritual attachment for the land itself.

The thin edge between romanticism and reality of that daily inner life, now past, seems as blurred as the landscape one moves through. This may be due to the constant changing light and frequent cloud-forms moving in from the sea, or from some hidden quality; as one local man put it, 'there is an attraction there . . . something in the hills that holds the people'. It is also possible that some of the encounters with the weird creatures of popular lore may not have been all that fanciful. If there was any truth in the assertion that Loch Suainaval was the abode of a Ness-type 'Beiste' then Seaforth's gilly must have had a good five-mile run over the moor to Gisla. A bird's-eye view of the full length of this deep loch can be had from the summit of Suainaval itself. The nearest accessible point on this road is a track opposite a small jetty beyond the thin straggle of cottages called Carshader. After a few hundred yards' walk beside the trickle of water, marked on the map as the River Uasaig, which is probably more impressive in winter, a left fork leads off in the general direction of the mountain. The other path continues to a radar installation, as we found out from a local chap who came careering down the uneven track on an old bike with his feet wide apart, coat flapping in the wind and a cap jammed on his head. He braked suddenly for a chat, and due to the late hour and the amount of wet-weather gear we wore, mistook us for soldiers. Suainaval is (400m.) above sealevel, but the climb against the blasting sleet was a bit more leg-stretching than we at first realised. However, from the top, awesome black clouds swirled in from the Atlantic with the evening light underneath them, and sudden squalls drenched us as they passed directly overhead. The wide girth of an eight-foot-high cairn gave a modicum of shelter from the fierce winds. Like most of them on these wild summits, this was almost a work of art with its small stones packed tightly into an upward spiral. This stone structure perched here in all weathers for goodness knows how many years seemed so locked into itself that it would almost take an earthquake to shift it. The view east towards Callanish, seemingly visible in the quick shafts of light through the dark clouds, had the appearance of a vast mist-covered pool, with Great Bernera and the smaller islands around Loch Roag protruding gaunt and indistinct.

Glen Valtos, Uig

At the entrance to Glen Valtos is a narrow drystone-rubble 19th-century pack-horse bridge over a stream that joins the road to Miavaig and Valtos itself. Even on a good summer's day the seemingly endless white sands of Traig na Berie are usually deserted. When tired of sunbathing, running your fingers through the fine silver grains or splashing in the sea, there are numerous midden heaps along the shoreline to be explored. The sheer quantity of cockle and limpet shells that leavened the sand into a solid brownish mass makes one pause and wonder who those people were nearly 2,000 years ago who seemed to live on little else but shellfish.

From a much earlier era of earth-time a volcanic fault caused the ground to split apart, and over millennia, wind, ice and water-erosion created the Glen Valtos valley. From the road the deep-brown and deep-greenish coloured hills are serated with matching natural indentations on both sides. In its almost indelible silence, a waterfall with patches of reddish stone on either side of it looks like a painted postcard. A straggling fir plantation curves with the slope of the hillside. A small stream trickles along by the road past the ruins of an old beehive house. This spot could almost have been paradise to its inhabitants. Sitting here meditating on the nature of time and the extraordinary capacity of our consciousness to perceive the changes in the world about us, even an occasional lorry or passing car does not distract from the deep peace of this fold in the earth's surface.

All too soon at the end of this mile-long beautiful valley one is confronted by a bewildering array of possible directions and destinations. North to Gallan Head? West to Uig sands? Or further south over the Red River bridge, by the sandquarries, to Mangersta, Islivig, Brenish; then to the end of the track and the ruins of the nunnery at Maelista? Like most of the minor coastal roads on the western side of Lewis, the many smaller tracks and paths have an irritating habit of disappearing so that one is forced to backtrack and begin all over again to somewhere else. I am clearly referring to my own mental ineptitude as a traveller, for as far as the islanders are concerned roads usually end at villages if they don't go down to the shore or up on to the moor nearest their peat-cuttings.

Uig Sands

It was near here that the hoard of ivory chesspieces was discovered in 1831. According to the RCAHM report, the exact spot was 'in a windswept gully in the sands of the southwestern face of Eornal and about 400 yards south of the highwater mark on the southern shore of Uig Bay'. There are a number of different versions about finding the chessmen. A contemporary newspaper report stated that a peasant of the place found them whilst digging at a sandbank. A cow is also supposed to have dislodged the sand, and a third version is that a storm carried away part of a bank and uncovered a small subterranean stone cist or oven and a local man broke it but thought he had found an assembly of frozen elves. However, his wife was of sterner stuff and induced him to return to the spot and carry away the little men. Whatever the original circumstances, the British Museum quickly acquired 67 pieces, a belt buckle and 14 plain draughtsmen for the sum of £84. The Edinburgh National Museum of Antiquities bought a further 11 pieces in 1888. So now there are nearly four complete chess sets (minus a knight, four rooks and 45 pawns), with each piece individually carved in walrus ivory, varying in height from the kings at four and a half inches to the

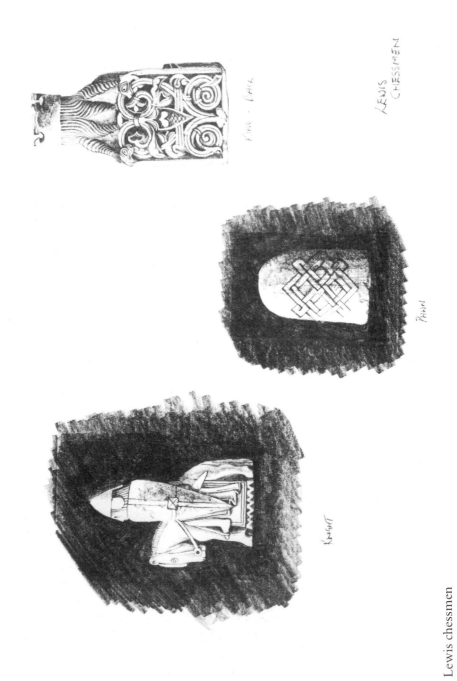

KING - BACK

LEWIS
CHESSMEN

Pawn

Knight

Lewis chessmen

pawns that are just over an inch tall. They are considered to be the work of a mid-12th-century Scandinavian master carver. None are broken or damaged and the British Museum booklet concludes, 'they belonged to some merchant who, travelling by sea or land, lost a part of his stock in circumstances we shall never know'.

The Gaelic term for second sight, an da shealladh, carried the connotation of 'two sights' or 'vision in two places,' incorporating a two-fold vision, one of the material world we all see and the other the spiritual or etherial realms. Other terms used to describe those with this gift were da radharc, 'power of vision,' and taibhsearochd, a combination of two words meaning 'the vision seen' and 'the seer', roughly translated as 'the gift of supernatural sight.' There were various degrees of this faculty, from hearing knocks at unusual times of day or night, or spirit voices, or seeing lights on lochs at night (known as corpse candles), to actually seeing the physical forms of people or apparitions. It was usually in connection with sinister events about to take place and the premonition of death—such as seeing a friend or relative being carried off in a coffin from the house, or being carried over the moor in blood-stained clothing. Its occurrence seemed not to be confined to any particular time or place, for even in the midst of a party one with the gift might see the 'other self' suddenly superimposed over a person and everyone present would be aware of some unusual occurrence for the phenomenon was often accompanied by a 'nerve-storm' bringing about an almost epileptic prostration of the seer.

Second sight is mentioned in most of the books about the Highlands. The Irish Franciscan missionaries to the Hebrides cited several instances in their reports home from the Isles between 1624 and 1640. There was a fairly widespread belief that the seventh child of a seventh child would have the gift, and Robert Kirk, the minister of Aberfoyle, was reputed to be one such. His treatise dated 1652 and called 'The Secret Commonwealth of Elves, Fauns and Fairies' was probably the first on the subject. Andrew Laing in his introduction to the printed version in 1815 said that by 1700 it was not so common as it used to be and quotes a letter from Lord Tarbat to Robert Boyle that 'it was a trouble to most of them who are subject to it, and they would be rid of it at any rate if they could'. In his *Voyage to the Hebrides* in 1822 the Swiss scientist, Mechor de Seusseure, wrote that 'second sight was the most well known and the most general superstition of the Gaels'. Pepys often corresponded about it, and John Aubrey in his *Miscellanies* of 1696 based his accounts on several questionnaires, with eight headings, which he had sent to various correspondents in Scotland. Martin Martin seemed to be aware of this intellectual discourse for he discussed second sight using a number of the common reservations of the period, namely that seers are visionary and melancholic, are not learned enough and that they are imposters who make it all up for vulgar attention. He points out that the faculty is not confined to the Highlands and Isles but was found in other places as well, and that the seers were usually quite cheerful and learned, and most of them would, if they could, get rid of the faculty.

   Although there is no actual record, Ceanneth Odhar is said to have been born at Baillenacille near Ardroil in Uig. Another tradition associates him with Ness but both the claims and confusions that accrued to these seers are understandable given the subject matter and the times, when credulity and brutality went hand-in-hand among the ruling clans of the West Highlands. The story goes that before he was born, his father left his young wife alone while out fishing one night. She heard strange cries outside and when she ventured out by the graveyard she saw the ghost of a drowned figure—a Norwegian princess—whose body had been washed up on the beach but who could not rest until the grave had been paid for. The young woman asked what to do and was told by the princess to cut a sheaf of ripe corn from the field and lay it on the grave. When this was done the ghost said she could now rest in peace and gave her a clear black stone in token of her gratitude and which the wife was to keep for her unborn son when he became seven years of age. By the time the baby was born, the young woman had forgotten all about the lady by the shore. On the boy's seventh birthday, he knocked over an old shell which had the stone inside it. As he picked it up, his mother remembered the words of the ghost, and when the boy looked at the stone, he saw a whale in the nearby Raven's cave. As a birthday treat and to humour his son, his father took him out in his boat, and of course they found a whale beached inside the cave.

Later, when they could not find any fish, the crew would take Ceanneth with them out to sea to tell them the best place to make a haul, and so Ceanneth's fame gradually spread. There are many well-known prophecies attributed to him, such as 'many a long waste 'fearineg [a once-cultivated runrig] will yet be seen between Uig of the Mountains and Ness of the Plains,' and 'the day will come when the big sheep will overrun the country,' which certainly came to pass. However there are some that still await the judgment of time—that Lewis would be the battleground against an invader of Britain, and that black rain would fall and destroy the island forever. Such riddles have usually been considered fanciful until now, when the Western Isles have become one of Britain's forward strategic areas against a possible nuclear attack.

Aird Uig was once a picturesque little village clinging to the lee of a hill above a shingle beach and a narrow Atlantic bay, but now it is an appendage to the road's end at a deserted World War II army camp and the futuristic steel 'n' cable radar mast towering a few hundred feet above Gallan Head. What is most objectionable about coming upon military rubbish of this scale is not only the inherent 'might is right' attitude, that permits any kind of desecration of nature, but also that when the military move on they leave it all behind them. They use the same arguments elsewhere, but masked by a very sophisticated public relations exercise—as with Stornoway NATO Extension. The spiritual blight on everything they touch is gradually creeping through the length and breadth of the Isles without any public outcry.

A turning to the left inside the gate of the army camp has a sign marked 'Tigh a'mhanaich', and this path winds across the moor to old peat workings. Beyond the loch, across the stream and through a walled enclosure, and there 'very sweetly and picturesquely situated in a small hollow, a mile or so short of the summit of Gallan Head, is Tigh Bheannaich, "Blessing House"'. The teampull ruin is much as it was described by Muir over a century ago, except that now the interior is filled with stones from the walls and the altar stone below the remains of the east gable window cannot be seen. Visited on a cold blustering showery November day, one could begin to understand why this little spit of land with its green grass and great gashes of pink crystal underfoot was known as a blessed place. The northwesterly winds which dominate the Isles towards the end of the year were sending white shoals of spray and foam up over Gallan Head itself. Yet on this particular shingle raised ten feet above sea level there was hardly any surge or movement of water to be seen. For the monks who once lived on this green sward with its spring and beehive dwellings, there would have been little to do except venerate and contemplate the awesome power of nature, God's divine handiwork.

Flannan Isles

Twenty miles west of Gallan Head, the 'Seven Hunters' or 'North Hunters' of the Flannan Isles were of special importance to the ancient men of Lewis, who referred to them as the 'Sacred Isles'. It is due to Martin Martin that we know anything of the rituals observed by fishermen in the 17th century on their annual visits for seabirds, eggs, down and quills. Their exactitude and formal character were almost obsequial. If the east wind dropped or changed course, very sensibly they would call the venture off and return home. If any one of the crew was on his first voyage, he was instructed precisely in the manner of the ancient customs and was accompanied by an experienced man at all times while on the island. They used special ladders to climb up from the boats onto the rocks. The first action was to visit the chapel of St. Flannan (an Irish anchorite reputed to have been a king's son), now a ruin on Eilean Mhor. Twenty paces from the chapel they stripped off their upper garments and laying them on a flat rock, recited their first prayer. A second was recited on their knees as they did a right–hand turn around three times, and the third recited inside the chapel. After this they could hunt the birds, but observing certain taboos. They were forbidden to kill any fowl from their boat or with a stone from the land or after evening prayer when the sun had gone down.

Two other curious prohibitions were mentioned by Martin. The first was that they could not urinate near to where the boat was moored as this was reckoned to be a crime against nature and of dangerous consequence for all the crew. The other was that they did not call the rocks, strand, water and any physical aspect by the usual names but rather with a special set of 'propee' words. A tentative deciphering of Martin's account indicates that water was called root, as in the source of a river; rock became hand; the shore was called a cave; fields became sand; sour was reversed to sweet, while sharp or slippery (as in rock) was soft.

The Flannans are also known for one of those intriguing sea mysteries that periodically resurface to exercise the public imagination accompanied by a new theory or explanation. The lighthouse, now automatic, was built at the turn of the century, but as the materials had to be hauled up 70-foot cliffs, it took four years instead of the estimated two. In December 1900, almost a year after it had been officially manned, a passing ship noticed that its light was extinguished, and sent a message to the shore station at Breasclete. The supply ship was actually loading supplies for the coming Christmas but got underway immediately to investigate what was wrong. When the crew landed they never found any trace of the three missing keepers. Inside the lighthouse, 280 feet above the turbulent waters, the clocks had stopped ticking and the final entry in the logbook was at 0900 hours, Saturday 15th December. Everything else was in order. The lamps with their 140,000 candle-power beam were trimmed and ready to be lit. None of the many theories that have been put forward to account for the complete disappearance of the three men has convincingly explained what may have occurred and so the mystery hangs like a cloud over that most sacred isle.

North Rona

This isle, barely one mile long by one broad, lies 44 miles north north-east of the Butt. Its primitive chapel, built with converging walls to meet the flat slab roof, is said to be the oldest example of Celtic church architecture in the Outer Isles. Within the small grave enclosure are a few beehive drystone dwellings and two crude crosses. There is a story that an anchorite, having built Teampull Ronargh, became so troubled by the voices of the women of Europie scolding and quarrelling that he prayed for God to take him some place where he might find peace. Early the following morning he heard a voice telling him to go down to the shore, where he found a large whale waiting for him. He climbed on her back and ended up on North Rona at Sron an Teinnteinn, the fireplace point. However he found the isle inhabited by wild beast-like dogs but they all backed away from him and drowned in the sea. As they went down they scratched a rock, still called 'the beasts' scrach,' which is where he built the little chapel.

Martin records that five families lived here up to the end of the 17th century. They each had their own dwelling houses made of stone, thatched with a straw, and with a porch to keep out the wind and rain. With separate barns for the cattle (unused in those days), they seemed self-sufficient. They took their surnames from the colour of the sky, rainbows and clouds. It is this kind of detail within a mass of observed data that makes Martin's travels so riveting. However, this garden of Eden was overrun by a swarm of rats, probably from a passing ship, that devoured everything and some months later sailors robbed the people of their only bull. 'These misfortunes and the want of supply from Lewis for the space of a year occasioned the death of all that ancient race of people.' Since then there have been spasmodic attempts at resettlement, including two men from Ness who took themselves off here as a form of penance—but a year later they were both found dead. It is now a Nature Reserve for colonies of seabirds and seals.

Sulasgeir, roughly three miles away, is also a Nature Reserve. One of its buildings is said to be called the 'House of Blessing,' and Brenhilda, sister of St. Ronan, is supposed to have died here. So perhaps the old stories of the saint fleeing from the women of Ness are a confused memory of the eremitic tradition when such small isles were used as refuge for individual prayer and meditation. They would in a sense have been an extension of the main monastery. The stacs or pinacles of rock nearer the coast of Lewis, such as Pigmy Isle off the Butt and those by the Port of Geiraha on the east coast were also utilised in the same manner.

At present the yearly guga slaughter here is the only surviving example of what was common practice in the Hebrides. The men of Ness have a special licence to cull the young gannets between September and January, for the solon goose is a protected bird and the tiny isle with its towering cliffs, 38 miles northwest of Lewis, is a bird sanctuary. Traditionally, ten experienced seamen spend three weeks killing and plucking nearly 3,000 birds before returning to the port of Ness; once the men have received their equal share of the birds as tradition dictates, the remainder are sold to a queue of eager buyers, direct from the pier. Regarded as a delicacy by island gourmets, the guga apparently taste like strong oily mackerel.

The account of the hunt in the *Stornoway Gazette* (19.9.81) by a reporter who went with the seamen contains some curious anecdotes. The hunters split into two groups to work in different parts of the isle. Using specially adapted rods, with clamps operated by levers, two men snare the young sea birds, which are then clubbed to death with a stick. A fifth man collects the dead birds. They work from dawn to dusk and live rough in old beehive stone houses that are so infested with insects that the men are forced to put cotton wool in their ears to get some sleep. In days long past, prior to the use of a chartered fishing vessel, the open sail boats and the uncertain weather gave rise to many a strange tale. None stranger than the one set about 150 years ago, when no word was received and the men were eventually presumed drowned. Many of the 'widows' had actually remarried when a few years later all the fishermen returned home, saying that they had been kidnapped and then marooned in Africa.

Last year's cull reaped its own tragic quota for on the calmest return in years, a seaman having an early-morning cuppa suddenly disappeared overboard. His body was never recovered but the broken cup and spilt tea were clearly evident on deck.

Great Bernera

Although now part of the parish of Uig since it was connected to the mainland by bridge in 1953, Great Bernera is in every other way still the largest isle in Loch Roag. The rest are all depopulated now, though over a century ago most of them supported small numbers of families, and on Bernera too there has been a steady drop in numbers to the present figure of over 300 people. In character it is much like the rest of the region: hilly, perforated with small lochs and with a thoroughly indented coastline on both sides of its five-mile length. Bosta, at the extreme northwestern part, is still a very beautiful valley, with remains of sheilings, mills and other ruins, as well as some interesting rectangular stone structures that may have been cattle enclosures. Although in conjunction with the large platform-type stone structures or 'altars' on the hills beyond, they may also have had a different function originally. Cairns dominate the skyline around this enclosed valley and there is a little stream that runs down to the beach which is now popular with local families during the summer. It was Donald the shepherd at Callanish who recounted the clearing of people from here during the early years of the 19th century. Most went to Kirkibost at the southeast end of the isle, but some moved over to the opposite shore of East Loch Roag. These were the first families of the stones. When Kirkibost was itself cleared decades later, the people joined the earlier exodus to Callanish. The indendations and the turf-covered remains of the old houses on the slope down to the shore are still evident, and listening to the passionate discourse of the shepherd brought some of the old ghosts to life again. Standing beneath the stones, Donald grabbed my arm with one hand and waving his crook in the other, shouted into the wind: 'They Tories moved us to Hell. You're no Tory I hope ,' and his eyes twinkled for a few seconds before the fiery vehemence returned to permeate his stocky frame with authority and absolute certainty. 'My people lived there in that croft under the hill,' he said, pointing to a grass-covered ruin. 'And they moved us away to Hell, you know.' It was difficult for me to understand such a long-cherished feeling of rancour when the distance to hell where his croft now resided was a few hundred yards.

Sometimes it seems as if the older people have a direct 'memory' of the past which encompasses all that has happened in the area for hundreds of years, and perhaps even

Dun Stuigh at the entrance to Loch Roag

earlier. Sitting in the intimacy of a front room with tea in the special china and plates full of scones and bannocks, a fire in the grate and rain lashing the windows, the talk threads through the current state of the weather and the peats into the old beliefs—so that certain areas and knowledge become almost ever present. Many times at Callanish we had been told to visit the graves of the dead on Bernera, and in one form or other that note was slipped into conversations. After a few years we finally visited Bosta and found that some of the standing stones could have been quarried from here, for the rocky outcrops are stratified at an angle and so would have split easily. Large nodes of crumbling black pegmatite are also in evidence, and these nodules are a striking feature of the main circle and avenue, especially the centre stone. So when we returned to our teller of tales filled with this discovery and full of theories, she merely smiled and said: 'Aye, well it took you a wee while.' The subject was never mentioned again.

From the right-hand side of the beach at Bosta you can climb up the rough steps of a rocky cleft into the remains of an interesting broch called Dun Stuigh. The outer walls can be traced all round and the base of the walling stands sheer, 30 feet above the high-water mark. The interior is now filled with stones but inside the massive walls are what appears to be part of the lintelled interior passage. Located at a strategic point by the entrance to East Loch Roag, a stone cairn now marks the summit of this rocky promontory. Opposite on Little Bernera a roofless chapel and the old burial ground are clearly visible. Martin mentions that there were two chapels here dedicated to St. Michael and St. Dondan. Beyond it, among the great rock stacs is a view of Bearasay, which was the stronghold of Neil MacLeod for three years before his capture and execution in 1613. He forced the Fife adventurers to leave Lewis but it was his friend and companion Donald Cham or 'Squint-Eyed' MacAuley—now buried on Little Bernera—who became a legendary local folk hero with many stories about his exploits heard along the west coast.

The deserted township of Kirkibost is quite an interesting place to visit. There are the remains of a church built and vacated during the 19th century when the people were cleared. Below the north wall are the foundations of what may have been a much earlier chapel site, perhaps the one mentioned by Martin as dedicated to St. Michael. Nearby are remains of sheilings, stone enclosures and a 'smithy'. Set into a platform of stone is its 6 by 6 foot (1.8m.) concave recess, rather like a stone cauldron with a squared flue below it, flush with the front wall of a waist-high stone platform. It is a remarkable example of its kind and illustrates, as much as the beehive houses and some of the hilltop cairns, that the tradition of drystone walling techniques had remained intact in the Isles since prehistoric times. This deserted township ought to be scheduled and restored before it erodes away completely, for it gives a unique glimpse into the life of the recent past.

Of course, the most outstanding ancient monuments here are the stones on the left bank above the bridge, seen when first crossing on the B8059, which itself is a turning off from the main Uig road. The three standing stones (C/8) are now arced in a most unusual position on the edge of a steep rock face 50 feet (15m.) above Loch Barraglom. The centre stone is nine-foot (2.7m.) high with a fallen one eight-foot-long

(2.3m.) nearby, while the west stone is seven feet (2m.), and the east one over 60 feet (18m.) away is three feet (0.9m.) high. Beyond the south side of the bridge in the ditch at the side road to Aird Earshader is a pillar stone that may have had some significance. Also some of the boulders high up on this mainland side were considered by Somerville to mark the Mayday sunrise when viewed from the standing stones. Recently a number of other megalithic features have been discovered on both sides of the loch and perhaps after they have been surveyed, some of the mystery surrounding the position of C/8 (at one of the entrances to the East Loch Roag but completely out of sight of the main circle at Callanish) may be clarified.

In relation to the 'entrances' to this loch, at least two of the small isles are known to be magnetic anomalies. One of these, Vuia Beag, is known as the 'salmon run', for according to local fishing lore the fish swim round and round this small isle 'until the dark side of the moon'. It is as if they are trapped within the orbit of the rock—about which a Garynahine man has said. 'Four men on oars with an outboard motor would find it difficult to land there'—and then only released by the new moon to continue their journey upriver. Murdo MacLeod suggested that the shoals moving down from the Butt after their long journey across the Atlantic would come in on one side of the Loch in a kind of figure-of-eight sweep before moving out through the other entrance to continue south along the coast for their 'home' rivers. It should be remembered that we are touching upon a very complex ecological cycle here: for the salmon to be able to move, a spate is needed from the hills of Uig to make the shallow rivers rise. May and June are usually the best months in the Outer Hebrides and so at the beginning of July, waiting for the weather to change, both fish and men would be at their most restless.

It was Murdo who first put us onto the idea of the standing stones by Bernera Bridge being somehow connected in terms of symbiotic magic to the arrival of the salmon. Towards the end of the driest summer in years the fish had been confined for days in the mouth of the loch waiting for a spate to take them up the Grimersta, one of the last salmon rivers left in

Lewis. Standing on the opposite shore in the early evening, we were spectators to a seemingly neverending choreography of sudden movement as three, four, and sometimes six, long silver bodies would emerge in unison with graceful arched leaps and tails scudding the surface of the still dark waters. The term 'somersault' comes from 'salmon-sault', so reminiscent and evocative of that hovering leap, once seen never forgotten. Half the male population of the area were also watching this dance, this constant preparation for their journey up river to spawn, as Murdo casually remarked that the stones on the cliff edge were used by ancient archers to hide from the fish passing below. This seemed a familiar transposition of an early sacred function to a more mundane event in the life of a mediaeval poacher, notwithstanding the fact that Murdo himself was once known as the best poacher in Uig.

There are many ways of catching the 'venison of the rivers' but the oldest is thought to have been in use in the Isles until the end of the 18th century when strict working of the Salmon Acts made it illegal. It was called 'An Garadh', or 'the Dyke,' built out into the water and along the coast most frequented by the salmon. Those left high and dry at ebb-tide in the bend would make an easy catch. Wicker nets and weirs were also used. It's all quite different now with explosives, wanton waste and horrific tales of summary justice in kangaroo courts on the large estates, who in fact are a law unto themselves where fishing rights are concerned. However, such thoughts were far away as we watched the dance on the loch in what for the salmon were probably the first still waters since they left their feeding grounds below the Greenland iceflows. It is impossible to escape the conclusion that this annual influx of so much nutritious food would have been one of the most singular events in the lives of the ancient islanders and those on the mainland. Perhaps this may be the significance underlying the carvings of fish on so many of the Pictish stones.

The most direct route back to Stornoway is from the A858 junction at Garynahine, but there is also a slightly longer one through Breasclete or from Carloway along the picturesque

Pentland Road. Any excuse to spend time at the Callanish stones should not be gainsaid, for however disposed one may be towards standing stones in general, there is no doubt that they are the most outstanding megalithic monument in the Hebrides. For the purposes of this book, however, our journey will continue up along the west coast road to the Butt itself.

The Callanish Township

A legend about Callanish says that it was here that the ancient inhabitants met in council once a year. They refused to accept the new Christ religion or build a chapel for St. Kiarnan, so the latter turned them all to stone—a familiar turn of events associated with many stone circles throughout the mainland. The old township around the stones can still be discerned, even with the stock fencing throughout the nearby croftlands and the rebuilding of the 'tighdubh' into a pretty little coffee house at the edge of the north avenue. It is not too difficult to imagine what the area was like before the peat cover was removed from around the stone circles during the middle of the last century. A few early photographs and the first Six Inch OS map showed the path that came up through the village and across the stones of the main circle below Cnoc an Tursa to the old harbour. There was also an inn on the site of the present farmhouse and this was the route taken by Lady Matheson and her summer house-guests after arriving by boat from Stornoway to visit the stones. The recent archaeological dig revealed traces of this path down to the loch which seems to have disturbed and added much confusion to the burial cairn inside the main circle. According to Donald the shepherd, the reasons the stones were finally cleared (after local peat-cutting had revealed their true depth) and the original families moved on from the sheltered lee of the hill between the western side and the loch, was that Lady Matheson kept soiling her dresses.

Callanish today is certainly not unique among Hebridean townships with its mix of bungalows, old shacks, post office, blackhouses turned into byres, mounds of newly cut and dried peats, car wrecks and discarded machinery sinking into the crofts, separated by makeshift fencing that does not seem

View from the Hill of the Bones

to prevent the bleeting sheep nibbling everywhere they can find a tuft of grass. However, having three major stone circles intervisible to each other has made it an essential stop on every visitor's itinerary especially for those dedicated trippers who pay their frequent respects to the 'Stones' almost as one visits a favourite aunt. The echoes of sheep, dogs, cars, bird sounds, and the interminable clattering of the weavers' looms inside small tin sheds, make a memorable sound cameo during the perambulation from circle to circle. Discovering other stones scattered in and around the village can be almost as exciting as contemplating the megaliths. At the turning by the side of the road towards C/2 is a fairly large round white stone which by day looks innocuous enough, though often in the moonlight its stark whiteness and luminous whorls can make it appear quite significant. However, it fell off the back of a lorry over a year ago and has now become part of the local scenery. At the bottom of the steep rise below the main circle are a number of large boulders that were probably blasted out of the bedrock for the making of the road, but again their placement by its edge becomes part of the immediate drama of plodding up the hill, usually harassed by a couple of sheepdogs, for the first close-up view of the tall grey standers. By car it is a fast zoom-lens effect but with the slight physical effort of the climb it is always memorable, no matter how often one has seen them before. Another good viewing point is from the top of the hillock at the south end, Cnoc an Tursa. From here the architectural quality of the circle and stone avenues with the village straggling off to the north is apparent. It is certainly the best place to view the grand tableau of the Clisham Hills, the cone of Roineval, and the unforgettable spread of the 'Sleeping Beauty' against an everchanging dome of sky.

Broch, Doune Carloway

The road around Callanish has been improved recently and as one passes along the estuary through Braesclete, the stark remains of a stone chamber on top of 'Phrionas' hill stands out clearly. It is a small oval structure of four stones set on edge to form a cist. Just beyond the school in the midst of a group of council houses is a five-feet-high (1.5m.) standing stone. By some strange quirk of bureaucratic good taste, this gneiss pillar was set up on a concrete plinth when the houses were built in the 1960s, mainly I suppose to position it roughly where it was originally revealed by peat-cutting more than half a century ago. The pier and disused fish-processing factory are at the seaward end of the B8010, which joins up to the Pentland Road three miles out on the moor. The road itself runs from Carloway to Stornoway.

Beyond Braesclete the character of the surrounding terrain changes quite dramatically, becoming much more rugged and with some spectacular geological faulting visible where the A858 road was blasted through. The village of Tolsta Chaolais is worth a visit but the main interest on this stretch is the licensed hotel at Doune Carloway. It is one of the very few refreshing stops on this side of the Lewis bogland, with a large bar which is usually full of animated fishermen and crofters, especially near to closing time at ten o'clock in the evening. The restaurant tends to be rather erratic—or perhaps it has set hours that never seemed to coincide with our ramblings through the area. Close by are the remains of a blackhouse that was lived in until a year ago when the roof collapsed. It was always a strange sight to see the small woman in black, standing by her door watching the steady stream of cars driving over the cattle grid and into the forecourt of the hotel, to get petrol and a drink.

Carloway Broch is one of the best-preserved examples of an Iron Age defensive fort in the Hebrides. At present it looks like an open-sectioned cone with the double drystone wall revealing its true broch structure. The galleries passageway and lintel steps are intact on the east side which is 30-feet (9m.) high. Sited on the crest of a steep rocky slope, 150 feet above sealevel, its walls are between ten and twelve feet (3–3.6m.) thick. There is a small doorway in the north wall just over three-feet (1m.) high, which leads into the central courtyard, with beam-holes on the inside walls indicating that it was roofed at some period. Local traditions say it was burned down by 'Squint-Eyed' MacAuley, who climbed the outer wall at night, using two dirks as climbing aids, and then dropped bundles of burning heather onto it to suffocate the Morrisons who were sleeping inside. It has been suggested that the diameter of the broch (47 feet/14m.) is nine megalithic yards and that perhaps there may have been a 'Broch yardstick' having a mean length of 0.839m., only 1cm. larger than Thom's megalithic yard; also, that several brochs were circular and elliptical in the same manner that has been shown to approximate to the geometry of the stone circles.

On the other side of Loch Carloway is a seven-foot-high (2m.) pillar stone called Clach an Tursa, or 'Stone of Sadness.' Martin mentioned three stones standing here, adding that: 'Some of the ignorant vulgar say, they were men by enchantment turn'd into stones, and others say, they are monuments of persons of note kill'd in battle.' The other two are now lying nearby, broken, but the fact that they measure 14 feet and 17 feet, respectively, in length (4m. and 5m.), indicates that this was indeed an important prehistoric site. The standing stone faces to the northeast and inclines slightly in that direction, but wherether all three formed an aligned row relating to the major moon standstill is impossible to ascertain. They may have stood as a triad above the head of the loch, similar to the group overlooking Bernera Bridge, and having some connection with the annual influx of the salmon.

Beyond Carloway, the first turning to the left leads to Dalmore beach which often has spectacular rollers whipping in from the North Atlantic. There are some interesting cliff walks on both sides of the sands. Midden heaps were recorded here since early in the century, but recently some remains of what may well turn out to be an important prehistoric building were uncovered during repair work to shore-up the edges of the cemetery from wholesale erosion by the sea. The site has since been covered over awaiting proper excavation.

Clach an Trushal, Shader

The route north to the tallest standing stone in the Hebrides passes some tourist set-piece reconstructions from the recent past, that help relieve the tedium of this dull road. Just before Shawbost to the west is a Norse-mill that was reconstructed by the local school children who were also largely responsible for the charm of the folk museum in Shawbost, essays and school-books on display side-by-side with the memorabilia of the 'old days'. At Bragar is an arch made from two whalebones of a mammal killed here during World War One. The harpoon is suspended from the jaws above the gate of a house that was the post office at the time. No. 42 Arnol, the next village along, is a blackhouse which has been restored by the DOE and turned into a 'museum', open all year except on Sundays. Everything inside is spick and span but gives little idea of what life inside a tighdubh might have been like. However, one can see quite clearly the outside part of the essential structure: the low thatched roof running into the centre of the four-foot-thick (just over 1m.) wall so that water would drain naturally into the rubble. The walls are curved as is the roof-ends, held down with ropes and flat stones, making this low-lying house with its smooth curves an ideal buffer against the strong winds that are usual in Lewis. Arnol is now almost a museum in itself, with its old blackhouses and ruins much in evidence. The village was originally situated by the shore around Loch Arnol, but in the 18th century began to spread back towards the road. The older houses were less regulated then, with many additional stables or byres added in ad hoc fashion when needed—whereas the houses like No. 42, which were built over 100 years ago, appear more elongated with a stricter division between living space and that for animals. Many of these were in use up to the 1930s but the last inhabited one in Lewis was at Callanish. When Annie MacLeod moved out last year, the roof almost immediately began to cave in. It seems that the constant peat fires day and night, which gave it its name as opposed to the chimneyed 'whitehouses' in Skye, helped to keep the structure intact, but with a radical alteration in temperature and increased dampness inside, it only needed one winter season to turn what had been a comfortable little house into a ruin.

Covered all over with sparse green lichen, so that it often looks like a hairy monster among the council houses, the monolith at Ballantrushal, a quarter mile from the main road, measures 19 feet by 6 feet (5·7 x 1·8m.). Its girth at base is over 15 feet (4·5m.), tapering to an elegant four feet (over 1m.) around the top. Sited on a hillside slope, 100 feet above the sea shore, facing east-south-east and slanting slightly south and west, Clach an Trushal would have been a stark and massive marker, especially from the open sea. This north-east coastline is very rocky and the beach here is one of the few landing places available for open craft. The pebbles have been ground into the most sinuous and round shapes and it is interesting to note that the pebbles found in the grave cairn inside the stone circles at Callanish (C/2), mentioned by its 19th-century excavator, may have come from this beach.

Various stories from each era have become associated with this 'stone of compassion.' It is said to mark the spot of the final victory of the Morrisons over their long-standing enemies the MacAuleys of Uig, and before that the burial place of a Norse prince. But the 'Lay of Truiseal' recited by an old Lewis man, and published by J.F. Camphall, as an imaginary recital between the singer and the stone, is rather whimsical. Here is a literal translation of two of the verses:

A tale with thee, thou Truiseal great,
 Who were the peoples in thy age?
 Wert thou (there) in time of the Fiann,
 Did'st thou see Fionn, Fial or Fraoch?

I am a Truisealach after the Fiann,
Long do I wish to follow the rest;
On my elbow here in the west,
Fixed to the root of both my wings.

The Megalithic Setting at Steinacleit, Shadar

This is certainly one of the more confusing and confused ancient sites on Lewis. It comprises an outer enclosure, lying east/west and measuring 270 feet by 183 feet (82 x 55·5m.) which was revealed when the area was stripped of three to four feet (1m.) of peat more than half a century ago, with an inner ring of kerb and loose slab stones whose diameter is 54 feet (16m.). The former are about four feet (just over 1m.) above the ground while the latter are at least seven feet, (2m.) high. There are also a few odd-shaped stones inside the ring and 140 feet (42·5m.) to the south-east is a 66 inch-high (1·6m.) stone. The site has been described as a 'circle and denuded cairn' (Ref. RCAHM No. 17) and a 'reputed chambered cairn' (*Chambered Cairns of Scotland*, Vol. 2), although Henshall seems to conclude that it could have been a building while nevertheless rejecting the idea because of the ring of stones set on edge. It was probably used as a cattle enclosure for without modern stock fencing and with smaller flocks it would have been a convenient place for a sheep fank. However, that does not explain what the original function may have been but if the area is viewed in a larger topographical overview in the manner that the Callanish complex is beginning to be understood, then I suspect that it might make more sense. Clach an Truishal is less than a mile across the Shader river, and 540 yards (491m.) away, only 4° off true north, is Clach Stei lin, a five-foot-high standing stone. There are probably other structures buried in the peat of the surrounding moorland.

St. Moluag's Chapel, Europie, Ness

The road up to the Butt had in the final stages of our periegesis become a kind of latter-day pilgrimage, with constant deviation from the main road along side turnings towards the sea to wander amid ecclesiastical ruins. It may well have been a retracing of an older peregrination up this coastal plateau for nearly 20 miles. From the chapel site at Kirwrig in Carloway; to the ruin at Dalmore; to Teampull Eoin at Bragar; to Teampull Mhuire at Barvas; to Teampull Pheadair at Shadar; to Teampull Bhrichid and holy well at Melbost Borve; to Teampull nan Cro-Naomh at South Galson; to Teampull Pheadair at Swainbost; to Teampull Thomais at Habost; and finally to Teampull Moluadh and Teampull Ronaigh at Europie near Ness.

Martin mentions a tradition in Lewis that was carried out as late as the mid 17th century of the people walking to the church of St. Malvay, the latter has not been identified as far as I know but may correspond to that of St. Moluadh at Ness near the Butt, which is quite flat. Each family brought a peck of malt that was brewed into ale. One person from the company then walked into the sea up to his middle and, throwing a cup of the brew into the waves, shouted out: 'Shony I give you this cup of ale hoping that you will be kind and send us plenty of sea ware for enriching our ground for the ensuing year.' After the invocation to the goddess of the sea, they went inside the church with a single candle burning on the altar and stood silent; then off to the fields, singing and dancing for the rest of All Hallows night.

Moluag was one of the Irish missionaries who acted independently of Iona and traditionally it was at Europie that he first preached Christianity and founded a chapel. He travelled extensively through what was then East and North Pictland, establishing chapels, and he died at Rosemarkie on the 25th June AD 592. Much loved, he was described by one of his disciples as 'Moluag the pious and brilliant, the gracious and decorous'. The existing church at Europie was founded by Olav the Black of Norway in either the 12th or 14th century according to different authorities and it became, like St. Magnus' Cathedral on Orkney, one of the pilgrimage places of the Western Highlands. It was recorded as being in a state of good repair in 1630 but it had become a roofless ruin when acquired by the Scottish Episcopal Church who restored it in 1912. It now stands in a field about 250 yards (227m.) north of the township, and its anonymous greystone exterior and tall slate roof blends well with the windswept flat landscape of the Butt.

Lying due east/west and oblong on plan, it measures externally 44 feet by 18 feet (13·4 x 5·4m.), with a projecting sacristy and a chapel. There is a semi-arched doorway at the southwest. The east window is round-headed and the west is slightly smaller. There are small windows on top of the wall and Muir pointed out that the originals in the side buildings were mere slits. The main walls are 33 inches (0·8m.) thick and nearly 16 feet (4·8m.) high, with rear arch pointed. The large Celtic-shaped stone cross which stands outside by the door was a war memorial erected in 1920. The relics that were inside for many years have been temporarily removed to St. Peter's Church in Stornoway.

On the summit of a hill 500 yards (455m.) northeast of the church is an irregular stony mound which is all that remains of Teampull Ronaigh (Ronan).

The four-foot-high (just over 1m.) stonecross from North Rona stood on the altar of St. Moluadh for many years until it fell and broke in half 'due to the vibrations of the door closing'. Inside the church is a very pronounced echo which is a poignant reminder of its use as a healing place for the insane which continued up to the 17th century but was discontinued after persistent pressure from the Presbyterian ministers. According to Martin, the lunatic was bathed after sunset at a nearby well then walked seven times around the church before being laid down and bound hand and foot with his head enclosed between two quern stones. The poor creature was then left in front of the altar all night in what must have been the equivalent of a megalithic straight-jacket resonating with the echo of screaming and mental agony. And all this on a full moon. If this was an ancient practice it is no wonder that the saint was driven to find some peace on North Rona.

The broken and blackened half of the quern stone from the church now lies at the front of the local schoolmaster's garden. Nearby at the end of this croft, covered in red and yellow mimulus, a spring is all that remains of the original well, which was buried under the ground when the modern road was laid down. St. Andrew's Well at Shader, which was filled in in 1914, was another well-known healing centre. Apparently, if someone was very ill a wooden dish was used to ascertain if they could be cured or not. The dish was laid on the surface of the water and if it rotated sunwise, then the patient would recover; however, if it did not, then death was imminent. This type of either—or divination was also known to have been practised at wells on the mainland. Tobar Brighid at Borve is one of the few wells throughout the Isles that is kept in good condition.

Before the advent of mains water, wells and springs were essential to life here. In the widespread respect for the necessity for fresh water, some wells, because of the generous sweet taste or accepted healing properties of their water, were deemed sacred. The energy emitting from the proximity of holy wells rich in minerals and trace elements, was used to exercise the malignant spirits arising from unbalanced states of sickness. In the Isles the waters from beneath the earth are considered the juices of the moon. In its strong connection with ancient wisdom, fertility and healing, the sacred water of these wells is still recognised by many people, especially dowsers and healers with the 'sight' who practised their natural gifts in a manner that is as necessary today as when they were swept aside by the reforming zeal of puritanism.

Five hundred yards northwest of the Port of Ness, on the brow of a hill, two great pillar stones are all that remains now of what must have been a most spectacular megalithic setting. Across their sloping tops a slab of enormous dimensions stood athwart them. This was reported by the RCAHM in 1914 as lying prostrate nearby, but unfortunately it was wantonly smashed by soldiers during World War Two, for their canteen material.

The dimensions of the northerly stone are five feet by ten (1·5 x 3m.) round the base; the other rough boulder standing 11 feet (3·3m.) to the southwest is 40 inches by nine feet (1 x 2·7m.) girth. Through the 'window' of the original structure the midwinter sun might be seen to rise from the hill at Teampull Moluadh to extend over the whole of the plateau.

Pygmy Isle, Butt of Lewis

People who live underground are part of the Hebridean tradition associated with souterrains, hypogea and caves. The natural feature by the Butt of Lewis is known as Luchaban, or 'Pygmy Isle', combining cell and oratory together, one of the more primitive dwellings of an anchorite. On top of the towering 80-foot-high (24·5m.) stac is an underground chamber. The original Gaelic word, Lusbirdin, meant 'pygmy' and Dean Munroe in his 16th-century descriptions of the Western Isles recounted the charming story in such a manner as to suggest that it was a well-worn theme:

> At the north point of Lewis there is a little island called Pygmies' Isle with a little Kirk on it of their own handiwork. Within this Kirk the ancients of that country of the Lewis say that the said Pygmies have been buried there. Many men of different countries have delved deeply the floor of the little Kirk, and I myself among the rest, and have found round heads of wonderful little size, alleged to be the bones of the said Pygmies. But I leave this far to the ancients of Lewis.

An official account drawn up in 1680 said the bones being measured proved to be not quite two inches (5cm.) long. Martin referred to 'low structured people living here called Lusbirdon (Pygmies),' and Bleau's map shows it as Yien Dunibeg, 'Isle of Little Men.' A certain Capt. Dymes who visited the rock in 1630 was more sceptical and did not think them big enough to be human bones but added 'that the Irish came to Ness for the sole purpose of digging up Luchbirden bones,' which conjures up a delightful picture of the leprechaun trade of that era. More recently the said bones were pronounced to have been those of animals and birds.

The end of the road is but the beginning of a new journey. The Butt and Barra Head are two points of a compass, defining and definitive of a scattered group of islands running north-north-east for 140 odd miles. Rich and imaginative is the mental map of the Hebrides but these two precipitous cliffs can never be encompassed in mere words. The sight of a storm petrel in flight or the sound of the sea surging against the rocks below can never be matched in verbal equivalents. It is at the point when the descriptive capacity of ordinary language looses its grip that music and song must emerge. As the American poet, Jack Spicer, put it in his own colloquial fashion, 'poetry is the image of the real'.

Many others have tried to reconcile the irrevocable in formulating the beginning of this scattering of islands only to

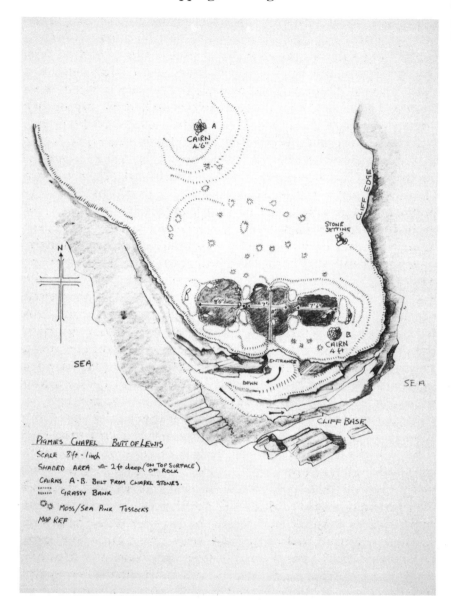

Plan of underground chamber, Butt of Lewis

show that the dreams of a perfect ordering are a small part of our perennial spiritual need. A Scandinavian tradition concerning the natural arch on the west side called Suil an Rodh, 'Eye of the Butt,' relates how the Hebrides acquired their present shapes. This promontory is now filled with nesting birds but the arch itself can be reached by scrambling down by a rope thoughtfully provided, to the rocks below when the sea is calm. When the world was young and fair and still attached to the mainland of Normandy, the Norsemen, encouraged by their repeated conquests, decided on the Herculean task of removing this jewel to the north. The preparations included making a huge cable of four strands and each strand made of a different material, one of heather, one of hemp, another of wood and the fourth of a woman's hair. When the cable was completed a fleet of ships, one for every day of the year, with gigantic sailors sailed south. A hole, like Suil an Rodh, was made in a rocky precipice and a cable passed through it. Then they all pulled so hard that the land was wrenched away from France and they began their journey home. Unfortunately, the seas were not favourable and a large part sank where Ireland is, then Scotland, and finally in a great storm the once green and beautiful land broke into a thousand rocky isle of all shapes and sizes as they are now.

Otta Swire relates another version of this tale. The Viking chief enquired of a passing mermaid what would be the best rope for the task and she advised him that the hair of a thousand maidens untouched by cold iron and twisted by the people of the sea caves would be best. He then carried off every maid he could find and offered them safety in return for their tresses. All accepted, so he gave them sharpened seashells. With much pain and tears they cut their hair, repeating runes of good omen—save one, who was so angry that she repeated a curse over every strand she hacked away. When the rope was prepared it was put through the arch and they sailed north. But the wind caught the hills and tugged them; and the sea waves broke the shores and cracked them, until bits of the Long Isle began to break away. First Barra and the southern isles, then the Uists and Benbecula, until finally the hair with the curse on it parted the rope, leaving Lewis and Harris as they are today.

The primaeval beginnings of the Outer Isles were due to the dragon-slayer. A fearsome nine-headed monster terrorised the land and carried off nine young maidens whenever he appeared from the sea. A young hero, betrothed to one of the maids who was taken by the beast, decided that unlike everyone else who lamented and hid, he would attempt to rescue her. He had once helped a waterhorse escape when the people tried to make it fish for them, so he went off to the mountain loch to ask for its help. The Easchuisge carried him over the ocean searching for the monster. They found it and after a long and terrible battle, the lad cut off the dragon's heads and stabbed it through the heart. Leaving the carcass for the seas to dispose off, the seahorse then carried him and the nine maids safely home to Skye. So the birds of the air and the fishes of the sea pecked and nibbled at it until there was nothing left but bones. However, these were so big that eventually they became home and shelter for both birds and fish. The bones turned to rocks and earth formed from the seawrack that gathered around them. So the indented body of the Long Isle is a fossilised dragon and the smaller isles of many different shape are its heads floating nearby.

Having reached the Butt and looked over the cliff on a wet blustering day with a cold wind whipping across the plateau, one could not envy the birds their unhurried flight. As the avifauna has evolved a manner of coping with the wild craggy wastes so too have the people who live and work here. Compared with the rest of the island it is relatively fertile. So the strip farms, houses and even the townships have a distinct pattern unique to Lewis that might be familiar to those from the south of England around the Fen country. The naturalist, Fraser-Darling, has pointed out that:

> the natural history of the Western Isles is a noble drama of weather and mountains and sea and plant and animal. Compared to the environment of the rest of Britain, the effect of people during the past 5,000 years has been minimal. Their visible presences from dilapidated stone burial vaults, chapels, defensive stone forts, ruined shielings and other domesticated dwellings can be read as a map with different structures representing blocks of time, as a time map.

The Outer Isles are special, too, in that the remains of this past have not been swept away by each subsequent era's struggle to cope with the present, but like the far older laycring of buckled land masses and gneiss swept bare by retreating ice or the machair building up from blown sand and the tenacious hold of grasses, all retain metaphorical reminders of a past. And yet because we walked the land and sensed its almighty presence it is in a real sense part of our present.

I can think of no better manner of expressing our vision of this presence than the song that manifested itself in dream by the ruins of St. Michael's Chapel at Grimsay on our way down to the southern cliffs to begin this mapping of the journey:

I am the ancient serpent that entwines the spirit of place
I am the green pinnacle of earth that lies fallow through time
I am the sharp split of rock that bleeds both man and beast
I am the pointed stone that burns the spinal root body
I am the breaking wave that once inundated the holy brethren
I am the salmon leaping in the loch preparing for a journey in spirit
I am the cuckoo spinning on a ledge ceaselessly singing for a mother
I am the moon who illuminates the bright maiden of the mound
I am the wind the flower the unwritten word
I am the dark lady who embraces the unwary poet and dreamer
I am the stone of emptiness on the Isles of Destiny

IS CRADH DIA

('God is Love') carved on stone on the moor, Cruilivig

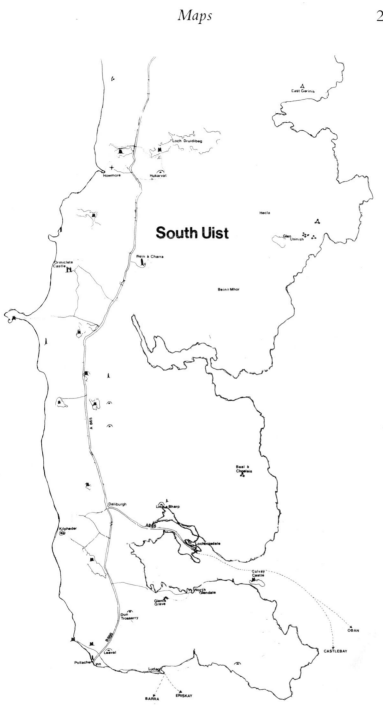

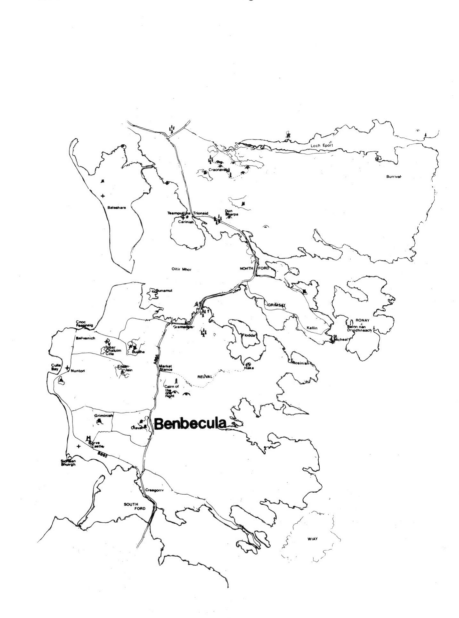

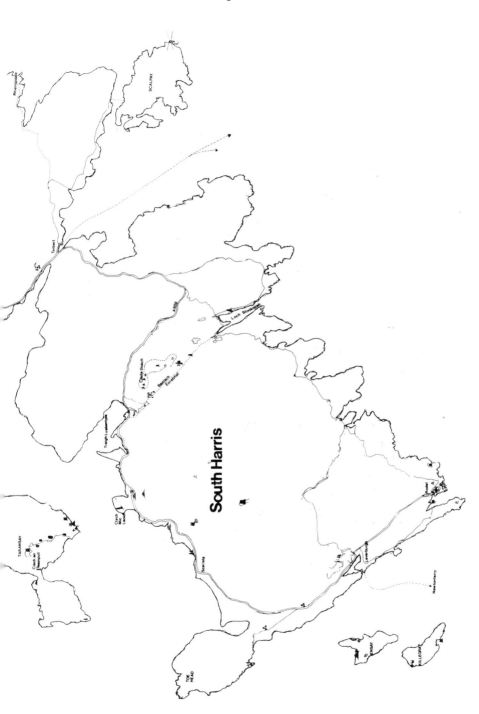

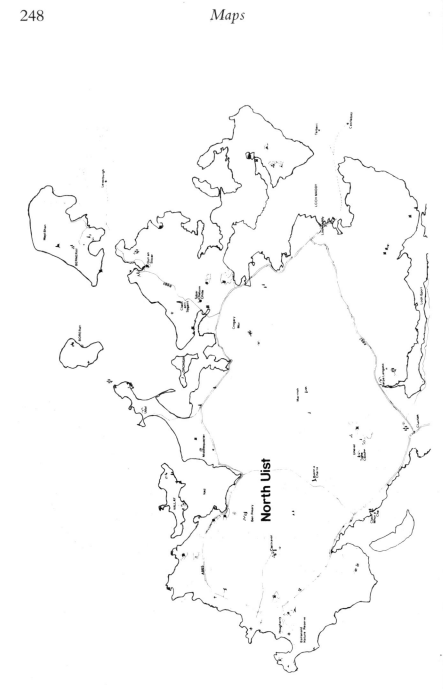

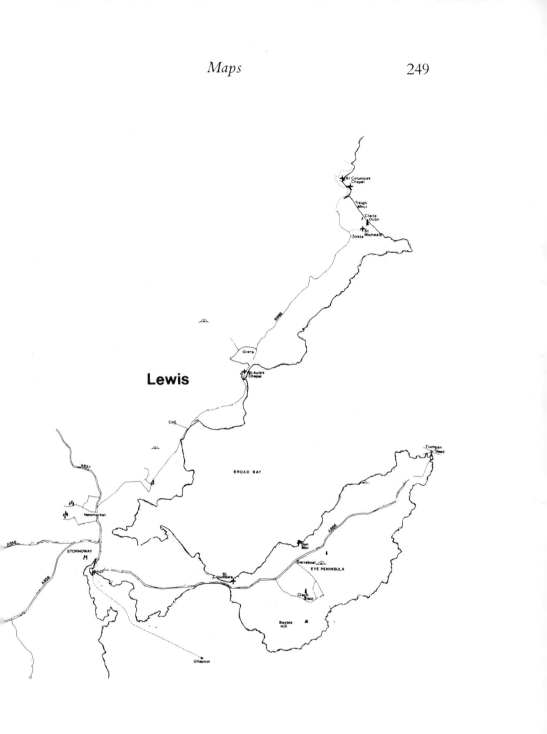

Lewis

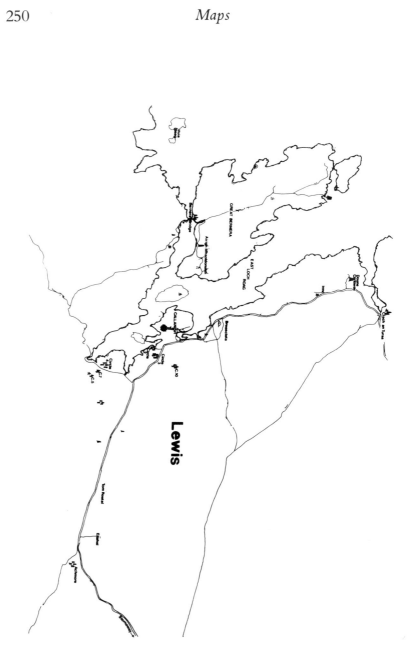

INDEX OF PLACES

*(Chapter and section headings are indicated in **bold**)*